D0948163

STUDENTS AND WORKERS

STUDENTS
AND WORKERS

*An Analytical Account of Dissent
in France May – June 1968*

JOHN GRETTON

MACDONALD · LONDON

First published in Great Britain 1969 by
Macdonald & Co. (Publishers) Ltd.,
49/50 Poland Street, London W.1.

SBN 356 02806 2

Printed by Unwin Brothers Limited
THE GRESHAM PRESS OLD WOKING SURREY ENGLAND
Set in Monotype Times
A member of the Staples Printing Group
(HL3986)

CONTENTS

DOCUMENTS

Introduction

PART III CHAPTER 9

Appendix 1 (iii)

FOR JUD AND HER FRIENDS

PREFACE

THE French are capable of as much hypocrisy as the British. *Les événements* no longer refers to the Algerian War but to the student riots and general strike of May and June 1968. For, like the Algerian War, they divided Frenchmen into two hostile camps, those who were 'for' and those who were 'against'. Those who wished to take an intermediary position, 'for' the workers but 'against' the students, or 'for' university reform but 'against' violence, were thrown willy-nilly into one or other camp by the general atmosphere and the election campaign. Having lived through those two months in Paris, having studied French society and having been in close contact with French students for five years, I was not exempt from this polarisation. I was, and am, 'for'. This being said, I have tried to present as objective an account as possible of what actually happened. In the rare cases where facts are given without supporting evidence, it is because the sources prefer for the moment to remain anonymous.

In comparison with France, Britain appears as a remarkably permissive society. But just as this permissiveness has its roots in a specific social and economic tradition, so those facets of the French cultural model which are most relevant to the 1968 explosion have deep roots. The book was planned and written with the object of making some at least of these roots apparent. The documents at the end of most of the chapters fall into two categories: some are intended simply to illustrate the text; the others have been chosen, with no attempt to aim either at exhaustiveness or a statistically typical sample, because they help to give an idea of the atmosphere of the period.

The responsibility for everything in the book is entirely my own. However, I would like to thank Renaud Sainsaulieu, Marie-Noël Thibault, Jacques Capdevielle and René Mouriaux who read and commented upon parts of the manuscript. In particular the last two very kindly let me use some of their interviews from a forthcoming doctoral thesis, *Les militants de la CGT et de la CFDT*. William MacLean was good enough to put at my disposal the as yet unpublished but invaluable material he amassed in the course of research into student perceptions and attitudes during May and

11

June 1968. Unless otherwise stated, all translations are by James Moore.

My thanks are also due to *New Society* for allowing me to make use of previously published articles. Finally, I would like to express my gratitude to Serge Hurtig of the *Fondation nationale des sciences politiques* for allowing me to continue to use the many facilities of the *Fondation* when I should in fact have been working on another project.

Le Moulin d'Andé
December, 1968.

STUDENTS AND WORKERS

INTRODUCTION

JUST as no man is an island so no historical event can be isolated from its economic, social, political and cultural context. The French student revolt and general strike in the early summer of 1968 was an historical event the measure of whose importance has yet to be accurately taken. This book does not pretend to predict its final consequences nor to give firm answers to questions concerning its causes. The object is simply to give an account of what happened while emphasising those aspects of the French context which appear to be most relevant and which will probably figure prominently in any definitive analysis. This inevitably means being very selective, and the image of France which emerges may well appear to many to be a perversely distorted one.[1] Yet it must be remembered that if in recent years there has been increasing student unrest of one sort or another in most of the advanced industrial societies, in Eastern Europe, in Western Europe and on the American continent, it is only in France that there occurred a gigantic social upheaval which at times took on the airs of a revolution and left many Frenchmen afterwards feeling that civil war had only been averted by a hair's breadth. It is clear therefore that either France is a unique case among advanced industrial societies, or that it is not unique but presents certain characteristics in common with other such societies but to a much greater (and more explosive) extent. Whichever alternative is preferred, it is worth studying the French case in some detail. Before embarking on such a study, however, a few words about the general rash of student agitation are in order.

1

Starting in the mid-1950s a wave of adolescent violence and brutality startled most of the advanced industrial societies. The 'hooligans' of Moscow, the *blousons noirs* of Paris and the British

1. A more optimistic account of contemporary French society may be found in John Ardagh's excellent account of social and economic changes since 1945, *The New French Revolution; a social and economic survey of France, 1945–1967*, London, Secker and Warburg, 1968.

'teddy boys' were part of a general revolt which also affected Sweden, Germany, and the United States of America, although the names have changed and the publicity has declined as the public has come to accept the persistence of a rebellious, and often violent, minority in its midst. No satisfactory explanation has yet been given, but it is difficult, in the light of later events, not to link it with the young bourgeois revolt. For at about the same time, or a little later, the 'beat' movement, which has since become the 'hippy' movement, went beyond its artistic and literary origins to become a vehicle for 'dropping-out'; in many Western countries[2] an increasingly large minority of bourgeois youth has abandoned a great many conventional norms and adopted a number of values diametrically opposed to the dominant ones of Western culture. Although many in both categories end up by being reintegrated into society, their place is taken by their younger brothers and sisters. The contours of the social fringe have been enlarged to take in not merely traditionally marginal groups (immigrants, coloureds, criminals, etc.) but also part of a certain age group who, unlike the others, are for the most part assured of a place in the sun if and when they choose to accept it. Social-psychological explanations in terms of adolescent role-conflict are certainly valid as far as they go, but doubts whether this is the whole story are increased when the student revolt is taken into account.

Student agitation is not a new phenomenon, and Latin-American governments have been toppled by it long before the French students posed a serious threat to the Gaullist regime. Even in Europe those countries whose twentieth century political history has been turbulent have seen students take sides for or against political movements. But if one excepts Japan it was not until 1964 that a sizeable minority of the student body of a university in an advanced industrial society raised the standard of revolt. From Berkeley in 1964 student agitation spread to the Free University of Berlin in 1965, and since then the momentum has increased to such an extent that during the academic year 1967–1968 there was scarcely a country in Western or Eastern Europe that was not affected by it.[3] Although there has

2. Although not in France, where for reasons that will become apparent in Part 1 this sort of non-violent, hedonistic revolt is not possible under normal circumstances. The French social equivalent were the *blousons dorés* who in dress as in violence modelled their behaviour on that of their plebeian counterparts.
3. J. Joussellin in *Les Révoltes des Jeunes*, Paris, les Editions Ouvrières, 1968, p. 13, has made a list based on press cuttings from *Le Monde* and including

obviously been a certain amount of cross-fertilisation, no evidence of conspiracy exists and no serious observer has pretended that it does.[4] Others have seen it all as a conflict of generations, which is to put the student revolt in approximately the same category as the ones mentioned above. And there is indeed some connection, if only because historically, and in some cases in membership (some rebellious students are 'hippies' and vice-versa), there is an overlap. However, the same reservations that were made about the role-conflict type of explanation apply to the basically similar 'conflict of generation' one.

There are two aspects of the student revolt which in particular distinguish it from the others. The first is that its expression has nearly always been political. Not only is protest against the Vietnam War the most effective general mobiliser of student opinion, but even where the first stirrings of revolt were concerned with purely university problems subsequent agitation has always had an overtly political character; and in the case of Berlin the first incidents in 1965 were directly connected with the twentieth anniversary of the end of Hitler's Nazism.[5] The second is that the phenomenon which student revolt in advanced industrial societies most closely resembles is student revolt in developing countries.[6] Many student movements have played an important role in the early stages of nationalism in the former colonies, and long before the Indonesian students played their part in the overthrow of President Sukarno, twentieth century Latin-American history is full of examples to show that student agitation was a factor with which governments had to reckon almost as much as with army pressure.

These two aspects have been noted before, particularly by some

references to non-student youthful revolts: Austria, Belgium, Czechoslovakia, Denmark, Germany (West and East), Great Britain, Greece, Holland, Ireland, Italy, Luxembourg, Poland, Portugal, Spain, Sweden, Switzerland, Turkey, USSR, Vatican, Yugoslavia.

4. Cf. Robin Davy's articles in *The Times*, 27 May–1 June, and below, p. 57, note 23.

5. Cf. Serge Bosc and Jean-Marcel Bouguereau, 'Le Mouvement des Etudiants Berlinois' in *Les Temps Modernes*, 265, July 1968. Despite the jargon in which it is wrapped up, this is the best study to date (at least in English or French) of the German student revolt; it contains a very useful fifteen page chronological table.

6. This term, like all those used to refer to non-advanced industrial societies, is ambiguous and unsatisfactory. The least 'loaded' is perhaps 'Afro-Asian countries', but as this term is most often used in the context of voting behaviour at the United Nations, it cannot be stretched to include Latin-America.

of the vast number of American scholars who since 1964 have turned their attention to the problems of student movements throughout the world. The majority have given special attention to student agitation in developing countries, but the links between the original stimulus (the student revolt at Berkeley University) and the research undertaken are tenuous, and often seem to have more connection with American foreign policy than with student agitation.[7] A great deal of relevant information is assembled, although it is sometimes rather dubiously classified, but the general theme is summed up in the title of one of the essays in S. M. Lipset's book, *Student Freedom and the Republic of Scholars*, the inference being that those universities which most nearly conform in practice to the ideals of the American university are least likely to be bedevilled by student agitation. This comforting conclusion does not take sufficient account of non-educational factors, although mention is made of them in passing. The most important of these may well prove to be the relationship between higher education and the different stages of economic growth.

That such a relationship exists is obvious now that the advanced industrial societies are crying out for an ever-increasing number of qualified scientists and engineers. It is increasingly recognised, for example, that the State, for purely economic reasons, has more need of its students than its students have of the State.[8] This was not so obvious in the nineteenth century and the first half of the twentieth century when industrialisation and the expansion of education went hand in hand. Higher education was confined to an elite large enough to provide for the needs of the bourgeois capitalists who furnished the financial and creative stimulus for industrialisation, but small enough not to upset the delicate balance between the economic and the social evolution of the countries concerned. However, this functional role of higher education was not recognised at the time; it was considered to be an end in itself. The result was that when the economic consequences of industrialisation impelled these countries to increase their hold on their existing colonies or to acquire new ones, cultural colonisation was added, partly as a justification, partly as a reinforcement, to economic and political colonisation. Higher education was also developed, for much the same reasons, in those countries, such as the Latin

7. Cf. Seymour Martin Lipset (ed.), *Student Politics*, New York, Basic Books, Inc., 1967, and the special issue of *Daedalus*, 97 (1), winter 1968.
8. Cf. Robin Davy, op. cit.

American ones, which although they had acquired political independence were still economically dependent and were kept, as they are today, in a state of permanent industrial under-development. The social and political disequilibrium which followed the emergence of elites with little or no economic function is well known; in colonial territories it engendered nationalism, and in independent ones it encourages chronic political instability. Students, at the pivotal point of the situation and most acutely aware of the difference between the values of liberty, equality, justice and democracy which they were taught and the social and economic reality surrounding them, tended (and still tend today) to react in the most obvious way, by claiming that the political reality at least be brought into harmony with their own expectations.[9]

If these remarks apply to the developing countries it is tempting to enquire whether one of the causes of contemporary student unrest in advanced industrial societies is not also to be found in a new internal disequilibrium. There are in fact some grounds for thinking that this is the case. In Britain, France, Germany and the United States (not to mention Czechoslovakia) there exists a political malaise which is perhaps only the reflection of a deeper problem, the fact that social and political institutions are out of tune with the economy, and the whole structure of society is under some degree of continual strain. One thing that is certain is that the idea according to which higher education is an end in itself, a value that is independent of economic and social needs, has been shown to be a sham. If the ever-increasing numbers of students remain a privileged elite, while they are students, they can no longer be certain of being able to exercise that wider choice which is the prerogative of all privilege. Their future careers and, to an increasing extent, their studies are dictated by the needs of an economy in the political conduct of which they are less and less sure of being able to have an effective say. This is true of all students; it is particularly true of liberal arts students. It is natural that, finding their future expectations frustrated in advance, they should concentrate first on seeing that the values they have been taught, and in particular that of effective democratic control, should be practised within their own universities, in 'the republic of scholars'. But the examples of Germany and France are there to show that this may only be a passing phase. Student agitation is fundamentally political, and as such is linked to problems which concern society as a whole.

9. Cf. Kwame N'Krumah's famous slogan: 'Seek ye first the political kingdom!'

Two of the characteristics of a contemporary industrial economy can be resumed as follows:[10] it is not susceptible of traditional democratic control (which is linked to the fact that the nation-state is no longer an adequate framework); and its effective running requires the mobilisation, in one way or another, of every member of society. In protesting against the first, students also refuse to accept the second, and it is in this respect that their revolt is similar to that of the 'hooligans' and 'hippies' mentioned above. In their different ways they all indicate a refusal to be mobilised, whatever the rewards society offers. Although many of the rebels claim to be protesting against a 'technological' or 'consumer' society, it is by no means certain that this is the real problem. It is equally possible that their basic protest is against the fact of being mobilised at all, and that if the cultural (social, political and educational) environment were different they would happily accept the very type of society they now condemn. In any case, the futility of value-judgements on 'consumer' or 'technological' societies is shown by the fact that alternatives can be envisaged only in terms of the past. This comes out very clearly in the works of Herbert Marcuse, whose writings are supposed to have had some influence on a certain number of student leaders. Although some of his analysis is relevant, and although he has seen clearly enough the importance of elite revolts in advanced industrial societies, much of his work is a plea for a return to the golden age of the independent craftsman. He is in fact as much in the tradition of William Morris and John Ruskin as in that of Aldous Huxley and George Orwell.[11]

If these remarks are valid, and the fundamental problem does turn out to be the fact that nineteenth century culture and its corresponding institutions are no longer in harmony with the economic organisation of society today, then it is likely that France is not a unique case, and that French society does illustrate this

10. Needless to say there are many others, but it is not the purpose of this brief Introduction to elaborate a coherent theory, which would require much more research; all that can be done is to touch on a certain number of ideas which appear to be relevant to the general problem of student agitation.

11. His best known work is *One Dimensional Man*, Boston, The Beacon Press, 1964. For a frivolous, but typical example, see the passage, p. 73, where he extols the merits of love-making in a field as opposed to in a car. This is romantic nonsense; *ceteris paribus* there is no reason why the pleasure should vary from one place to another—provided, of course, that the car is big enough (Marcuse was writing in America). It is only fair to add that Marcuse is aware of the trap, but that does not mean that he always avoids it.

contradiction more fully than others. Nevertheless, like every other country, France presents a certain number of unique features which mean, at the very least, that what happened in France is unlikely to be repeated in exactly the same way elsewhere. Those characteristics of French society most directly relevant to the student revolt, the general strike and the election are described in the appropriate place. A certain number of more general remarks follow in the second part of this Introduction.

2

Looked at from one angle France is a country with a history no longer than that of the United States of America; which explains, among other things, why she has so often given the impression of being in search of a national identity. The French Revolution marked the successful revolt of the bourgeoisie against the *Ancien Régime*, but more than that it was a nationalist revolution, and it is as such above all that reference to it has become the stock-in-trade of revolutionaries throughout the world. The nationalism which so alarmed France's neighbours was first and foremost an internal nationalism. Up to 1789 the various provinces of France were referred to as *nations* and although as a result of a long series of bitter wars, diplomatic marriages and cultural onslaughts they had all become subject to the royal authority in Paris, they had preserved their own dialects, *patois* and even, in some cases, language as well as memories of an independent and not inglorious history. Many of them joined the Revolution, but any hopes they may have had of a minimum of autonomy were soon dashed. A system of elective government at all levels was instituted, but was never put into practice; the intermediate representatives between the people and the central Parliament were not elected but nominated from Paris. French was imposed as the official language, and the injunction that all school lessons should be in French was interpreted in the strictest sense to exclude all local languages from the syllabus.

This process of internal colonisation was continued by Napoleon, who created an extremely efficient and durable but highly centralised administrative system, and by the Third Republic, in the early days of which children who spoke *patois* in class were punished and their parents victimised. The result was not the immediate destruction of all local culture; as late as the 1930s a President of the Republic

21

like Gaston Doumergue was happy to speak *patois* in his provincial home, and in the early 1950s it was still possible for a Frenchman to travel in parts of Brittany without being able to understand a word of what was being said around him. But the fact that social and economic advancement was only possible in French meant that local culture could only survive in backward areas. Today there is little trace of the immense cultural, and even ethnic, diversity that was France apart from the still discernible differences between the land and the people north of the Loire, the country of the *langue d'oïl*, and those south of the Loire, the country of the *langue d'oc*.

It was perhaps necessary and inevitable that some degree of cultural homogeneity should be imposed in order to give an appearance of unity within the arbitrary geographical frontiers, but the manner in which it was carried out was extremely brutal and definitive. A trivial but significant example is the history of the French flag. Unlike the Union Jack, which is composed in equal proportions of the flags of the three members of the Union, the French national flag has always been that of one or other of the towns or dynasties imposed on the whole of the country. The Tricolour, which in its composition although not its present form dates from 1789, symbolises a compromise between the royal white and the red and blue of Paris. But the white is also the rest of France, and the manner in which it is sandwiched between the colours of Paris illustrates well enough the stranglehold that the capital city has maintained on the rest of the country.

The process by which Paris extended its influence over the whole of France had of course been going on for some time, but the Revolution put a seal on it. From then on the term *nation* was used to refer to the country as a whole, and history books were written in a teleological light; everything that happened before 1789 converged towards the creation of the French nation. As time went on this period began to be considered as a sort of pre-history; real history began in 1789. Although every French schoolboy learns the pre-history along with the rest, he rarely refers to anything that happened before 1789, and he is in general much better informed on nineteenth and twentieth century history than his British counterpart. Political references never go beyond the French Revolution, and very often do not stop short of it. The ritual of left-wing parties includes references to Marx, 1848, 1871, and 1936, but 1789 always tends (implicitly or explicitly) to occupy pride of place. Right-wing parties are less historically minded, but the

22

nationalism of the right is also influenced by the Jacobins. The French Revolution and the Declaration of the Rights of Man occupy the same place in French political mythology as the Constitution, the Declaration of Independence and the Gettysburg oration do in American political mythology.

Inordinate emphasis was also placed on the French language (the rules of which, for the sake of uniformity, rapidly hardened to the point of becoming inflexible) and French culture. By a natural but unjustifiable extension, France's internal cultural mission became a universal one, and it thus was possible to be both left-wing and colonialist, to be against capitalism and for imperialism. Once the idea became accepted that there was only one way to be French, it was not long before the idea took root that there was only one way to be. The race which has a reputation for excessive individualism was able, with a quiet conscience and by a policy of assimilation, to deny all cultural relativism; which among other things made the very notion of decolonisation extremely difficult to accept.

Within the frontiers of France the domination of Paris became one of the facts of life, but the cost was high. Since no deviation from the norm could be tolerated, the administrative structure was not only all-pervasive; it was rigidly inflexible. So magnificent at the time, Napoleon's achievement now seems more of a handicap than an advantage. Moreover, it inspired in a great many Frenchmen an excessive mistrust of all centralised authority. Although the Frenchman could be aroused to intense patriotism at times, his loyalty was to his immediate environment or to the country, but never to the President of the Republic or the Government. This loyalty could be commanded by a single man, a king or an emperor (and, as will be seen in the chapter on Gaullism, this explains a lot), but never by the President of the Republic or the Government. But should that king or emperor abuse his power, or even simply use it, he was overthrown. Regional revolts were rare, but so was civic loyalty. And as the suspicion with which the Frenchman regarded the central authority was reciprocated, the system has tended to perpetuate itself and decentralisation has become doubly difficult.

The French Revolution was also an agricultural revolution, although not in the same sense as the term is used in Britain. A great deal of land was parcelled out to small farmers, and the stringent Napoleonic laws of equal inheritance (which also limited the birthrate among the nineteenth century bourgeoisie) ensured that farms, instead of becoming bigger and more specialised, became smaller and more general. As much of French soil is extremely fertile and general farming, even at subsistence level, is always feasible, farmers did not have the same incentive to leave the land as did the British ones. As recently as 1946, on the eve of what may be termed France's second industrial revolution, there were still as many people employed in agriculture as in industry, and the farming methods used were hopelessly antiquated.

This is one of the reasons why the first French industrial revolution, in the first half of the nineteenth century, was (comparatively speaking) a half-hearted affair. This is true geographically as well as economically. For the line which divides France in two is no longer the historical and cultural one of the Loire, but an economic one which runs approximately from Le Havre south-east to Marseilles. To the north and east of that line France became industrialised, and all the growth areas, in both economic and demographic terms, are to be found in that part; on the northern and central plains farming itself has become an efficient and specialised industry. To the west and south France has remained predominantly rural with a population which is relatively prosperous in some parts, such as the Dordogne, but in others abysmally poor and backward. As late as World War II, for example, it was still possible to find peasant families in the Sarthe department eating off bare boards without plates or cutlery. The population has continually declined, and in recent years this has assumed drastic proportions as more and more abandon an impossible struggle for existence. Despite attempts to persuade or bully industry to go there, the future of France seems irrevocably tied to what is happening the other side of the line.

Other factors connected with France's limited industrial expansion include the fact that, being rich in natural resources and able to feed her population herself, she was not under the same pressure as, for example, Britain, and was able to produce and consume for her own needs behind high tariff barriers. This comparative stagnation was reflected in the relatively slow growth of her population. In 1800 France was the most populous country in Western Europe, but a century later she had fallen behind both Britain and Germany, while in the 1930s the number of deaths registered in France was greater than the number of births. However, since World War II and at the same time as she embarked on her second industrial revolution, France has participated in the general baby boom, but to a greater and more consistent extent than any other non-Communist industrialised country. A glance at the population diagrams (pps. 27–8) shows that since 1946 the number of members of each annual age group regularly exceeds the number of members of any age group born before 1946. In this, with the exception of the USSR, France is unique, and it means that the whole structure of her population is in the process of changing. For example, in June 1968 there were 28,171,635 voters on the electoral roll out of a population of some 50,000,000, but every year during the following five years between 800,000 and 900,000 will become eligible to vote. Although this will be partly offset by deaths, it does mean that the average age of the electorate in 1973 will be considerably less than it was in 1968, and will go on decreasing thereafter.[12]

The consequences of this for employment are also obvious. It means that in every sector France must continue to expand at a rapid rate if she is to keep pace with her demographic expansion. It is possible to see in this one of the causes of the May revolts. For not only is there a great solid wave of youth pushing at the bottom rungs of the social and economic ladder, but there is another wave pushing higher up, immediately after the very small age groups caused by the losses in World War I. But if this is indeed a factor which will have to be taken into account in any final analysis, it is only one among many, as what follows is designed to show.

12. The 21–24 age group formed 8·5% of the electorate in 1967 and 1968, but if the electoral lists had been revised before the June 1968 election the figure would have been nearer 10%.

DOCUMENT 1

France

Seats of Region ●

1	Lille
2	Amiens
3	Rouen
4	Caen
5	Châlons-sur-Marne
6	Nancy
7	Strasbourg
8	Rennes
9	Orléans
10	Nantes
11	Dijon
12	Besancon
13	Poitiers
14	Limoges
15	Clermont-Ferrand
16	Lyon
17	Bordeaux
18	Toulouse
19	Montpellier
20	Marseilles
21	Paris

Mentioned in text ○

22	Avranches
23	Sochaux
24	Flins
25	Cléon
26	Le Havre
27	Arras
28	Vendôme
29	Le Mans
30	Quimper
31	Périgueux
32	St. Brieux
33	Decazeville
34	Grenoble
35	Nice
36	Reims

26

DOCUMENT 2

Population Graphs (Source: INSEE)

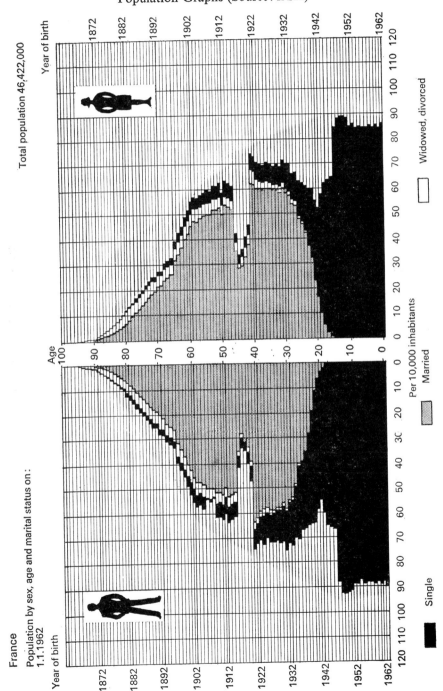

France

Population by sex, age and marital status on:
1.1.1962

Total population 46,422,000

Year of birth

Age

Per 10,000 inhabitants

Widowed, divorced

Married

Single

Population of France by sex and age on:
1.1.1968

Year of birth

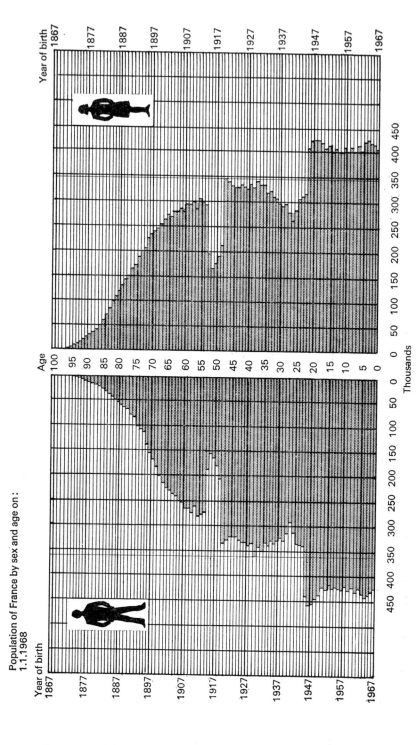

Thin vertical lines denote pre-1945 maxima)

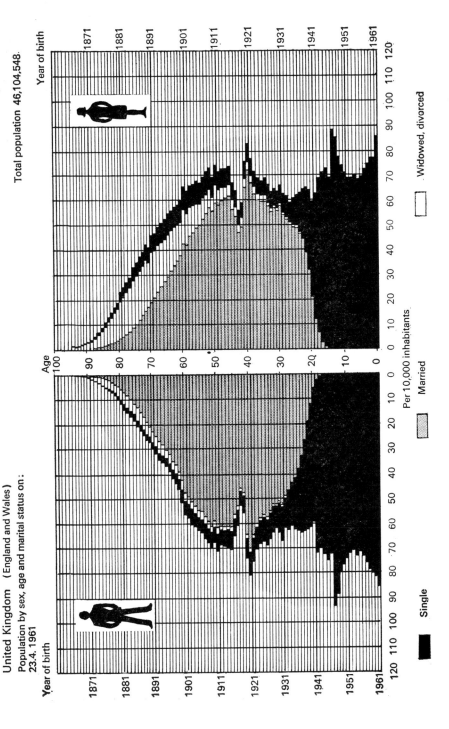

United Kingdom (England and Wales)
Population by sex, age and marital status on:
23.4.1961

Total population 46,104,548.

Year of birth

Age

Per 10,000 inhabitants.

Single   Married   Widowed, divorced

Western Germany

Population by sex, age and marital status on:
6.6.1961

Total population 53,977,400

Year of birth

Year of birth

Age

Per 10,000 inhabitants

Single

Married

Widowed, divorced

Year of birth

1871 1881 1891 1901 1911 1921 1931 1941 1951 1961

1881 1891 1901 1911 1921 1931 1941 1951 1961

THE STUDENT REVOLT

'Ce n'est / qu'un début, / continuons le // combat'*

* The rhythmically chanted slogan finally adopted by the students; earlier they had chanted, to the same staccato rhythm, 'Fouchet, assassin, libérez la Sorbonne!', which was directly taken from 'US, assassin, libérez le Vietnam!'.

INTRODUCTION

THE French educational system did not, like some Minerva, spring fully-armed from the head of Napoleon. In some respects very much a piecemeal affair, it did not receive its final, coherent shape until the 1880s and 1890s. In the form it then took it survived, with only minor alterations occasioned by the massive increase in the school and university population after World War II, until May 1968. At least until 1940 the system functioned remarkably well, insofar as it corresponded well enough to the social and economic infrastructure of French society. Without creating the dominant characteristics of this society, it served to perpetuate and consolidate them in such a way that, while France's second industrial revolution is still having profound effects on her economy, neither the educational system nor the social structure can easily be changed independently of one another.

Louis XIV had already done much towards centralising the French administration. Napoleon extended this policy to education, and the process was continued throughout the century. This meant that the increasing number of children who were taught the three 'r's learnt to speak French and to use the metric system; but as primary education passed beyond the stage of bare literacy, it also meant that the young Breton and the young Provençal (and later the young Algerian and Vietnamese) learned the same history, botany, etc., even if they had little or no connection with their own immediate environment. But perhaps the greatest disadvantage was that changes could only come from above; as many realised, including those who along with Professor Louis Liard attempted in vain to decentralise the University in the 1890s, reform and progress were rendered, if not impossible, at least ten times more difficult.

Up to the French Revolution education had been the exclusive preserve of the Catholic clergy. Napoleon took over from them the idea of consciously using education as a means to an end.[1] He needed officers and cadres to continue his work, and his skeleton outline of

1. Many of the characteristics of the present system were formulated at this time: the unity of secondary and higher education, the tolerance of a private (i.e. Catholic) system alongside the state one, and the overall authority of the State over both systems.

B

a secondary and higher education system was directed towards this end. But the universities, with the exception of the faculties of law and medicine, scarcely existed after 1795, so instead of attempting the huge task of giving life to them again, he created the military school at Saint Cyr, reorganised the Polytechnique (the first of the *grandes écoles*, devoted to forming a highly qualified industrial elite but with no provision for research), and resurrected the *Ecole Normale Supérieure* founded by the Convention, for the education of secondary school teachers. The primary task of the university faculties became to produce examiners for the *baccalauréat*; students were practically an unknown quantity until the 1880s, and if lectures had not been thrown open to the public and become social occasions, there would often have been no-one to listen to them.

However, it was in the field of primary education that the ideological struggle and objectives were most apparent. At the beginning of the nineteenth century primary schools as such did not exist; here and there a teacher, dependent for his living on what suspicious parents would give him and extra work done for the *curé*, did what he could without any proper facilities. In 1833 Guizot, the man whose advice to a cautious bourgeoisie was '*Enrichissez-vous!*', did much to spread education, particularly by making it compulsory for every department to have at least one primary teacher training school. But the influence of the clergy remained preponderant; attendance was irregular, and the precarious financial and social position of the teacher laid him open to all sorts of pressures which the Church did not hesitate to use. Even so, illiteracy fell from over 50% in 1830 to under 20% in 1880, by which time there were only 159 communes in France without a primary school. Thus when the founders of the Third Republic turned their attention to education, they did so less with the object of making France literate than of making her Republican. For this purpose it was necessary to eliminate the influence of the Church. Primary education became free and compulsory[2], and teachers' salaries were raised to make them independent of the local *curé*, although they were still allowed to take the extremely influential (and 'Republican') post of secretary to the Mayor. These men who then went out to 'republicanise' the countryside, were loyal, dedicated and austere. For them the enemy was less religion than the clergy, and their undoubted liberalism, based like that of John Stuart Mill on a predominantly classical

2. Up to the age of twelve to begin with, later increased to fourteen, and in 1959 theoretically, although not in practice, increased again to sixteen.

education, was tainted by more than a streak of Kantian puritanism. The combination of transcendence (the Republic is more than the sum of its local representatives) and of the categorical imperative (a very strict moral and physical discipline) corresponded to their ideals. To this must be added the intense patriotism inherited from the Revolution. Their task, which they willingly accepted, was to form ideal citizens of the French Republic.

The nature of the ideal may have changed somewhat over the years, but the notion that the child is something to be fitted (forced, if necessary) into a pre-determined mould, while it did not originate in that period, found then its fullest expression, and has never been seriously questioned since. Teaching methods are different in the primary and secondary schools, but in both cases it is taken for granted that *educere* means not to 'draw out' the innate and infinitely varied qualities of the child but to 'lead' him 'up' to conform as closely as possible to the cultural model proposed and exemplified by the teacher. This approach is shared by parents: the French love small children, but once the child has reached 'the age of reason' (seven), he is expected to forget to a large extent that he is a child and to behave like a miniature adult. Such an attitude, typical of the nineteenth century bourgeoisie everywhere, is still much in evidence today, and it is reasonable to suppose that one of the factors contributing to its survival is the French school system.

For the French system was, and is, essentially bourgeois. While the precise nature of the political regime was disputed by a large and influential minority of Frenchmen there could be argument about the exact contours of the cultural model. But at no time was the basic structure of society questioned. From the beginning the primary school was considered to be the school of the 'people', and such it has remained ever since. The *lycées* and the universities, to all intents and purposes, have not ceased to be the exclusive preserve of the middle classes (the upper classes tended to patronise the Catholic schools). Many a son of an agricultural worker became a primary school teacher; beyond that there was little opening apart from the civil service. The examination sanctioning the end of compulsory education took place two years after entrance to the *lycée*. For those who wished to stay on at school, 'complementary courses' were introduced. These later became *Collèges d'Enseignement Général*, but remained part of the primary system. Teachers still address pupils as 'tu' in primary schools and the CEG, but not in *lycées,* and if the subjects taught lack much of the pretentious superfluous-

35

ness that characterised the *lycées*, no attempts were made until after World War II to remedy the crying need, which was noted as far back as the French Exhibition of 1878, for something to replace the lack of an effective apprenticeship system. Moreover, the primary schools were free, but the *lycées* did not become so until 1933, and even then, to replace the economic filter a system of 'pupil counselling' was introduced which served much the same purpose.

Further, the education dispensed by the *lycées* gives an enormous advantage to the child from a 'cultured' home. There are of course exceptions, and they are increasingly numerous, but the 'swot' has as much difficulty in a French *lycée* as the grammar schoolboy at Oxbridge. For if the education is no longer as uniformly classical in content as it was,[3] it is still to a large extent so in form. The most important item on the programme is the general essay, for which the subjects are mostly taken from French literature. The teacher will give the outline, and the pupils have only to fill it in. But what matters far more than what they say is how they say it. When he comes to the 'fair copy' the teacher will give a sort of public performance, *un cour magistral*, in which by his stylistic virtuosity and purity he will show what it is to be a cultured, civilised Frenchman. This serves not only to underline the goal to which his pupils should aspire, but to demonstrate, by making it plain that he has already reached it, the teacher's invincible superiority and indeed his very *raison d'être*.

The reason for this attitude is to a large extent to be found in the internal coherence of the system. From the end of the nineteenth century onwards the main function of the universities has been to perpetuate the secondary and higher educational systems. Although enormously expanded and reorganised in the 1880s,[4] research and career-oriented teaching was subordinated to the need to provide professors and teachers who would continue to propagate a 'disinterested' general culture. From the basic *licence* (licence to teach) to the prestigious State Arts Doctorate (which usually involves at least twenty years' work), every degree gives the right to teach at the appropriate level in the hierarchy. The exact level depends entirely

3. By 'classical' should be understood the classical Latin language. Silver Latin was ignored as much as Roman history, and Greek occupied, and still does, a relatively minor place.

4. Napoleon had created 29 university regions (the same as the 29 judicial ones), and these were reduced to 15. Strasbourg was added after 1918 and since 1962 Nantes, Orléans, Rheims, Amiens, Rouen, Limoges and Nice.

on the amount of knowledge accumulated and in no way on the ability to communicate it to students or pupils (with the sole exception of the *Certificat d'Aptitude au Professorat de l'Enseignement Secondaire*, created in 1950 to supplement the supply of teachers and which includes one year's probation). The *agrégation*, the highest teaching diploma and one of the most exclusive examinations in France, involves giving a model lesson; but this is not judged from the point of view of the candidate's future pupils, but in terms of how his peers would judge his future 'fair copies'.

Although it is certainly legitimate to judge this system very severely in terms of the 1960s, it worked very well, within its limits, up to World War II, and certainly some of its products have given it a reputation which perhaps it never quite deserved. Moreover, it should not be isolated from other, particularly economic, factors. Much more research would be needed to establish causal links, if they exist, but it is a fact that the growth of primary and secondary education in France coincided with France's first industrial revolution. From the 1880s onwards the numbers of secondary school-children in France remained fairly stable; and France's economy and population had both ceased to grow as well.[5] The abolition of secondary school fees put the curve of secondary education into another steady climb, and after the war the new economic boom and continual population expansion produced a situation with which the system was unable to cope. Like the French economy and French culture in general, it had too long remained closed and class-bound; when it was forced to become more democratic it did so quantitatively rather than qualitatively, with the results that May 1968 brought home to everybody—gross overcrowding combined with a fundamental inability to adapt to post-war needs.

Such modifications as were brought about will be illustrated in Chapter 1, which is in the main devoted to showing how the system works from the point of view of a child. Given the political reper-

5. In the nineteenth century the educational growth areas also corresponded with the economic ones: in other words there was a clear split between the dynamic and backward parts of the country (cf. Introduction, p. 24)—although as this equivalence no longer exists today (for reasons which remain obscure) it would be rash to draw any conclusions from it. For these comparisons and much else the author is indebted to Antoine Prost, *Histoire de l'Enseignement en France, 1800–1967*, Paris, Armand Colin, 1968. It is a mine of intelligently presented information and documents; cf. also F. Ridley, 'The French Educational System; policy and administrative aspects', in *Political Studies*, 11, 2 June 1963, pp. 178–202.

cussions of the May revolt, it is also important to take at least a brief look at the political socialisation of Frenchmen, both in general and in terms of student politics. Chapter 2 is a straightforward account of recent student unrest and its culmination in the events of May and June, while Chapter 3, it is hoped, will give some idea of how the schoolchildren and students perceived their own revolt, and what it was they were after.

DOCUMENT 3

Growth of Education in France

(Source: A. Prost, *op. cit.*)

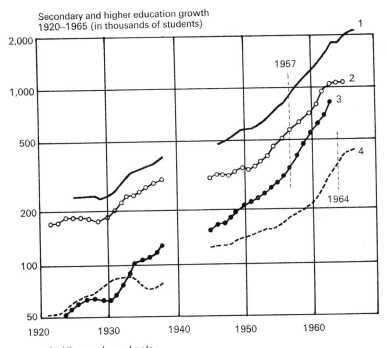

Secondary and higher education growth
1920–1965 (in thousands of students)

1. All secondary schools
2. *Lycées*
3. Prolonged primary education
4. University faculties

DOCUMENT 4

French School and University Population
(Source: A. Prost, *op. cit.*)

French school and university population by age
and type of establishment 1965–1966
(including private schools)

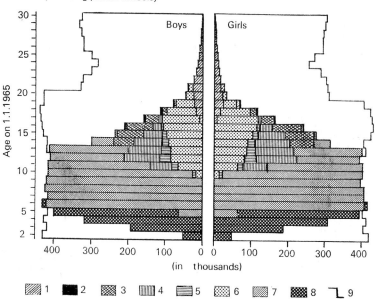

(in   thousands)

1. Universities
2. Primary Teacher-Training schools
3. Elementary technical schools
4. C.E.G. (public and private)
5. C.E.S.

6. *Lycées* and private secondary schools
7. Primary schools
8. Pre-primary schools
9. Total population

DOCUMENT 5

Growth of University Population, 1957-1967
(in thousands of students)

UNIVERSITIES	1957–58	1958–59	1959–60	1960–61	1961–62	1962–63	1963–64	1964–65	1965–66	1966–67
Paris	68·8	70·5	69·9	77·8	81·6	93·9	106·7	110·7	105·8	130·0
Lyon	9·9	10·7	11·3	13·3	15·3	17·3	20·1	21·6	24·7	29·3
Bordeaux	10·7	11·3	12·6	12·3	13·8	16·0	18·9	20·8	21·8	25·8
Lille	9·4	10·6	10·8	11·5	13·1	14·6	16·7	16·1	19·0	21·7
Toulouse	9·4	10·1	11·0	12·1	14·6	17·2	20·5	21·2	23·2	26·8
Nantes	—	—	—	—	4·2	4·7	5·8	6·8	7·9	9·3
Strasbourg	6·3	6·9	7·7	8·5	11·7	13·4	14·1	14·1	15·7	17·1
Grenoble	6·1	7·1	7·7	10·0	10·5	13·0	15·3	14·3	15·5	18·4
Nancy	6·3	6·8	6·8	8·3	8·7	9·8	11·1	11·1	12·9	15·3
Clermont-Ferrand	3·4	3·7	4·3	4·7	5·5	6·0	7·0	8·1	8·8	10·5
Rennes	9·7	9·9	10·5	11·1	9·3	9·8	11·7	13·4	14·7	17·3
Dijon	2·8	3·1	3·4	3·7	4·6	5·3	6·2	6·6	7·7	8·8
Reims	—	—	—	—	1·3	1·5	2·3	3·0	3·4	4·8
Orléans	—	—	—	—	1·6	2·5	3·4	5·4	6·2	7·6
Montpellier	8·3	8·9	9·6	10·5	13·4	15·7	17·6	19·3	19·2	21·5
Caen	4·8	5·3	5·5	6·4	7·4	8·5	10·5	8·0	9·0	10·0
Besançon	2·0	2·2	2·7	2·2	2·9	3·4	3·8	4·7	5·3	6·4
Poitiers	5·6	5·9	6·6	6·8	6·3	7·4	8·6	9·4	8·6	9·1
Aix-Marseille	12·0	13·1	14·4	15·5	19·0	22·2	26·0	28·6	23·5	28·7
Amiens	—	—	—	—	—	—	—	1·6	2·8	3·7
Rouen	—	—	—	—	—	—	—	4·1	5·1	6·0
Limoges	—	—	—	—	—	—	—	—	1·9	2·4
Nice	—	—	—	—	—	—	—	—	5·9	7·1
Total	175·5	186·1	194·8	214·7	244·8	282·2	326·3	348·9	368·6	437·6

B*

CHAPTER ONE

A FRENCHMAN'S UPBRINGING
AND EDUCATION

'*Dans le personnage pirandellien, l'intolérable prison des formes se dramatise dans la souffrance de la forme la plus intimement inutile mais pourtant la plus constitutionnelle de son chaos intérieur, la raison: et entre ses illusions grotesques affleure la plus risible et la plus pénible de ses illusions, la vaine logique. Dans ces moments, qui couvrent en grande partie la soi-disant surface rationnelle, le soi-disant artifice de la dramaturgie de Pirandello, la raison est passion et condamnation de l'homme, cri de l'existence qui invoque l'essence: contemplation et poésie et en définitive pirandelliennement théâtre.*'

This untranslatable—and deliriously incomprehensible— nonsense was given in 1968 to candidates for the *agrégation* in Italian to discuss in a seven-hour essay.

ALL generalisations are to some extent abusive, and this chapter will inevitably be full of them. France is an extremely varied country, and customs and traditions vary from one region to another, not to mention the differences which exist between the country and the town and between the various social classes. However, the one thing which is uniform everywhere is the educational system, and as there is a certain amount of interaction between the attitudes it engenders and those which parents adopt towards their children, some degree of extrapolation is perhaps legitimate. For example, one such attitude, and probably the most important, concerns the recognition of a hierarchical system of authority. In certain country regions after the War the swaddling of babies in such a way that they could not move their legs was still common practice.[1] It is probably much less so today, but although Dr Spock's books are now obtainable they tend to be bought as works of reference rather than for the liberal precepts they contain, and even the most progressive young

1. Cf. Lucien Bernot and René Blancard, *Nouville, un village français*, Paris, Institut d'Ethnologie, 1953, pp. 112–14. Geoffrey Gorer has somewhere remarked on the importance of swaddling in Russia, a country which has a long tradition of centralised authoritarian government.

couples are amazed at the amount of freedom young British and American parents allow their children. And from their earliest days most French children will see their mother do all the housework, with or without the help of a maid, even if both parents work. Although there are a small but increasing number of exceptions, the male in the French family does not lift a finger except for odd jobs (the 'man in apron' cartoon image scarcely exists), and the mother will even wait on grown-up student or working sons. The father appears to the child as the exact replica of the 'father figure', an image itself drawn originally from nineteenth century bourgeois society.[2]

The hierarchical authoritarian nature of his relationships with adults is confirmed for the child when he goes to primary school, but the spread of pre-primary education has made this transition much more difficult. *L'école maternelle*, or kindergarten, received its final form in 1921, and is in many ways a model of its kind. Due largely to the efforts of one woman, Pauline Kergomard, the children are not taught but learn through 'exercises' and games, and the teacher is not separated from the children but works among them. No one method is dominant; for example, extensive use is made of Montessori material, although not always in the same spirit in which she designed it. Its freedom to develop and experiment has meant that French pre-primary education is very eclectic, and as long as it was restricted to a small number of children it was very successful. But by 1965 roughly 75% of children between four and six years old took advantage of it with the result that classes became too big and teachers (in the majority of cases primary school teachers with a special diploma) too conscious of the problems of their colleagues in the primary schools; to an increasing extent the older children find themselves in a traditional classroom setting being taught the rudiments of the three 'r's. However, the free open atmosphere is still very different from that which the child will encounter in the primary school, and many who go from one to the other have to go through a long and painful period of adjustment.

For from the moment the child enters the primary school his life there is regimented. Every day the children wait for their teacher

2. For a detailed account of the bringing up of children, attitudes towards cleanliness, discipline, etc., see Laurence Wylie, *Village in the Vaucluse*, Harvard University Press, 1957. Although the study was made in a small country village much has universal relevance and can be confirmed by anyone who has lived in France.

in the covered courtyard, line up in crocodile formation when he arrives, and follow him in silence to the classroom where he takes his place on the raised dais in front of the class. From there knowledge is dispensed and order kept by a discipline which the fact that the most severe punishment is all too often public ridicule only renders more effective. The child is quickly made to realise that he is no longer a small person whose individual qualities are to be developed but an object to be moulded according to a certain pattern, and any variations from the norm are quickly suppressed. A spirit of competition is also inculcated; if the child is not immediately aware of the importance of the marks he gets, the reactions of his parents, his teacher and his schoolmates will quickly enlighten him. And the highest marks do not always go to the most intelligent child; the way the work is set out, the neatness of the handwriting and so on count for a great deal, and even trivial mistakes in dictation and sums are heavily marked down. Moreover, the syllabus, any connection of which with the future *lycée* syllabus is quite fortuitous, is worked out in some unreal world where children are not children but IBM machines which only need programming. Far too much is expected of them, not only in quantity (until ten years ago even the tiny tots were taking back written homework to do), but also in quality. Nearly every arithmetical and grammatical concept appears in the French syllabus one or two years before it does in that of other countries.

Under these conditions the recommended pedagogy inevitably goes by the board. Confronted by an impossible syllabus and by larger and larger classes, and to an increasing extent untrained,[3] teachers tend to opt for the easy way out, to teach from the book and make the children learn by rote. A few, especially in the country where there is less control from above and fewer pressures from anxious parents and harassed colleagues, try to apply the principles laid down by Ferdinand Buisson and Paul Lapie (1887 and 1923 respectively), divide their classes into smaller work-groups, and encourage the children to learn by experience and experiment. But in general the intuitive, inductive method gives way to the deductive one, so much more akin to the French cultural model. A general rule is enounced, and one or two examples are learnt by heart;

3. In 1964 roughly one teacher in three had not had any teacher-training. These are expected to learn their profession on the spot and by following courses on Thursdays (there is no school in France on Thursdays, in theory so that the Church may organise religious instruction for those who want it).

when this has been done often enough the child learns to identify every particular case by the general rule under which it can be subsumed. This principle is applied, *mutatis mutandis*, in every field, including history and geography. One is what one is because one's historical and geographical environment has made one so. The idea that one might want to look outwards, to explore, master and possibly change the environment is quite alien. The best that can be hoped for is to preserve one's situation against outside intrusion ('*Ca va?*' '*Ca se défend.*').

The system works for some, but by no means for everybody. It often happens that the child who is top of his class in the primary school goes to the bottom in the *lycée* which, for all its faults, does demand some sort of positive intelligence. Further, at the beginning of the century the illiteracy rate settled down at 4% of every age group; today it is still 3·4%, a figure which can no longer be explained away by social phenomena such as agricultural absenteeism, immigrant children, etc. But it is the long term social and political consequences of primary education which are the most important. Primary teachers and headmasters are intensely loyal to the primary system and make themselves doubtless unwitting tools of the class system by explaining to parents whose children are considered apt for further education that they will be much happier with the CEG, which is part of the primary system, than they will with the *lycée* (see Document 6). But they are immensely aided in this task by the primary education itself, which tends to make both parents and children suspicious of the unknown, of a radical change in their social situation ('the *lycée's* not for the likes of us'). Once again it becomes apparent that the weeding-out process depends as much on the content of what is taught as on any artificial barriers. The result is that whereas there is no question but that every bourgeois boy and girl goes to the *lycée* only 45% of workers' sons do, and probably considerably fewer of their daughters.[4]

However, the most vicious part of the system becomes apparent when it is realised that, while children are obliged to remain in school until they are fourteen, secondary education is not compulsory.

4. It is only at the pre-primary and university levels that the sexes are not systematically segregated. In the provinces the primary schools are sometimes integrated, but for financial and administrative reasons, not as a matter of policy: in general the same goes for the *lycées*, although the policy now is to make them all integrated. It was not until 1924 that girls could take the same *baccalauréat* as boys, and their syllabus did not really become identical until 1930.

In October 1966 there were just under 850,000 boys and girls of eleven years old, the age at which secondary education normally begins. Less than 25 % of these went to a *lycée* or Catholic secondary school; roughly 40 % went on to some form of secondary education within the primary system (CEG or CES); which leaves 35 % to be divided among the few technical schools, the special schools for handicapped children—and the primary schools, where probably the majority just sit out their time until they can join the already overcrowded labour market.[5]

The consequences of all this for the continued stratification of French society in nineteenth century terms is obvious. The influence of the primary school on the political socialisation of the French child is no less great, although somewhat less evident. This influence is for the most part indirect. For, despite the rules and regulations, 'civic instruction' takes up on average only a quarter of an hour a week of class time (this rises to an hour every fortnight in the *lycées*), but it is nevertheless significant that the teacher, in order to respect the 'neutrality' of education, confines himself to describing the bare outlines of French political institutions without attempting to give an idea of how they work in practice (no French schoolboy has ever taken part in a mock general election, for example, and the very idea would produce shrieks of horror). A recent study of four hundred or so Grenoble schoolchildren[6] shows that the process of political socialisation is rather more devious. The replies of the children show that political concepts like authority and justice are familiar to them, but also that as soon as politics intervenes openly the second term becomes much less important than the first.

The very principle of the use of coercion by those with political power is accepted by the members of the community from their earliest years; in a way it is the continuation of the coercion which is accepted within the more intimate framework of the family.[7]

(And, one might add, of the school.)

5. The percentages are rough calculations based on figures published by *le Service Central des Statistiques et de la Conjoncture du Ministère de l'Education Nationale*. The situation would doubtless be slightly improved if there were more CES, but local councils, for example, prefer for prestige reasons to build a *lycée* even though a CEG or a CES would be more useful.

6. C. Roig and F. Billon-Grand, *La socialisation politique des enfants: conribution à l'étude de la formation des attitudes politiques en France*, Paris, A. Colin, 1968.

7. Ibid., p. 111. Author's translation.

This acceptance of authoritarianism in others and submission in oneself is reinforced as soon as the motherland is in question; for the seeds of an intense patriotism are sown very early.

The origins of the great symbolic value attached to the motherland, of the patriotic myth, should probably be sought first of all in national traditions (holidays, public ceremonies, the respect or ritual with which everything touching the motherland is enveloped), and secondly in the way history and geography are taught. . . . There can be found the image of a country to whom nature has been partial—a country with a good geographical position, well-balanced and harmonious—the image of a France who is a mother to all her children, the image of a France whose destiny places her above all others.[8]

But perhaps the most important aspect is one which has been noted by all acute observers of the French scene,[9] the emptiness of the political arena. There are only two important social entities in the life of a Frenchman, the family cell and the State. Intermediary institutions, whether they be schools, clubs, trade unions or political parties, count for nothing, and this comes across very clearly in the study. Politics are perceived as essentially a question of private, individual conscience. The classic defence of this state of affairs[10] is that the absence of commitment to anything but an abstract authority, symbolised by the State, leaves the individual with the greatest possible degree of liberty of thought and action. The first is true but not the second. The Frenchman reserves his judgment, and often voices his disagreement (nothing resembles one Frenchman grumbling about his taxes so much as another Frenchman grumbling about his taxes), but he ends up by accepting and obeying the central authority. A coercive force (teacher, factory-situation, the State) exists and is obeyed; to participate, directly or by intermediate institutions, would be to deprive oneself of the freedom not to commit oneself. This combination of private judgment and public obedience is very much an aristocratic virtue,[11] and is very difficult to practice. It is in fact only possible for those who can define themselves independently of, and in isolation from, others—for example, the aristocracy. As this is impossible for the great majority,

8. *Ibid.*, p. 72. Author's translation.
9. Such as Laurence Wylie, *op. cit.*
10. E.g., Antoine Prost, op. cit., pp. 343–4.
11. For the persistence of aristocratic values in French society see Jesse Pitts' contribution to Stanly Hoffman, *et al.*, *France: Change and Tradition*, London, Gollancz, 1963.

small atomised islands of group solidarity are formed, school-children against the teacher, the workers on a particular shop-floor, etc. These groups are quite uninstitutionalised; unspoken, unconscious even, their function is to fill the void between family and external authority, while keeping up the pretence of untrammelled liberty. This does not, of course, mean that normal democratic institutions are not used, or serve no purpose; but it does explain in part why Frenchmen find it so natural to vote negatively, for instance.

To sum up, the classic defence of non-commitment in terms of the maximum degree of personal liberty which it allows overlooks one thing which the Greeks never forgot: that man is first and foremost a social animal. The primary school is not alone responsible for this state of affairs, but its role is a very important one. As one trade union militant has put it,

The fact that the workers have difficulty in persuading themselves that a meeting can have any effect on a decision does not say much for the education they were given or for the way they have been conditioned since childhood. At primary school they had barely learned to read, write and do sums, skills quite inadequate for a world as large and as pretentious as ours. No one has ever taught them to think for themselves nor above all how to behave in a group, that is to say to acquire the rudimentary notions of living in society. They have to learn that at their work-place, and it must be admitted that the modern factory, with its robot work-system, is not exactly the ideal place for that. As for the trade union movement, it is far from filling the gap left by the primary school and does not prepare the militant for the spreading of this civic culture among the working class.[12]

*

At the *lycée* this process of socialisation continues, but it affects a smaller number, and in any case the most effective and durable socialisation always takes place in the pre-pubic years (from this point of view the British private preparatory school is much more dangerous than the public school). It is at the *lycée*, however, that the elitist bias of the system becomes most apparent.[13] The principal

12. D. Mothé, *Militant chez Renault*, Paris, Le Seuil, 1965 (author's translation), quoted in Roig and Billon-Grand, op. cit., p. 165. For a discussion of the implications for the political system, see Part III, Introduction.

13. Edgar Faure's 1968 reforms have changed the situation here described to some extent, but not a great deal; cf. the author's article in *New Society*, 14 November 1968.

function of the *lycée* is to prepare for the *baccalauréat* which gives the right to go to university, but by a process of direct and indirect selection the fall-out rate is extremely high; a worker's son for example has only a 2% chance of becoming a university student.

The process begins, as might be expected, at the beginning. As soon as the child enters the sixth form (the bottom class) he has to decide whether or not he is going to do Latin. The great majority, especially those whose parents have done Latin, decide to do it, while the few who opt for the 'modern' section (leading to a modern languages and mathematics *baccalauréat*) are looked down on by everybody; for Latin, the great sign of a 'cultured' background, was until very recently demanded at the *baccalauréat* level of those who specialise in physics and chemistry. At the end of two years the child can take the *Certificat d'Etudes Primaires*, but few *lycées* bother with it; there is however a counselling session in which in theory the weaker members are weeded out and encouraged to continue their education elsewhere. In practice, this does not often happen partly for administrative reasons (frequently the nearest CEG is not in the same administrative district as the *lycée*) and partly because teachers are well aware of the fact that there is nowhere to send them; all other educational institutions are full to overflowing.

Two years later, at the end of the first cycle, there is an examination which entitles the successful candidate to the *Brevet d'Etudes du Premier Cycle*, which also sanctions the end of a career in a CEG.[14] Those who are going on to the second cycle (leading to the *baccalauréat*) are not obliged to take it, and many do not; for the vast majority, on average nearly two-thirds of the total, who leave school then, it is essential. With the increasing number of children staying on at school its function has changed; whereas twenty years ago the BEPC was enough to ensure entry into a technical college, this is no longer the case and employers demand it for jobs for which twenty years ago a CEP would have satisfied them. This, combined with the still prevalent, but increasingly (and for the same reasons) false idea that the sole purpose of the *baccalauréat* is to grant access to the university, is one reason why there is such a heavy drop-out from school at the end of the first cycle. Those who see no point in going on to the second cycle unless they intend to go to university, even if they are capable of doing

14. The CES and the CEG, as well as the *lycée*, take children up to the end of the first cycle, but only the *lycée* goes on to the second one. The remarks in this paragraph therefore concern all three types of establishment.

so, prefer to opt either for such jobs as they can get with the BEPC or for such technical and professional schools as luck and the BEPC can get them into.[15]

Although many leave school at this stage, few leave the *lycée*. Many who have little or no hope of passing their *baccalauréat* continue either because there is no other educational alternative or because their parents hope nevertheless that they will eventually succeed in scraping through and thus distinguishing themselves from the rest of the population. A few brave ones come into the *lycées* from the CEG but in view of the difficulties they have to overcome certainly not as many as are intellectually qualified. For they almost certainly need grants, and grants are comparatively hard to come by and usually inadequate. To justify their parents' sacrifices they must be certain of succeeding, but the education they have received up till then is not the same as that of the *lycéens*; in particular, they do not have the same stylistic mastery of their own language. Before the Fouchet reforms of 1966, the *baccalauréat* was taken in two parts, the first after two years and the second after another year. Although cumbersome, this system at least had the merit of enabling the less gifted, or the less well adapted but persistent, pupils to come away with their 'first bac.' Under the present system there is only one examination, for which an average of 50% in every paper is required, and the failure rate is extremely high (40–45%). Those who fail have little to show for the fact that they have stayed at school until the age of eighteen. There is no reason why they should, since theoretically the *baccalauréat*'s function is still to serve as a passport to university. In practice, however, employers demand it for nearly every 'middle-class' type of job. The degree of callous wastage inherent in the system is obvious.

15. Pierre Bourdieu, 'L'Ecole conservatrice; les inégalités devant l'école et devant la culture', in *La Revue française de sociologie*, 7 (3), September 1966, claims that with a matrix consisting of cultural and environmental variables alone (i.e. irrespective of any differences in infant IQs) it is possible to predict accurately at what point any given child's educational career will end, and with what degree of success. One such variable would certainly be the existence of a local *lycée*. For in the nineteenth century, under the Napoleonic system, *lycées* were scattered in a regular pattern over the whole country. Since the 1880s, when education became a matter of political concern, and up to 1960, the majority of new *lycées* were built in areas which vote radical or socialist, such as the south-west of France. In industrial areas, where a regular supply of semi-skilled labour was required, far fewer *lycées* were built—cf. Y. Legoux, 'Disparité de la formation des adolescents: l'exemple des petites villes', in *Etudes et Documents*, 21, 1968; the study was carried out by MM. Sceaux and Châtelain.

Before the war this did not matter very much; the bourgeois parent could usually be sure of finding a job for his son or a husband for his daughter, *baccalauréat* or no *baccalauréat*. Nowadays, from the moment a child enters the *lycée* he is under constant and in some cases intolerable pressure to succeed. At home marks and reports are cause not only for comment but often for sanctions as well. At the same time the child has to face a school environment which, if different from that of the primary school, is no less authoritarian and restrictive. Greater demands are made on the pupil's intelligence, but everything is directed towards passing the *baccalauréat*, an examination which requires a considerable amount of knowledge, but even more the mastery of a particular way of expressing it. The basic method in philosophy and French which, with Latin, are the key subjects, is that of commenting on a given passage from a well-known author. Such passages are collected together in text-books, and the traditionally brilliant pupil is the one who can expound, in the most stylistically harmonious way, the received view on an isolated passage of Montaigne, Descartes, or Pascal.

No attempt is made to divert the eyes of the pupil from this goal, even for a moment. Few *lycées* have libraries, which in any case are optional and may be abolished by the next headmaster. No attempt is made to teach pupils how to use them or, where one does not exist, the municipal library (an institution which is sadly neglected and underdeveloped in France). No newspaper is allowed inside the building, and extra-curricular activities, where they exist, rarely go beyond a theatre group or choral society. In short, it is assumed from beginning to end that culture is in every home (for are not all equal?), that the school is neutral concerning religious, social, and political problems, and that its only purpose in life is to turn out standardised intellectual products according to a given pattern.

The teachers also are prisoners of the system. Brought up themselves to believe in the overriding virtue of reason, they seek to disseminate the ideal of a disinterested culture by the most rational means. Because it is all most rational, there is no room for alternative methods, no room for cultural relativism (hence the number of Frenchmen who still believe in the universal value of the French language and French culture much as the British once did in that of British justice). This, at its worst (or best) gives rise to a classroom attitude which has been cruelly but not inaccurately satirised:

In the classroom he was like a schoolmaster in his church, among the faithful; or a shepherd playing the flute for his sheep. In actual fact, the shepherd plays the flute for himself, but the sheep may, if they wish, become music-lovers.[16]

Moreover, their freedom of action is strictly circumscribed.

It should not be forgotten that the object of Napoleon's university system is not only to teach young Frenchmen, but also to supervise the school-masters. A certain amount of distrust was inevitably created by the political positions adopted by the teaching body during the nineteenth century and after. Napoleon III forbade schoolmasters to wear beards and made them take an oath of allegiance. Whether or not it is necessary to restrict the 'inopportune initiatives' of schoolmasters by a centralised system of programmes and regulations is a matter of opinion. But the system exists.[17]

And it is not only a question of politics. Enmeshed in a professional and administrative hierarchy from which they cannot escape, they are continually supervised, marked (by the Headmaster) and inspected once a year by an Inspector who sits in the back of the class and has a private chat with the teacher afterwards. Under normal circumstances this goes off without incident, but should the teacher let it appear that (as in not infrequently the case) he knows more about teaching his subject than the Inspector, or should he refuse to start the lesson over again (each lesson is a carefully constructed model from which no part should be missing) if the Inspector arrives late, he will be made to suffer for it. He cannot be dismissed, but his application to teach elsewhere will be refused, his salary may arrive late, and his overtime be paid months in arrears. Added to this are all the problems posed by a jealously guarded status and a rigid professional hierarchy; those with the highest academic qualifications (and not the best or the most experienced teachers) are not only paid more but do less work. The teacher is therefore very much a cog in a machine, with little or no control over either his own destiny or that of his profes-

16. M. Toesca, *Hommage à Alain*, Paris 1952, quoted in Gérard Vincent, *Les Professeurs du Second Degré; contribution à l'étude du corps enseignant*, Paris, A. Colin, 1967. Author's translation.
17. Ibid., p. 62. Author's translation. It should be added that Napoleon III's suspicion of the political attitudes of the teaching profession is fully shared by the Gaullists today.

sion.[18] As elsewhere, his social status in the community is not clearly defined; the only place where he can feel really secure is the classroom—on condition that his status there is never challenged by his pupils.

The normal tension common to any classroom is thus multiplied considerably by the exceptionally brittle nature of the relationship between the teacher and his class. If this relationship breaks down, the results is *le chahut*. *Le chahut* is not the same thing as rowdyism, which is a normal, and probably healthy, release of a generally bearable tension. It is much more the implicit recognition by both sides that the system is in fact unbearable,[19] and the teacher who loses the enforced respect and control of his class to the extent of allowing it to happen is pilloried with a cruelty and mercilessness which must be unique.

An increasing number of teachers are aware of the unsatisfactory nature of their own position and of the system in general. According to the survey conducted by Gérard Vincent,[20] only 15% declared themselves positively dissatisfied with their lot, but 35% complained that they knew nothing of psychology or pedagogy and, perhaps most significant of all, only 15% wished the same fate on their children. This suggests that the number of dissatisfied teachers is considerably greater than the number of those who were prepared to admit it openly to themselves. The majority react in a classical manner, by clinging with obstinate faith to what they have been taught and what they teach; for them salvation, or at least some measure of tranquillity, lies within the system as it is.

However, although no accurate data exists on this point, a certain number of younger teachers have been trying, over the past ten years, to improve the system from within by introducing a minimum of human contact. This has usually taken the form of founding co-operatives, clubs, societies and groups run by the pupils themselves. But although these flourish in the few modern 'pilot' *lycées*, elsewhere they are few and far between and, where they do exist, they encounter considerable suspicion and opposition. Despite the fact that they were recognised by the Ministry of Education in

18. According to Gérard Vincent, op. cit., p. 301, this is one reason why so many secondary school teachers have entered politics. As a deputy they can at least have the illusion of being somewhere near the decision-making centres.

19. Of all professions secondary school teachers hold the record for the percentage of mental illnesses. The psychological effects of the system on the children have not yet been the object of a systematic study.

20. Op. cit., pp. 150 and 165.

53

1965, headmasters and the administration remain extremely sceptical. The reason is not hard to find. Those teachers who inspired the movement are almost without exception agreeably surprised by the maturity, sense of responsibility and intelligence of the pupils who take part; the rest see in this a threat (which it undoubtedly is) to the established order. There are also a very few young ones who reject the system altogether. Students during the later phases of the Algerian War, they followed, or took part in, the great debate within the student union on the educational system in general. Their action is inevitably very limited, and for the most part takes the form of attempting to shake their pupils out of the attitude which consists of considering everything the teacher says as holy writ, and of establishing as much personal contact as possible; their great moment came in May 1968 when they were able to canalise the dissatisfaction both of their pupils and of a fair number of their fellow-teachers.

The basic problem is the same at every level. Piecemeal reform from within comes up against the rigid, centralised structure of education in France and the conservatism of a profession which fears change more than it dislikes the *status quo*. And radical changes from above would necessitate a more agonising reappraisal of French society as a whole than most people, let alone teachers, are willing to accept.

*

The young Frenchman who leaves the *lycée* with his *baccalauréat* finds that in many ways his problems are only just beginning. He has little idea of what the real world is like; if he is lucky he will have some elementary notions of economics and perhaps of sociology, although in France the latter has a tendency to resemble philosophy more than anything else. But above all, he will have no idea of what it is to be part of a community, to live in society. Like the workers, he has to learn this on the spot, the hard way, and not always very successfully. For those who do not go to university this may not matter too much; once they have got a job (which is not always easy) their problems are, more or less, solved.

Those, the majority, who do become university students find themselves members of an antiquated and heavily biased institution. Only approximately 10% of French students are from workers' families, as opposed to 25–30% in Britain, although there are twice as many French students as British ones. Moreover the Frenchman

54

stands only a 50–60% chance of coming away with a degree as opposed to the nearly 90% chance of the British student. This 'wastage' is partly due to the appalling student conditions prevalent in France: gross overcrowding (the number of students has quadrupled since 1950 and doubled since 1962, while additional facilities have been provided for only a fraction of the increase), the anonymous situation of the student due to the lack of any contact, let alone a 'human' one, between teachers and taught, and the real poverty of the majority of students without independent means (although tuition fees, food and cultural activities are cheap for students, grants are not only rare but well below subsistence level). But another cause of the failure rate is that little or nothing exists in the way of technical colleges, or junior liberal arts colleges, for those who rightly feel that a couple of years' higher education cannot but do themselves (and in the long run their country) good but do not feel capable of, or tempted by, a traditional degree.[21] This becomes apparent to the future student when he has to decide what he is going to study and where. For, since the French university has always been totally divorced from all social and economic reality (except the teaching profession), there is not much to guide him. It is not therefore surprising that there is an enormous structural imbalance between what the statisticians consider necessary for a modern economy and the choices made by the majority of students, choices dictated in part by the possibilities open to them, and partly by a persistent cultural tradition of which the roots have already been examined.

But the student also has acute social problems. Although fewer now tend to be attracted to Paris, many students have to go outside their home town to find a university. The usual problem of living away from home for the first time is complicated by the acute isolation of French students, both as regards the community in which they live and one another. They themselves have not been taught to live as part of a group, and no integrative structure exists to help them do so; it does not occur to French students to join together to share a flat, and it is not only the high cost of housing that is responsible for this. Neither the parents' home nor the tiny maid's room, which is the lot of many, is conducive to spending

21. The Fouchet reforms of 1966 go some way towards remedying this particular defect, but leave most of the major faults of the system untouched. For an account of them as well as of the academic *cursus honorum* leading to a class of mandarin professors, cf. John Ardagh, op. cit., pp. 322 *et seq.*

the evening at home, either alone or in company. The French café, with its atomised tables and expensive service, is far from fulfilling the integrative role of the British pub. The student's life is spent in one long round between library and lecture-hall (when, which is all too seldom, he can find a place in either), cafés, student canteens and the cinema (it is no accident that French students are so fond of, and so knowledgeable about, the cinema). Neither his own nor others' lodgings can provide the essential environmental base which will give him a minimum of security (hence, during May 1968, the importance of the Latin Quarter as such).

Few can put up with this situation unaided; hence the phenomenon known as *la bande de copains*, which is a much more tightly-knit group than the circle or circles of friends common to most students everywhere. The band does everything together, from meeting regularly every day in the same café to going to see the same films. Often, but not always, it is mixed. A boy and a girl may sleep together, but it rarely becomes a regular affair; they will not in any case separate from the band to live together as far as circumstances will allow, but will continue to form part of it. For it is the band which gives the student his identity (one can only find one's identity through others), and at the same time a protective shell against a society that is seen as generally hostile. It is not uncommon for such a band to exert a strong influence on its members long after they have ceased to be students.

Many find the band enough, but others whose eyes have been suddenly opened to the political and social realities of the world in which they live need to give expression to this new awareness, and find further integration in one or other of the various student movements. This has been particularly true since the Algerian War, which not only brought home to many the realities of political, moral and social conflicts but also coincided with the overt disintegration of the university system. Thus the *Jeunesse Etudiante Chrétienne*, the *Union Nationale des Etudiants de France* and the *Union des Etudiants Communistes* came to have the same function for the student as the political party for the older militant: they provided at one and the same time a means of protest against society, and a secure (but, for students, temporary) haven in which doctrinal answers to all society's problems could be formulated.[22]

22. This is not to denigrate either the sincerity or the usefulness of the work done by party and student militants. However, it is enough to have accompanied, as the author has done, a party of student volunteers in Algeria to realise that

The various small student movements, such as the Trotskyite *Jeunesse Communiste Révolutionnaire* and *Fédération des Etudiants Révolutionnaires*, the Maoist *Union de la Jeunesse Communiste Marxiste-Léniniste* and the various Vietnam Committees, which gained such publicity during May and June 1968, should not be seen in any other light. They arose as a result of the realisation by a fraction of the UEC and the UNEF in the later stages of the Algerian War that the Communist Party was acting more as a brake than anything else on the student movement. A concerted effort was made to destroy the influence of the Communist Party among students. The effort was successful, and resulted in 1965 and 1966 in the formation of these small movements—and the UEC has been reduced to a mere puppet organisation. This in itself was to have important consequences in May 1968, but, this having been said, their basic function remained the same. Their doctrinal differences are comparatively unimportant; all that need be said is that the more powerless they felt to exert any influence on the course of events in the real (i.e. non-student) world, the more extremist the positions they adopted. But that did not change their political impotence. To take just one concrete example, despite the fact that it was what he had always preached and longed for, no one was more surprised than Alain Krivine, leader of the JCR, when news was brought to him in the Sorbonne that the workers at Cléon had occupied the Renault factory. These movements were not even, in any meaningful way, at the origin of the student revolt, the immediate antecedents of which are discussed in the first part of the next chapter.[23]

the social and psychological sources of their missionary zeal are more important than the political ones. Indicative of the student's difficulties is the traditional way he is referred to by non-students, particularly parents: 'he is doing his studies', and not 'he is a student' or 'he is at university'. Studying is not seen as conferring any status on the student, but as a goal-oriented activity.

23. It is sometimes suggested that there is an international student plot to overthrow Western capitalist society. In practical terms, this is nonsense. Student leaders from different countries certainly meet at regular intervals, but it should be remembered that students have always been very internationally minded, and that the existing international student organisations are both devoted to serving the interests of either the American or the Russian alliance. Not surprisingly a certain number of student unions have been trying to create a more independent and effective international movement. Nevertheless, it is certain that a considerable amount of tactical knowledge, particularly concerning street-fighting techniques, have filtered through from the Japanese Zengakuren *via* the German SDS etc.—but in the world as it is today, that is not very surprising either.

DOCUMENT 6

The barrier at the entrance to the lycée.

THE following text is taken from *Orientation Professionnelle, informations des services publics d'orientation professionnelle de la Seine*, (No. 28), October, 1959. The broadsheet is given free to primary school pupils in the Seine department. The author has been assured by teachers and parents that this is still typical of the tenor of advice given by primary school headmasters and headmistresses to the parents of children in the top form.

Secondary education demands from the child a considerable effort of adaptation

Secondary education is not easy and if the child is to have any chance of success he must have a solid grasp of the necessary basic knowledge. Yet even where this knowledge has been acquired, experience shows that the change-over is not always easy.

The child is no longer so closely guided in the organisation of his working day; he must organise it himself within the limits of the time he has available. Lessons will have to be learned and homework done as required. This means that on some days he will have neither homework nor lessons to do, whereas sometimes he hill find himself with several lessons and a lot of homework to do in one day.

The parents' role in getting the child used to a new scholastic life is far from negligible. Their job, whether or not they themselves had a secondary education, is less a question of helping the child to do his homework correctly than to see, as far as possible, that his personal work is properly organised.

The effect of the last paragraph in particular on someone who has *not* been to secondary school is not hard to imagine.

DOCUMENT 7

How the barriers can be surmounted—and with what result.

THE following text was written at the author's request by a 38 year old junior mathematics lecturer in a provincial university. The ironic bitterness of the tone renders any further comment superfluous. By definition, the case is not typical of university lecturers; but the cry is typical of the cry of many people (in many countries) who have expended all their energy on forcing themselves through a mill which was not designed for them, and find themselves at the end with no motivation to make use of it.

MY ACADEMIC CAREER

Obviously an exceptional individual, my career began at kindergarten age—but this only left me with the memory of an unhappy love affair with a doctor's daughter—whence my marriage later on with a girl from a good bourgeois family and the energy necessary to succeed, in bourgeois terms (even now the dolls from the 16th *arrondissement* between seventeen and twenty years old plunge me into a state of erotic-social subjugation)—on the other hand, having learnt to read in three months with my mother's help (using an adult method), I find myself in primary school, a brilliant pupil—the mistresses' favourite. One of them almost melted because I'd been able to quote my sources (a universal Larousse dictionary that the concierge had saved from the dustbin)—so a suburban primary school where my teachers were of the old type (they'd been to one of those puritan 'teacher training colleges' which just don't exist any more)—nine years old in 1939—*'puta de refugia'* in the Dordogne —barefoot sheep watcher—back to my mother's native village, where I go on looking after sheep (studying shorthand at the same time, with the aid of a book I stole in a small neighbouring village— that wretched shorthand, I never used it and never forgot it) and also go to the village school—another 'old style' school—three divisions per age—a couple of secular teachers, (therefore atheists, town-hall secretary and always arguing with the village priest, in spite of the use of radio detection) impressed by the clever little lad from the suburbs—corrupted[1] by this nice couple, I find myself

---

[1] Because my class position changed progressively as I solved problems for classmates who were older than myself.

going in for the CEP two years in advance if you please—first in the district; this was the beginning of my triumphal progress. France then steadies herself in the midst of scarcity and Petain's stupidity; I find myself at Bagneux (in the suburbs of Paris), put in a class for those who are finishing their studies—this through error and my parents' ignorance.

A communist master then became indignant about this state of affairs, and there I was, shot into the slot machine—that is to say teacher training college; there I come a brilliant first, only to be told by the head at the end of the oral that I don't 'make the grade' (concrete sense of the term)—henceforth I shall never make the grade (moral sense). So I turn to another competition, quite by chance (I mean I heard about it by chance)—the entrance exam to the local *lycée* (200 entrants, 30 places); I naturally come first (from now on this is always the case), but my confounded family get indignant about it with my arse-licking parents: 'What, but the lad *must* become a worker, must earn his living as quickly as possible; and you want to send him to *lycée*, where he won't learn anything useful, and then once he's big he won't want to look at his own mother.' So there I was back in a 'complementary course', destined for the modest glory of the lower middle classes. Three not unhappy years—I came a brilliant first again in the BEPC (with English), thanks to the bourgeois virtue of a good catholic lady, whose son I used to play with, and also a personal desire not to get caught in the proletarian rut (piece work, which was threatening, was already not particularly attractive to me), and so I went in for the entrance competition for the second cycle in a *lycée* (500 entrants, 3 scholarships), and came out top, which meant I could go to the *lycée Henri IV*—first real confrontation with the upper classes—apart from the other three scholars (who have remained friends), the rest of the modern section is naturally made up of dunces and the school riffraff (which is supposed to have a good reputation though). I'm first in all subjects except . . . languages! My first feelings of humility at being a simpleton—forgetting that the others have already been doing languages for four years, while I only possess the rudiments. I concentrate very hard on French, and the fact that I've already read a great deal (the wrong stuff of course, out of my parents' and the municipal 'libraries') enables me (with the help of the pink pages in the 'petit Larousse'), to acquire a considerable knowledge of 16th *arrondissement* French and to move up a few places again—alas my swine of a headmaster uses my disastrous marks in English and Spanish as a pretext to make me do my 5th form year again. My family, who still humbly respect bourgeois disorder (in spite of or because of the period when the 'Left' was in power from 1946 to 1947?), asks me if I really want to see them go on sacrificing themselves (and sacrificing two sisters for me), so I have to change over to the technical side—and as this is not altogether unattractive to me (it has the advantage of ignorance), I take the entrance exam to the School of Optics at the end of the year, and since I come first again, I have the right to choose my section—the one which leads to the technical *baccalauréat* rather than the CAP, and since I still have my grant, I stay there for two years—wasting my time for fifteen hours workshop per week by playing at being Spinoza, and (such is the thirst for knowledge of youngsters of that age) I follow evening classes at the 'Arts et Métiers' school (technical). Moving memories of workers, after seven years misery, coming to obtain a wretched, pseudo engineering diploma. The poor devils, who were half-dead with fatigue, used to fall asleep at nine o'clock in the very '*ex cathedra*' lectures given by an old idiot of a professor. I—being fresher—find myself at the age of seventeen with a very strong pass in the technical *baccalauréat* and a mathematics certificate from the 'Arts et Métiers' (just pre-university level); as well as with the firm conviction that I'm not so bloody stupid as to become a technician, even a higher technician—and anyway, damn it, I like maths. Consumed with this novice's ardour, I take things into my own hands and enroll in 'the maths section' at the *lycée* St. Louis. There the headmaster doesn't want to know about me, but is somewhat put out by the diplomas I have; finally he hits upon the solution by asking me to give up my grant (which is now technical!). But I immediately agree, and so he's cornered and I'm sinisterly ostracized by the shit from the 16th *arrondissement*. Yet again I come out top and win the general prize; my maths teacher, who is a good fellow, gets me straight into the class preparing 'Polytechnique', and there the ostracism really becomes vicious (the only friend I make is of course a Jew).

I then go down with suspected TB, and nearly kill my father, who was on the dole; I refuse the grant which I have a right to because of my half finished 'Normale Supérieure' competition, cancel my military deferment and do my national service. When I come back to France I have to earn my bread and butter; I get a job in a road-building firm where I have to give orders to the poor unfortunate foremen, who cordially detest me. I can't stand it any more, and still being spurred on in my ignorance of the world by the fascinating universe of science, at the age of 25 I enroll at the Sorbonne. Quite keen studies—I take part in seminars and . . . along comes the war with Algeria—called up for 18 months—come home in a pretty traumatic state. A famous professor finishes me off by telling me 'I had you in mind as an assistant teacher, but X was at the *Ecole Normale* . . .'. I start to cordially detest just about everything, beginning with maths—do nothing—get a job as junior lecturer in a provincial university (they were taking on anybody at that time) and ten years later here I am, a bad Frenchman, a bad teacher and a bad father, with nothing left but the small amount of pleasure that comes from having the time—gained by systematically sabotaging what ought to be my profession—to indulge my tastes for music, literature, friends and children.

DOCUMENT 8

A comment by the Radical philosopher Alain, written on 1 July 1910

There exists a monarchical conception of teaching, by which I mean a conception whose aim is to separate those who will be in possession of knowledge and will govern, from those who will be ignorant and will obey. In my imagination I can see once again my mathematics teacher, who was certainly not lacking in knowledge, humiliating one of our school-fellows with his crushing irony because he happened to be as short-sighted as it is possible to be. The child could only see what was right at the end of his nose. Thus he had to follow a line from one end to the other with his nose in order to have a precise conception of it: he could not even begin to think of seeing a triangle as a whole. I suppose that ideally he should have been given all sorts of small figures to work on, none of them bigger than the end of his nose; in this way he would have been able to see the whole triangle at the same time, grasp connections, and reason as well as the next person.

But the crux of the matter was really there. People rushed him. He used to hurry from one top of the triangle to the other, while talking to fill in time, he used to say A when he meant B, a straight line when he meant an angle, all of which made what he said perfectly ridiculous and had us helpless with laughter. The child was publicly condemned then to be a fool simply because he was short-sighted.

This crushing of the helpless is symbolic of an entire political system from which we have not yet completely freed ourselves. It would seem that the teacher's job is to choose an elite from amongst the crowd, and then to discourage and cut down the others. And we think we are good democrats because we choose without taking birth or wealth into account. You may be sure that monarchies and tyrannies have always acted in this way, choosing from amongst the people the most gifted of them, such as Colbert or Racine, to crush them.

What do we do nowadays? We choose a few men of genius and a certain number who are very talented; we make them presentable, we stamp them, we marry them comfortably off and we turn them into an intellectual aristocracy, which allies itself to the other and governs tyrannically in the name of equality, admirable equality, which gives everything to those who already have a great deal.

In my opinion we ought to proceed in an altogether different way. Educate all the people; bear with shortsightedness, with stupidity, goad idleness, at all costs wake up the people who are asleep, and show more delight in seeing a peasant who has cleaned himself up a bit than an elegant mathematician who soars with ease to the very summit of the *Ecole polytechnique*. According to this theory the State authorities ought therefore to make every effort to educate the masses from underneath and from the inside, rather than glorifying a few magnificent men at the top, a few kings born amongst the people, who lend an air of justice to the inequality. But who thinks about such things? Even the socialists have no very clear idea on the subject; I see them corrupted by tyranny, demanding good kings. There are no good kings!

DOCUMENT 9

The Productivity of Higher Education

A
The chances of obtaining a university education in France

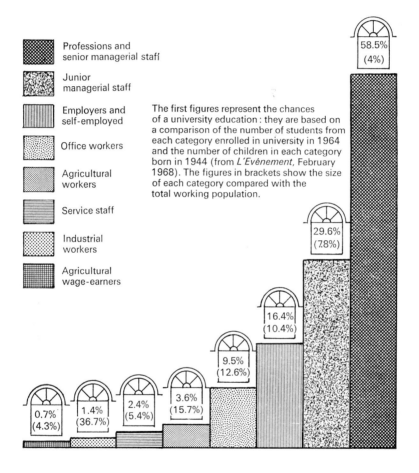

Professions and
senior managerial staff

Junior
managerial staff

Employers and
self-employed

Office workers

Agricultural
workers

Service staff

Industrial
workers

Agricultural
wage-earners

The first figures represent the chances
of a university education: they are based on
a comparison of the number of students from
each category enrolled in university in 1964
and the number of children in each category
born in 1944 (from L'Evénement, February
1968). The figures in brackets show the size
of each category compared with the
total working population.

58.5%
(4%)

29.6%
(7.8%)

16.4%
(10.4%)

9.5%
(12.6%)

3.6%
(15.7%)

2.4%
(5.4%)

1.4%
(36.7%)

0.7%
(4.3%)

C

B

The productivity of higher education in the Common Market, Britain, USSR and USA

1. Percentage of members of an age-group in higher education

COUNTRY	YEAR	FULL TIME %	PART TIME %	RATIO OF GIRL STUDENTS %	
USA	1963	34	—	38	(1961)
USSR	1963	7·3	9·7	42	(1962)
England and Wales	1961	8·5	6·6	⎧ 25 (university) ⎨ 70 (training ⎩ colleges) ⎬	(1962)
West Germany	1963	7·3	—	⎧ 24 (university) ⎨ 62·5 (training ⎩ colleges) ⎬	(1963)
Belgium	1963	17·4	—	24	(1963)
France	1963	13·8	0·8	42·1	(1963)
Italy	1960	6·0	—	27	(1959)
The Netherlands	1961	4·6	—	18	(1962)

2. Degrees obtained

COUNTRY	DEGREES		DEGREES AND DIPLOMAS	
	number	% of age-group	number	% of age-group
USA (1963)	450,594	19·6	—	—
USSR (1959)	338,000	8·2	—	—
Britain (1962)	37,514	5·68	59,394	9·0
West Germany (1963)	37,899	3·94	—	—
Belgium (1963)	9,275	8·0	12,586	10·9
France (1964)	27,877	5·06	—	—
Italy (1963)	23,019	2·86	—	—
The Netherlands (1962)	3,016	1·8	4,977	3·0

(Source: R. Poignant, *L'Enseignement dans les pays du Marché Commun* Paris, *Institut pédagogique national*, 1965.)

CHAPTER TWO

THE OPEN REVOLT

1 Before 3 May 1968

'Quand la France s'ennuie. . . .'
Pierre Viansson-Ponté, *Le Monde*, 15 March 1968.

T HE *Union Nationale des Etudiants de France* is made up of *Associations Générales* of students from the various university faculties. The first one of these, called at the time a student society, was founded by the students of Nancy in 1877, but it was thirty years before the different AGs came together to form the UNEF. In the early days it seems to have resembled a mixture of an Oxbridge Union and Dining Club more than anything else, and it was not until after World War I that it began in any way to represent the interests of the students. Apart from taking the lead in founding the first international student organisation in 1919, its activities between the wars were mostly inspired by the social conscience of the time. For the relative impoverishment of the middle classes, in part reflected in the abolition of fees for secondary education in 1930, and the economic depression meant that fewer and fewer students were able to rely for support entirely on their parents. An important beginning was made in providing hostels and restaurants, travel and health services, mostly out of private donations, but although the UNEF was largely responsible for their creation, their administration passed into the hands of the State or the University.

The student body had remained more of a guild than a union, concerned exclusively with the material conditions of its members. Despite certain outstanding exceptions, this attitude persisted throughout World War II and the Occupation, so much so that when forced labour[1] was introduced in 1943 the UNEF contented itself with trying to obtain deferment for students. Although it never actually collaborated, this passive attitude (much more widespread in France than the enthusiasm of the Liberation would ever

1. The hated STO (*service du travail obligatoire*) by which many young Frenchmen were sent to work in Germany. Its introduction swelled considerably the ranks of the Resistance.

have suggested) brought it into discredit at the end of the War. Those students who had been active members of the Resistance first formed a rival body and then, led by the Lyon AG, decided to change the UNEF from the inside. Their representatives were finally elected in 1946 and succeeded in getting voted the famous Grenoble Charter (see Document 10). The importance of the Charter lies in the definition of a student as a 'young intellectual worker'; from which it follows that the student is an object of interest and responsibility to society as a whole, and that he has a right to a say on those aspects of society which concern him and his future, directly or indirectly. These principles, although sometimes disputed within the UNEF and, more often, by non-student organisations and institutions which it inevitably came up against, have not been abandoned, and the UNEF as it is today remains very much marked by the Resistance and the Grenoble Charter.

Its post-war history centres around a few dates and figures. The first big student strike took place in June 1947 to protest against the raising of university fees and a cut in grants; as a result, the proposals were withdrawn. Social security was extended to students in 1948, and in 1951 a Bill came before the National Assembly which, although it was not voted for economic reasons, publicly stated the principle of a fixed grant for all students. In 1955 the students obtained an active share in the running of the organisation which looks after student welfare, restaurants, etc.[2] Since the war the UNEF had maintained permanent, if sometimes tenuous, contacts with student organisations from the French colonies, and its courageous struggle against the atrocities of the Algerian War was crowned by a huge protest meeting held on 27 October 1960 in conjunction with one or two workers' organisations.[3] By the following year its membership had climbed from 29,000 in 1946 (approximately one in eight students) to 100,000 (approximately one in three).

But this is not the whole story. Until the early 1960s the UNEF was essentially a Catholic movement. Those who were responsible for the Grenoble Charter were simply a younger version of the left-wing Catholic members of the Resistance who, for example, founded

2. What students still refer to as COPAR, although its present title is the *Centre Régional des Oeuvres Universitaires et Scolaires*.

3. The Communist Party and the CGT at first refused to have anything to do with it, but after long and sordid negotiations which shocked the politically naïve students, agreed to take part. However, when the Government banned the demonstration they climbed down, and only the CFTC and the metal-workers' branch of the CGT finally took part.

the new political party, *le Mouvement Républicain Populaire*. In 1950 (at about the same time as the MRP began to move further to the right) a more moderate tendency began to show itself in the election of leaders whose conception of the role of the union was at times closer to that of the 1939 generation than the 1946 one. However the left-wing militants, many of whom were formed by the *Jeunesse Etudiante Chrétienne*, again took control in 1956, largely as a reaction against the nationalist positions of the outgoing leaders on colonial questions and as a result of their own effective work at grass-roots level.

Both these reasons for the success of the new leaders throw some light on the future. The first meant that out of solidarity for the Algerian students and from a deep moral, even more than political, repugnance for the methods used by the French,[4] the UNEF came to take a courageous, and at first very solitary, stand against the Algerian War. This inevitably led the students into a political arena where the issues were far wider and deeper than those which they had handled up to then, and the Government was not slow to react. Its subsidy from the Ministry of Education was withdrawn in June 1960,[5] and in January 1961 a rival student union, the *Fédération Nationale des Etudiants de France*, was formed with Government help. Even if account is taken of the drastic decline in membership of the UNEF during recent years, the right-wing FNEF, despite its considerable following in the provinces, has never had anything like as many members, but the Government has always considered it as a 'representative organisation',[6] sometimes to the exclusion of the UNEF. Thus the UNEF's immense task of finding a new policy and strategy after the end of the Algerian War was made much more difficult by the Government's systematic policy (applied equally to unions and political parties) of undermining any elective body other than itself.

4. Although the basic facts are now widely known, it is worth recalling that French atrocities in Algeria far exceeded anything the British did in Cyprus or Kenya: torture was freely used against both Frenchmen and Algerians, in France as in Algeria, on anyone suspected of harbouring sympathies for the FLN, and the same unscrupulous methods were later employed against the OAS.

5. Withdrawn by Louis Joxe when Minister of Education in 1960, it was restored by Christian Fouchet in January 1963, but was again withdrawn by him in February 1964 when the UNEF's increasing hostility towards the Fouchet Reforms took the form of a street demonstration during the President of Italy's state visit.

6. See below, p. 155.

This task was further complicated by factiousness, which is perhaps inevitable in a movement whose members and leaders are continually changing, and in which only those who are prepared to sacrifice a year or more of their studies can take an active part. It is relatively easy, as was shown in 1956, for such people to gain control of local AGs and thus possibly of the union, and in the early 1960s members of the UEC (*Union des Etudiants Communistes*) succeeded in getting a foothold. The end of the Algerian War produced a crop of crises throughout the French Left (the JEC and the UEC were both taken in hand by their parent organisations,[7] while the earlier split in the non-Communist Left had produced the *Union de la Gauche Socialiste*, later to become the PSU to which Mendès-France was affiliated), and the UNEF became the battle-ground for all these student factions, to which must be added the Trotskyites and the 'pro-China' Marxist-Leninists. None of them, however, had more than a handful of followers among the students as a whole.

In the circumstances it is not surprising that the UNEF had some difficulty in formulating a coherent policy acceptable to the students, even on such important questions as university reform. But even though its annual conferences presented an increasingly sorry spectacle, a great deal of serious work was done in the background. Some of the material in Bourdieu and Passeron, *Les Héritiers*, comes from UNEF files, and a UNEF memorandum which Marc Kravetz published in *Les Temps Modernes* of February 1964 contains much which, although it appeared revolutionary at the time, had by May 1968 become widely accepted.[8] Little of this, however, reached the student rank and file to whom the UNEF, as a result of a combination of factiousness and Government policy, appeared less and less capable of effectively representing their interests. Various protest movements grew up independently of the national union, of which one of the most important was that which demanded free mutual access to boys and girls hostels. The problem had been simmering for nearly three years before the UNEF decided to use

7. On the JEC, cf. John Ardagh, op. cit., pp. 387–8: on the UEC, see above, p. 56. The motives and tactics of both the Catholic Church and the Communist Party were strikingly similar.

8. Bourdieu and Passeron, *Les Héritiers*, Paris, Editions de Minuit, 1964, is a sociological study of the student condition. Marc Kravetz is an ex-militant of the UNEF and in March 1968 helped to form the *Mouvement d'Action Universitaire* which played a minor role during the events of May.

it in order to regain some of its lost influence and organised a nation-wide anti-segregation protest on 14 February 1968.

*

The problem of the French university hostel and campus illustrates perfectly why in May it took such a small spark to set off such a big explosion. The idea of a hostel, and still more of a campus, is very recent; in 1958 7,000 students were so lodged, in 1962 18,000 and in 1968 67,000 or 12% of the total student population. From the beginning the very principle of a campus was criticised by those who considered that the American model was inappropriate to France, and a certain number of cases of depression and suicide lent weight to their arguments. To some extent these people were right, although not for the reasons put forward. The problem is not so much whether the university should be separate from, or integrated into, the town, but the fact that the Frenchman has little idea, and less experience, of community living. As was pointed out in Chapter 1, the Frenchman's world tends to consist of the family cell and the State, with nothing in between. Nothing prepared him for campus living, and, once there, nothing in the conception of the campus does anything to facilitate his adjustment. Professors and their families do not live on the campus (sometimes they do not even live in the town, but come from Paris for a couple of days a week), links with the town depend on private transport or an unmodified public system, sports facilities are rarely included in the plans for a new campus (the famous swimming-pool at Nanterre is an exception, but it was built before the library!), recreational and social activities are usually limited to what can be obtained from a cafeteria, a film-club, a ping-pong table and a television room, and of course any meeting or activity which has the faintest aura of politics about it is strictly forbidden, as are any independently organised art exhibitions, lectures, etc.

Although there is the occasional exception,[9] the hostels were conceived of first and foremost as dormitories and not in any way as communities. Rules and regulations governing conduct within them are taken lock, stock and barrel from the boarding sections

9. Such as Grenoble, for a description of which cf. John Ardagh, op. cit., pp. 330–1: cf. also Appendix 1 (ii). Students on grants generally have priority in the allocation of rooms in university hostels; since such students are regarded as an inferior species, this might in part account for the official view that they must on no account be allowed any freedom or responsibility.

of *lycées*, and of course they are the same everywhere. Thus students dispose of a room but are not considered as renting it, and so have no more rights than a secondary-school boarder; no visitors are allowed in a student's room, but only in the hall or recreation rooms; no alteration of any sort may be made to a student's room (this includes the hanging of pictures); all notices and posters inside a hostel must be vetted by the administration; and no propaganda of any sort is allowed.

With the possible exception of the last one, all these rules are equally ridiculous, and when Pierre Viansson-Ponté, the political correspondent of *Le Monde*, wrote in the article quoted at the head of this chapter that the protest against the rigid segregation in student hostels revealed a somewhat limited conception of the rights of man, he showed some wit but little understanding.[10] For, far from being accidental aberrations, they are typical of many French institutions, in the widest sense of the word. Under French law it is illegal for anyone of either sex to seduce a minor of either sex, so that, to take an extreme example, a girl of twenty-one could be prosecuted for sleeping with a boy of twenty. Article 93 of the legal family code reads: 'Any minor lodged in a group away from his parents' residence is put under the protection of the public authority.' The last term refers to the State, and as in France power and responsibility are rarely if ever delegated except in the most formal sense, every hostel warden throughout the whole of France feels obliged, and is expected, to interpret the law in the most restrictive and literal way. Moreover, in the unlikely event of a French warden following the example of the Dean of an Oxford woman's college, who is reputed to have declared herself in favour of a course of sexual education for her young charges to avoid the spate of early marriages followed by swift divorces, there would

10. This judgement may appear both severe and inspired by hindsight. On the second point, the author, in private conversations, argued in exactly the same way when the article appeared. On the first, Pierre Viansson-Ponté is an excellent political correspondent, and his articles during May stand up remarkably well to re-reading after the event. But like so many of his compatriots (and they include political and social scientists) he interprets '*la spécificité française*' to mean that none but a Frenchmen is really competent to criticise France (his curious review of John Ardagh's book, *Le Monde* 30 March 1968, is a case in point), and that none but negative lessons are to be learnt from studies and experiences in other countries (in this case, on the relative coherence of the social and political system). The idea of a French Fulton Commission drawing positive conclusions from another country's system is scarcely credible.

have been a fearful outcry. For France, unlike her non-Catholic neighbours, is still riddled by sexual taboos, inhibitions and conventions,[11] and the role of these in maintaining a closed, stratified and authoritarian society should need no emphasising. There was thus no question of young students being encouraged to exercise some kind of responsible control over their own lives, whether sexual, educational or administrative, and any demand for such control was bound, as the obstacles in the way of achieving it became clearer, to lead to more radical and 'political' demands.

A brief historical summary of the conflict will illustrate this. The residential campus at Antony in the southern suburbs of Paris was relatively free from discipline, partly because it contained the only students married quarters, and had a bad reputation for abortions, etc. (a natural enough result in a country where contraceptive information is unpublicised and hard to come by). In the autumn of 1965 it was decided to build a porter's lodge from which the comings and goings in the girls hostels could be surveyed. The students occupied the site to prevent it being built, and for three months there were fierce battles, with the authorities resorting to increasingly severe measures. Finally a compromise was obtained whereby the lodge was built, but a new Director of the campus was discreetly authorised to introduce his own regulations. Visiting by the opposite sex within certain hours was authorised for everybody, although minors had to get written permission from their parents (obtained by 90% of them). But there was never at any time any question of Antony being anything but the exception which confirmed the general rule. When in 1967 the agitation, which usually took the form of a symbolic occupation of the girls hostel by the boys, spread elsewhere—to Nice, Lille, Rennes, Montpellier, Aix-en-Provence, Toulouse, Orléans, Dijon, and Nanterre— the authorities resorted to the police, but never to negotiation. Finally, after the UNEF's campaign on 14 February 1968, when the regulations were declared 'abolished' throughout the whole of France, sometimes to the accompaniment of violence (in Nantes the Rector's offices were invaded and considerable damage done), Alain Peyrfitte, the Minister of Education, produced proposals which did

11. Objective evidence on the subject is rare: most of what little there is has been summarised by John Ardagh (op. cit., pp. 247–9). His accurate and pertinent remarks are confirmed by the difficulties of the family planning organisation in France, reference to any article in the French press on the 'pill', and the furore created by the mildly reforming Neuwirth Act of 1967.

not even go as far as those of the *Centre National des Oeuvres*, on which students and the university administration are represented: boys over twenty-one could entertain girls in their rooms.

Why could the Ministry not follow the example of Antony and introduce more genuinely liberal reforms? After all, the 90% of parents of minors who gave their permission for visits showed that opposition was not likely to come from that quarter. But in France authority exists to reinforce (and not to give a lead in changing) the social norms it has itself helped to create. Those 90% form part of the minority of younger middle-class parents who at the end of World War II had their eyes opened to alternative methods of bringing up children by the Americans. In a generation or so their attitudes will probably spread to most Frenchmen, but the younger generation sees no reason why it should wait. In the meantime the State, supported by the majority of Frenchmen, in a manner rendered more obnoxious by Gaullist authoritarianism and contempt for negotiation, continues to impose the traditional and hopelessly out-dated French norms. Negotiations had not produced any results, in this or in any other field, and the proof was there that a little violence could open a tiny breach. Before May was to see greater violence open the flood-gates the lesson was learned and the technique refined at Nanterre.

*

Much, probably too much, has already been written about Nanterre.[12] If it was highly probable that the French university system would burst at the seams sooner or later, it was by no means inevitable that the explosion occur when it did nor that it take the form that it did. Nanterre was only exceptional in minor respects; there was unrest, and ample legitimate cause for unrest, in nearly every faculty in France.

For example, in November 1966 at Strasbourg a small group, calling themselves the International Situationists, ousted the UNEF from the AG and systematically set out to destroy the existing social organisations and structure of the university. As far as can be gathered from their published works,[13] they are more akin to the

12. A racy, but essentially accurate description of Nanterre and account of earlier agitation there can be found in chapter 1 of Patrick Seale and Maureen McConville, *French Revolution 1968*, Penguin Special, 1968.

13. Although they had no more consideration for the UNEF than for anyone else, the latter published in 1966, as a supplement to No. 16 of their magazine

surrealists than anything else, and their avowed object was to create a situation such that any step back towards the preceding order became impossible. Despite protests from some of the students and staff, as well as legal proceedings, they remained in power. The majority of the students may not have actively supported them but they were too apathetic to oppose them and turn them out. That the Situationists found an echo of some sort is shown by the fact that the students of Strasbourg were among the first to occupy their buildings (before the Sorbonne—see below p. 176, n. 1) and fly the red flag.

Everywhere there was evident an increasing awareness of the injustice and inadequacy of the French educational system as a whole, and of the university one in particular. The debate on the Fouchet reforms, the Colloque de Caen in November 1966 when professors produced intelligent analyses and reform proposals for the University (appreciated, but ignored, by the Ministry), the Colloque d'Amiens in March 1968 when teachers did the same for secondary education, a series of books and articles on the elitist nature of both the secondary and the university systems;[14] all these contributed to awaken public, and in particular student, opinion. The result, as a glance at the chronological table will show, was an impressive series of protests, demonstrations, and strikes by students, school teachers and professors. To these should be added a number of minor incidents which never got into the press. In short, if 1967/1968 ended violently, it began turbulently, nearly everywhere and not just at Nanterre.

The campus at Nanterre is one huge building site put down more by accident than design (the land was offered as a joke during the course of a Cabinet meeting in 1963 by the Army Minister to the Education Minister, who accepted) in the centre of a vast redevelopment area. On two sides there are ugly modern blocks of council-type flats, on one the railway, and on the fourth the remains of a shantytown. Nothing has been built except lecture halls, hostels, a canteen

21–27 a Situationist tract entitled; *De la misère en milieu étudiant considérée sous ses aspects économique, politique, psychologique, sexuel et notamment intellectuel, et de quelques moyens pour y remédier.* Written in a way calculated to offend everyone, from the extreme right to the extreme left, the few pages of analysis of the student condition are pertinent and by now all too familiar. More literary statements of their position can be found in Raoul Vaneigem, *Traité de savoir-vivre à l'usage des jeunes générations*, Gallimard, Paris, 1967, and Guy Debord, *La société du spectacle*, Buchet/Castel, Paris 1967.

14. In particular, Bourdieu and Passeron, op. cit.

and a swimming-pool; there are no cultural or recreational facilities, not even a library.[15] Among the faculties farmed off to Nanterre was that of letters, with its philosophy, psychology and sociology sections. And it was in the sociology department that the trouble began, which is not surprising. For sociology students are taught something of the structure of society, and how to criticise and question it, but in France the social sciences scarcely exist outside the university and the sociology graduate does not have the opportunity, which exists in most other countries, of doing something about improving a small section of the society he has begun to understand. The best he can hope for is to teach or, if he is lucky, to obtain one of the all too rare research posts; otherwise he is as likely as not to find himself doing market research. In either event (except research) he will be perpetuating the very system he has been taught to criticise.

But the originality of Nanterre lay not in the environmental conditions of the students there, but in the tactical sense of Daniel Cohn-Bendit and some of his fellow-students. Their genius lay in drawing the conclusions from the failure of all traditional forms of protest. It was not enough to try to force concessions or negotiations by, for example, the temporary and symbolic invasion of girls' hostels. Their answer lay in taking, and keeping, what they demanded, and so forcing the authorities to choose between total surrender and forceful repression. Since they were only a tiny minority, and had no very clear idea of what they would do with their conquest, their energy was directed towards obliging the authorities to make the second choice, and in this they succeeded remarkably well. Because their basic demands were essentially reasonable, and did not differ very much from what an increasing number of 'responsible' and 'respectable' people and organisations had been demanding for some time, the mass of students rallied to them as soon as there was any sign of repression. Their avowed object was *casser la*

15. The first year students of the Institute of Political Science were scheduled to go to Nanterre in October 1968. The Ministry was asked for temporary library facilities, but categorically refused on the grounds that the main library would be ready in 1970! As the Institute has some funds of its own it provided itself the money needed to strengthen the floors in one or two places so that a surreptitious temporary library could be installed without the Minister's official knowledge. This is a typical example of *le système D* (*débrouillard*) in practice, and it is in fact the way red tape is normally cut. But when such a system becomes, as it has in France, a social institution, there is something radically wrong with the country.

baraque (to destroy the whole works), but whatever they may have said after 13 May the works for them was the university and not the whole capitalist system. Yet their tactics, their gift for publicity and above all their success made them appear as more genuine 'revolutionaries' then all the 'pro-China' and Trotskyite grouplets (*groupuscules*) put together, even though the latter compensated for the lack of immediate efficacy by a real interest in the workers and Utopian visions of what society would be like after the proletarian revolution.

The movement started after the failure of the 'teach-in' strike by the sociology department of Nanterre on 17 November. The strike soon spread to the whole of the arts faculty, but ten days of discussions on all the problems of the university produced no concrete result. The Doyen of Nanterre, Pierre Grappin, an honourable and liberal-minded man who certainly did not merit the insults to which he was later subjected, met the students and promised to do what he could; but his hands were tied by Paris and he could do nothing. Agitation began soon after and reached its first climax on 8 January when the Minister for Youth and Sports, François Missoffe, came to inaugurate a huge new swimming-pool, and was insulted to his face by Cohn-Bendit.[16] This was followed by rumours of Cohn-Bendit's impending expulsion from France, of police informers and black lists of students (at least the first two seem to have had some foundation in fact). The students reacted by increased agitation, and the administration was provoked into calling in the police, who were lured into the centre of the campus where they were attacked and forced ignominiously to flee. And so the agitation and provocation went on. On 22 March a meeting was held at Nanterre to protest against the arrest of some students after anti-Vietnam War demonstrators had broken the windows of the American Express; at the end of the meeting the administrative block was occupied and *le mouvement du 22 mars* was born. On 28 March the Doyen suspended all lectures at Nanterre and two days later Alain Peyrfitte, the Minister of Education, in an interview on

16. A full account of the exchange, which concerned the relative merits of sport and sex, can be found in Seale and McConville, op. cit., p. 33. It is difficult not to sympathise with Cohn-Bendit insofar as the magnificent swimming-pool, in the context of the total cultural barrenness of Nanterre, was shown up for what it was, a gesture of pure propaganda. The very fact that anyone could have thought of giving *panem et circenses* to the students, given the far more crying needs of the university, only shows the Gaullists' culpable ignorance of the internal realities of France.

Radio Luxembourg spoke of *les enragés*[17] (the 'mad dogs'), a term which they did not reject and which gave them even more publicity.

Les enragés were no longer isolated and they now had in their train a certain number of grouplets, particularly those which had taken an active part in anti-Vietnam War demonstrations. These had become increasingly frequent over the previous couple of years under the auspices of the Comité Vietnam National. The CVN, founded in 1966, included a certain number of people, such as Jean-Pierre Vigier as well as Alain Krivine of the JCR, who considered that as de Gaulle's position had not had any noticeable effect on American policy nor stimulated any other major ally of America to dissociate itself from the war, more active measures were needed. In fact it is probably not unfair to say that they were people who lacked the logical (if, even in revolutionary terms, somewhat misguided) courage of Régis Debray;[18] unwilling to follow his example, and unable to influence the course of events from France or elsewhere in Europe, having no contact with the working-class in their own country, they were reduced to more and more violent demonstrations in Paris. In this they were, for a time, shielded by the Government and helped by the vocal and often violent opposition of those who supported South Vietnam, and above all of the extreme right-wing collection of student and non-student thugs which goes by the name of *Occident*.[19] Fights between the two groups became a common occurrence, both in Paris and the provinces. The arrest of some of their leaders after attacks on American property in Paris on 18 and 20 March led to the combined protest at Nanterre on 22 March. Commando raids on each other's

17. '*La rage*' means 'rabies', and '*enragé*' is used of dogs suffering from that disease and, by extension, of certain 'frenzied' people. However, it also has a precise historical reference, of which Peyrfitte was probably aware even if the majority of those who have used the term since were not. *Les enragés* were a motley assortment of half a dozen extremist revolutionaries who, under the leadership of Jacques Roux, a defrocked priest, enjoyed a certain popular esteem in Paris in 1792 and 1793. The movement was finally crushed by Robespierre in September, 1793.

18. A brilliant student philosopher from the *Ecole Normale Supérieure*, the son of wealthy and influential parents, Régis Debray went to Bolivia to offer his services to Che Guevara but ended up by, unwittingly, betraying him.

19. A descendant of *Action Française*, *Occident* was founded in 1964 by Pierre Sidos, of '*Jeune Nation*'. It has usually been at the service of M. Tixier-Vignancourt, one of the Presidential candidates in 1965.

property followed, and it is probable that if the faculty of Nanterre had not again been closed on 2 May *Occident* would have launched a full-scale attack. As it was, they threatened to turn their attention to the Sorbonne.

But probably the most important part of the CVN's activities was its spread to the *lycées*, in a few of which local CVN committees were set up. At the end of 1967 these were renamed *Comités d'Action Lycéens* (CAL) which were to play an important role during May. Yet this is not to say that the *lycées* became a breeding-ground for revolutionaries. For they would probably never have existed had it not been for the total absence of any kind of window on the world, and indeed on France, in French schools (see Chapter 1). As it was, all normal forms of political discussion and expression being denied them, some took the only outlet open to them and became extremist militants. The real nature of the problem can be grasped from a correspondence that appeared in *Le Monde* (25 January and 6 February 1968) following the expulsion of a schoolboy from the Lycée Condorcet for distributing leaflets, as well as from the almost unanimous praise which the by then far more numerous and popular CALs earned for the seriousness and pertinence of their discussions of education as a whole during the months of May and June (see the following Chapter).

Thus support for the extremists was growing, and it came not only from students and schoolboys. On 2 February Professors Alain Touraine and Michel Crozier, France's leading sociologists and both at Nanterre, signed a motion protesting against the threat of expulsion hanging over Cohn-Bendit, and later Alain Touraine wrote a series of articles in *Le Monde* (7 and 8 March) entitled 'The birth of a student movement'. But Daniel Cohn-Bendit and his friends remained resolutely independent and hostile to any established left-wing movement. At a meeting at Nanterre on 26 April Pierre Juquin of the Central Committee of the French Communist Party barely escaped being manhandled by 'pro-China' elements, and Laurent Schwartz, the mathematician, and André Gorz of *Les Temps Modernes* were only just given a hearing. This incident served their cause, if only by the publicity it provided. And so when, after a further series of provocations (of which the last was the taking over on 2 May of a lecture hall in which Professor René Rémond was due to give a history lecture in order to show a film of Che Guevara) the faculty of Nanterre was closed indefinitely, an activist meeting was held in the Sorbonne on 3 May and the majority of student grouplets were represented, however much they may have been opposed to Cohn-Bendit in the beginning.

However, it cannot be too strongly emphasised that none of the activists planned any of the consequences of their actions. Decisions were taken on the spur of the moment. The meeting at the Sorbonne was a natural result of the decisions, announced the previous day, to bring seven students from the faculty of Nanterre before the University disciplinary council and to close the faculty. Some of those present at the meeting were armed, since an attack by *Occident* was expected. All the grouplets put together represented only a very tiny minority of students and they could never have hoped by themselves to bring about the events of the next ten days. For the vast majority of students, although increasingly aware of the problems, were content to try to struggle through, in the hope that someone some day would bring about the necessary changes. They reacted at first out of a natural feeling of solidarity, and only later, in increasing numbers, did they at last see a real opportunity to do something about forcing through these changes themselves. The tactics of Cohn-Bendit and his friends were to succeed beyond their wildest expectations, but it was the students as a whole who, during the next ten days and even more in the discussions that took place in the occupied faculties, were to show to a perplexed Government and an amazed audience throughout the world to what their success was really due.

2. The student barricades

'The year will certainly be a difficult one, but I do not think there is any reason to fear a big catastrophe.'

M. Georges Pompidou, 11 January 1968

In the early afternoon of Friday 3 May approximately four hundred students were gathered in the quadrangle of the Sorbonne to protest against the closing of the faculty of Nanterre and the threat of disciplinary action against Cohn-Bendit and six other students. The majority were from Nanterre, although most of the grouplets were represented, including the *Mouvement d'Action Universitaire*, formed in March somewhat on the model of the *mouvement du 22 mars* (their first public action was to hold their first meeting in the main lecture hall of the Sorbonne although permission to do so had been refused by the authorities) and composed of senior students and junior professors from the Sorbonne. The meeting was relatively calm. There was a good deal of verbal violence, but nothing more. Some, perhaps as many as one in four, were armed as an attack was expected by members of *Occident*, and one or two chairs were broken up to provide clubs, but that was as far as the destruction of property went. The Rector of the University, Jean Roche, sent several emissaries to ask them to leave, but to no avail. Finally, after consultation with Alain Peyrfitte, the Minister of Education, he signed the warrant allowing the police to enter the Sorbonne. The quadrangle was evacuated peacefully, but with no attempt at discretion on the part of the police. All the four hundred students were bundled into police vans waiting outside, an operation which took some time, and driven away under the very eyes of the students who had begun to gather outside. They began by attempting to prevent the vans leaving the Place de la Sorbonne, and the escalation of violence had began in earnest.

The authorities certainly had every reason to take action of some sort, if only to avoid what promised to be a nasty fight taking place inside the Sorbonne, but it is doubtful whether they had fully weighed the consequences of calling in the police.[20] For while it is true that this was not the first time that police had entered university precincts (they had on more than one occasion intervened during the anti-segregation protests, and at that very moment there were five hundred police guarding the faculty of Nanterre), the Sorbonne was different. Throughout its long and venerable history it had always been considered as sacrosanct, and there had been times when this privilege had been of real importance. Further, the Sorbonne has great symbolic value for all French students, even for those who have never set foot inside it; for it is at once the sign and the confirmation of their somewhat precarious status. What made the authorities take the chance was probably the desire to nip the movement in the bud, to prevent the cancer spreading from Nanterre to the whole university. But such preventive action, if it was to have any hope of succeeding, should have been taken long ago at Nanterre. The

20. According to some accounts the Rector had strong reservations but was overridden by the Minister. The meeting, at which UNEF leaders were present, had been authorised. It is possible that the Government welcomed, if it did not provoke, the pretext in order to deal once and for all with student agitation before the arrival a week later of 2,000 foreign journalists to cover the Vietnam talks.

Ministry, although kept regularly informed by the Doyen and staff of all the incidents throughout the year, had adopted a policy of '*laisser pourrir*',[21] a policy designed to show to all and sundry, and in particular the open-minded Doyen and his staff, that a liberal attitude towards a university, most of whose members the Gaullists had with some justice always considered as being systematically hostile to them, would not get anyone anywhere. By 3 May, however, the situation had been allowed to deteriorate to such an extent that if the authorities had not taken the action they did, similar or even more repressive measures would have been forced upon them before very long.

The consequences of this policy are now well known. On that first Friday some militants had remained outside the Sorbonne all the time, perhaps to give advance warning of *Occident's* arrival, and they were joined by those who left the Sorbonne when, in the middle of the afternoon, lectures and seminars were suspended. This 'lock-out', the decision for which was taken after the activists had refused to leave, meant fewer people inside the building when the police arrived; but it also meant more outside to witness the police invasion. Once the trouble started it lasted for nearly six hours until 22.30. At the height of the riot fifteen hundred policemen were fighting little over two thousand students, and they took a long time to master them. Cobble-stones and iron railings, etc., proved remarkably effective against a police force that, despite its tear-gas and truncheons, was clearly taken by surprise.

All eye-witness accounts confirm the spontaneous character of the student riot, and many photographs were taken showing students with books and satchels in one hand and a cobble-stone in the other. And Maurice Grimaud, the Prefect of Police who throughout the riots did all he could to control his own troops and avoid the worst, admitted as much when interviewed in the heat of the battle the following Monday afternoon, as had police witnesses at the trials the previous day. At the same time all agreed that the leaderless students (their leaders had all been arrested inside the Sorbonne) had acted with an unparalleled violence which in its turn provoked

21. For the use of this policy in the industrial field see below, p. 198. The interpretation given here is confirmed by Epistémon, *Les idées qui ont ébranlé la France* (*Nanterre novembre 1967–juin 1968*), Paris, Fayard, 1968, pp. 72 and 115–16. It should perhaps be emphasised that the discussion here is concerned uniquely with tactics and not with the rights and wrongs of the Nanterre students' demands.

the beginning of a long series of inexcusable acts on the part of the police. By the end of the evening there were many wounded on both sides, and nearly two hundred arrests were made in addition to those which were the immediate cause of the riot. Most of them were released in the course of the following day.

The course of events the following week was more or less determined by the reactions and attitudes expressed on the morrow of the first riot. The Ministry of Education decided to close the Sorbonne indefinitely (exams were only three weeks away), a decision which had the inevitable result of forcing (psychologically, although not materially as other faculties, such as the science one, remained open) the students to make any further protests in the street. At the same time the Ministry of the Interior decided to make the courts sit over the week-end to try the twelve students and one baker against whom charges were preferred. Four students were sent to prison, one was acquitted, and the rest were given fines and suspended sentences. The manner in which the trials were conducted, as much as the sentences passed, could not have been better calculated to incense the students,[22] who were at the same time provided with two ready-made slogans, 'Open the Sorbonne!' and 'Free our comrades!'

At that stage the Government still thought it was possible to stop the rot before it spread any further, as Alain Peyrfitte's references to a 'handful of troublemakers' on both the Sunday and the Monday showed. But when this interpretation was no longer remotely feasible, the Government vacillated and thus revealed its real dilemma. On Wednesday, 8 May, Alain Peyrfitte announced that the Sorbonne would be opened the following day if the situation warranted it; there were no riots on Wednesday or Thursday, only a calm protest march and an announcement from the student and professors' unions that the strike would continue until the imprisoned students were released. Yet the Minister of Education did not make the gesture which would at least have had the merit of avoiding further bloodshed in the short run, even if it did not solve all the problems. The reason for this is not so much that there was nobody to take

22. For details, see the report in Le Monde, 7 May 1968. In general, the impression was given, both then and later when the Prime Minister promised that the students would be amnestied, that the judiciary was at the service of the executive. This is probably no more and no less true in France than in any other country: what is certain is that in France the unwritten rule, which represents a real safeguard for the British accused, whereby justice must not only be done but be seen to be done, is frequently violated.

overall command of the situation,[23] although this certainly did not help. The basic trouble was that no-one had the slightest idea what to do if the policy of repression was rejected. The students would not have stopped there, so what was the Government to do? To continue to let things slide was impossible; something had to be done towards profoundly reforming the university and schools, and that would have involved obtaining first the confidence and cooperation of those students, the great majority, who were not *enragés*, and secondly getting the reforms accepted by the majority of teachers and professors. This was a herculean task for anybody;[24] it was impossible for the Gaullists who have done much to modernise certain sectors of French society, but from above and without proper consultation—in just the way, in other words, most likely to reinforce and harden those hierarchical, authoritarian and secretive norms of behaviour which make French society so resistant to any but superficial change. When Georges Pompidou came back from Afghanistan on 11 May, aware at last of the size of the problem, he met all the immediate student demands, and thus avoided further bloodshed, but his other proposals, made three days later in the course of the special debate in the National Assembly, were more than too late (the Sorbonne had already been occupied by the students); they were quite inadequate. His 'study group' composed of students, teachers, parents and public figures, presumably intended to produce a report comparable to the Crowther, Robins, and Newsom reports in Britain, would have been admirable eighteen months earlier; coming when it did it could not help looking to the students like a diversion. Yet the praise with which it was greeted by nearly everybody else shows just how difficult even that

23. The Prime Minister was out of the country, in Afghanistan, from 2 May to 11 May. He was certainly kept informed, and probably let his own opinions (most likely in favour of standing firm, at least in the early stages) be known. The President of the Republic would not intervene personally in such a minor affair, but his views were made known by members of his personal cabinet, and his general secretary Bernard Tricot, and probably Jacques Foccart, responsible for security, were present at Ministerial meetings on the night of 10–11 May. The acting Prime Minister, Louis Joxe, Minister of Justice, although supported by other 'doves' such as Christian Fouchet, Minister of the Interior, and Michel Debré, Finance Minister, did not have enough personal authority to override the 'hawks'—but above all he had no coherent alternative policy to offer.

24. In *Le Monde* of 9 May Jacques Duhamel, President of the centre parliamentary group, *Progrès et Démocratie Moderne*, published a sensible article entitled 'Désarmer et dialoguer'; but would he have been any more capable than the Gaullists of putting this into practice?

limited step was, and underlines the fact that the Government's policy was forced upon them more by lack of an alternative than by pride or bloody-mindedness.

The first reactions of the press were no less significant and showed how future events were to be interpreted.[25] *Le Figaro* of 4 May was extremely violent and treated the rioters as juvenile delinquents rather than students (which provided the students with yet another slogan 'Figaro fasciste!'). Although obliged to somewhat modify its tone during the following week, it never showed any real understanding either of the students themselves or of what caused their revolt. *Le Monde*, on the other hand, castigated the Government and the university authorities from the beginning and consistently showed itself favourable to a profound revision of the university and educational system. At the same time it continually warned the students against the dangers of nihilism, and was, as might be expected, far less at ease during the general strike. Nevertheless it was the only source of information that came anywhere near maintaining a reasonable standard of objectivity. *Combat* took the same position as *Le Monde* but with a much more limited and selective news coverage; moreover its motives were doubtless influenced by a virulent anti-Gaullism dating from the Algerian War.

But by far the most interesting reaction, both for its immediate and long-term consequences, was that of the Communist Party newspaper, *L'Humanité*. On 4 May Georges Bouvard wrote: 'The Government, whose avowed object is to limit, as much as possible the number of university students, had every reason to be happy yesterday . . . . Yet how is one to describe those who by their irresponsible acts, their violence and their insults, have brought about this situation? The great mass of students including, we are convinced, many of those who allowed themselves to be manipulated, can now assess the serious consequences which are the inevitable result of political adventurism, even when it is masked by a pseudo-revolutionary phraseology'. The same day the Communist town council of Nanterre issued a statement containing the following: 'Certain grouplets (anarchist, Trotskyite, Maoist, etc.), whose members for the most part come from the upper middle class,[26] and which are

25. For a more detailed study of mass communications in general, including radio and television, see Appendix 2. *La Nation*, the Gaullist mouthpiece, published a remarkably mild article; for once it attempted to influence, not merely express, Gaullism.

26. 'Fils de grands bourgeois'. The full text may be found in *L'Humanité*, 6 May.

led by the German anarchist, Cohn-Bendit, . . . (They) thus objectively aid and abet the government and its policy.'

During the week that followed the Communists turned from the students to attack with increasing vehemence the police repression. But it was these first reactions, even more than their later policy (which was quite consistent with their early statements), which lost them a lot of support among the students who, even if not Communists themselves, naturally expected some encouragement from that quarter in their struggle against the established order. Many of them, even if they did not entirely approve of his timing or choice of words, sympathised with Cohn-Bendit's sentiments when, immediately after marching with the leaders of the CGT in the huge protest demonstration of 13 May, he referred to 'the Stalinist scum'. Yet how many of them stopped to wonder why the Communists were so lavish in their strictures?

The Communists have always had a horror of being overtaken on their left, and to the extent that they feared lest the student movement come under the control of one or all of the grouplets, their attitude was as reasonable as it was comprehensible. But it was less reasonable to try to separate the majority of students from the grouplets while at the same time continuing a series of virulent attacks against those whom most of the students, whatever their political positions, recognised as their spokesmen and whose orders they in the main obeyed.[27] This is probably to be explained by a reflex of class hatred, based in this instance on the opinion, certainly justified, that had the demonstrators been workers and not students (and therefore—in France—by definition the children of influential middle-class parents) police methods would not have been the same. As it was they were not pretty to watch, but it must be remembered that from beginning to end, and however often the police were forced to retreat and however many their wounded, not a single shot was fired, not even in the air. [28] The Communists had led enough workers' demonstrations in the past to know the difference.

This interpretation is confirmed by those who were able to form some idea of the atmosphere in the offices of L'Humanité during the period of the student riots. With one or two exceptions the general attitude was one of intolerance verging on hatred. Not

27. One young reporter who nevertheless sent in enthusiastic pro-student reports found himself relegated to covering women's conferences in Montpellier.
28. Except of course at Sochaux, where only workers were involved—see below, p. 199 and Appendix 3.

87

only were the students not taken seriously as a revolutionary movement, they were treated with the contempt and loathing reserved for the false friends, as opposed to the true enemies, of the working-class.[29] A further confirmation was the attitude of Georges Séguy, secretary-general of the CGT, during a television interview on 17 May. The general trend of the interview was, to all appearances, planned beforehand, and when he was asked about Cohn-Bendit, Georges Séguy replied with undisguised anger and loathing. His emotion, which was certainly genuine, was visible on his face, and was clearly intended to be shared by his audience. It was, in short, an appeal to the baser instincts of the workers, not excluding racialism.

It is true that the Communists did, to a certain limited extent, come to the help of the students both in word and deed, if only by their call for a general strike and demonstration on 13 May. But, as is shown on page 175, their motives were not unmixed. Moreover, at no time did the Party lend the full weight of its prestige and influence to the student cause. In this they were not alone. Several public figures made noble attempts to understand them, such as the left-wing Gaullist Edgar Pisani in a remarkable speech in the special debate in the National Assembly on 8 May, Pierre Mendès-France who visited the barricades on the night of 10 May, and the Archbishop of Paris who, although he later refused to confirm this, visited the wounded in hospital the same night. Yet no-one of any importance, except a few brave professors (they included five of the six French Nobel Prize winners), intervened in any active way to help them.[30] And this despite the fact that on 8 May the *Institut Français d'Opinion Publique* announced the results of a poll that showed 80% of Parisians to be favourable to the students. Although much of this sympathy was certainly dictated by traditional dislike

29. One exception was the Editor, René Andrieu, whose tone, perhaps because he had once been a student himself, was much more moderate. However, not even he took them seriously, since it was not until Wednesday, 15 May, when the first reports of the Sud-Aviation workers' strike came in, that for the first time he was seriously worried. In believing that the news indicated the beginning of something much more serious he was of course perfectly right.

30. Apart from the usual crop of petitions and statements from left-wing intellectuals and writers, on 8 May the following five Nobel Prize winners, MM. Jacob, Kastler, Lwoff, Mauriac, and Monod, sent a telegram to de Gaulle: 'urgently request you take personal action to calm student revolt. Amnesty convicted students. Reopening of faculties. Profound respects.' On 11 May Laurent Schwartz, Henri Cartan, and Maurice Clavel (ex-Gaullist philosopher and writer) resigned their posts, the first two as university professors, the third as a schoolteacher.

of the police, especially in action, and the results would probably have been exactly the opposite in the provinces, it does serve to underline the effective isolation of the students.

On Friday 3 May the students were quite unorganised, without leaders or spokesmen. Over the week-end three spokesmen emerged, Jacques Sauvageot, Alain Geismar, and Daniel Cohn-Bendit. The demonstrations and riots on Monday 6 May were rather sporadic and undisciplined, but by the following evening these three had also become the acknowledged leaders of the student movement. This is not to say that they in any way imposed themselves on the students, or that they were demagogic rabble-rousers. It means that, either because of the organisations they represented or because of what they stood for, they were accepted as delegates, negotiators, and tacticians. They did not control the movement so much as canalise it, and they were as often obliged to lead from behind as from in front.

The most important of the three was Jacques Sauvageot, the twenty-five year old vice-president of the UNEF. The union's conference on 21 April, provoked by the resignation for personal reasons of the President, was disrupted by violent altercations between left-wing and right-wing students, so that it was unable to complete its business and elect a new president. The existing vice-president, a law graduate from Dijon and engaged on a post-graduate thesis on the history of art, thus became temporary acting President. The UNEF was extremely divided and Jacques Sauvageot belonged to the PSU[31] fraction. To begin with, his position was not very secure. The student strike called by the UNEF on Saturday 4 May to take effect on Monday was followed in many provincial faculties, but by no means all. Where communist students had control of the local AGs they refused to strike, following the line of all Communists in the teaching professions that the essential task was to present a united front against the Government and that this would best be achieved by demanding salary increases and better working conditions. However, students everywhere rallied to the UNEF as being, in spite of everything, 'their' union, and under pressure of their reactions to events in Paris by the end of the week the union was not only united but representative of student opinion to a degree that it had not been since before the Algerian War.

31. *Parti Socialist Unifié*, a small, mainly intellectual but active splinter group of Socialist Party dissidents—for details, see Part III.

Alain Geismar is a twenty-nine year old chemistry lecturer (*maître-assistant*) in the Paris science faculty who had graduated from one of the *grandes écoles* (l'Ecole des Mines). He was also until he resigned on 27 May secretary-general of the *Syndicat National des Enseignants du Supérieur*, the university teachers' branch of the *Fédération de l'Education Nationale*, which comprises the *Syndicat National des Instituteurs* and the *Syndicat National des Enseignants du Secondaire*. The exact membership of the SNESup. is uncertain, and such figures as exist have been hotly contested. However, it seems reasonably certain that it is the largest university teachers' union and that it represents approximately a third of the profession. But unlike its smaller rival, the *Syndicat autonome de l'enseignement supérieur* which has an older and more conservative membership, the great majority of its members are, like Alain Geismar himself, young lecturers who have been recruited in vast numbers to cope with the expansion of higher education. They see clearly enough the inanities of the present system, and criticise it, without being certain of being able to benefit from its undoubted advantages at the top of the ladder.[32]

Like the UNEF, the SNESup., is subject to factiousness, and the PSU tendency, led by Alain Geismar (who had been one of the leaders of the PSU in Paris), had defeated the Communist tendency by a small margin at the 1967 conference. However, unlike the student union, its membership was not seriously affected by this, and the majority, few of whom were politically active, took no part in it. The disadvantage of this was that the leadership could not always count on its orders being followed. When Alain Geismar announced a strike on 3 May before the UNEF were able to announce theirs, he acted partly out of solidarity and partly because he saw a chance to force through a radical reform of the university. This was not understood by all his followers, many of whom did not strike on the following Monday, particularly in the provinces. During the week they tended to rally, but the role played by Alain Geismar during the night of 10–11 May once again created doubts. These doubts, which sprang from the feeling that the SNESup.'s solidarity

32. Many, probably most, of the rank and file are to be found, again like Alain Geismar himself, in the science or mathematics faculties. The reason is that in these rapidly developing fields the most outstanding research is often done by young men. Yet, under the French system, this brings few rewards. Advancement can be obtained only by climbing, slowly and painfully, the rungs of the traditional ladder. For an example of an earlier critique of the system see Alain Geismar's article in *Niveau 3*, **2**, September 1967.

with the students was going too far and becoming too overtly political, increased as time went on and it is probable that if Alain Geismar had not resigned when he did there would have been serious ructions. Nevertheless the union's position and actions did an enormous amount to mobilise opinion, both inside and outside the university, in favour of the students.

Daniel Cohn-Bendit was the only one of the three spokesmen who was not the elected representative of a movement. *Le mouvement du 22 mars* refused from the beginning to give itself any formal structure, but the striking looks of ginger-haired Danny 'le rouge', his candid charm, his political intelligence and tactical sense, not to mention his gift for publicity and fund-raising, marked him out, whether he liked it or not, as not merely spokesman but leader. Twenty-three years old at the time, he was born in France of a German Jewish father and French mother. Brought up in Germany after the war (he spent one term on an exchange in an English school), he opted for German nationality (after his father had died), but chose to do his higher education in France. All who taught him, including his sociology professors at Nanterre, appear to have had a great respect for his ability and intelligence, and during May everybody fell under his spell. Even staid columnists like Jean Ferniot, of *France-Soir* and Radio Luxembourg, could say after meeting him: 'I thought I was in the presence of Lenin.'[33]

But Daniel Cohn-Bendit is not a Lenin; he is not even a revolutionary in any meaningful sense of the term. His genius lay simply in this: by a series of relatively minor, but timely mocking and provocative acts and words (the swimming-pool incident at Nanterre, crossing the frontier at will, etc.) he cast on certain isolated aspects of French society a glaring light which neither the parts nor the whole could stand. Allied to this was a remarkable sense of what could and could not be done in the street (see, for a typical example, Document 11). But in any more flexible, more 'permissive' society than France, the tiny catalyst that he was would not have had the same effect; and even as it was his role after the night of 10–11 May was negligible.

Even before then, once the riots had started, his role was largely a symbolic one. The various grouplets who had allied themselves with him at Nanterre were much more inclined to go their own ways

33. *France-Soir*, 17 May 1968. Cf. also the account of several days spent in his company by a *Paris-Match* reporter in Philippe Labro *et al.*, *Ce n'est qu'un début*, Paris, Denoël, 1968, pp. 30–5.

in Paris. The Trotskyite JCR's primary role was to act as the *service d'ordre*[34] of the UNEF, with which Cohn-Bendit was not always in agreement. They did this remarkably well and, although they certainly joined in the fray once fighting started, on several occasions they did all that was humanly possible to avoid a head-on clash with the police. The other Trotskyite faction, the FER, was much more violently inclined and is almost certainly to be counted among those who, along with Cohn-Bendit's 'anarchists', sought to provoke the police into action; however, unlike the *mouvement du 22 mars*, it did not take part in the 'Gay-Lussac' battle on 10–11 May having correctly judged that from a tactical point of view the barricades were a death-trap.[35] Similarly, as early as Monday 6 May the young 'pro-Chinese' UJCML abandoned the march about 13.00 when it turned away from the right bank of the Seine to go back to the Latin Quarter. Thinking that a clash was inevitable they decided to go off in small groups to the working-class districts to explain the students' point of view.

However, these defections were more than compensated for by other groups which, if they had openly announced their presence, would certainly have been disowned by the demonstrators. *Occident*, for example, joined the fray out of hostility to the Government, even though some of its members later took part in counter-demonstrations and attacks on occupied faculties. And from Monday 6 May the hundred or so members of the *Mouvement de la Jeunesse Révolutionnaire* were there in force, armed for the most part and ready for combat. Their motives also were purely political; the only genuinely fascist movement in France,[36] the fact that the MJR had

34. *Service d'ordre* has no exact equivalent in English, although it can easily be defined by its functions. The first and most important is to marshal and control meetings (party conferences, for example), demonstrations or protest marches. Its secondary function is to resist attacks by rival organisations. In certain circumstances the minor function may become the dominant one, but in general a *service d'ordre* is something quite respectable.

35. The FER was intensely jealous of the JCR, and this doubtless influenced its tactical appreciation of the situation. It justified its pacifism on this occasion by the need to persuade the workers to come to the help of the students but, as Appendix 1 (i) shows, where the germs of such an alliance already existed, it was as violently extremist as anyone.

36. The term 'fascist' is often misused. The clandestine MJR, whose leader M. Sergent is in exile in Brussels under sentence of death for OAS activities, merits the term. A glance at Document 10B, which a member of the MJR has assured the author still represents the basis of its doctrine, will show that it corresponds closely enough to the traditional doctrines of national socialism.

its roots in the OAS meant that its hatred of de Gaulle was greater than its hatred of Communism. These were the groups who, together with the FER and some at least of the Nanterre 'anarchists', comprised the 'uncontrolled and uncontrollable elements' which, despite the orders of the leaders, sought clashes with the police whenever possible; it was they, for example, who formed the core of those who started a fight with the police at the end of the long march on 7 May. Yet it is worth remembering that none of the attempts by the authorities to discredit the student movement by driving a wedge between the violent goats and the reasonable sheep succeeded —at least insofar as the students themselves were concerned.

The events of that week are by now sufficiently well known and need only be briefly recapitulated.[37] On Monday, as was to be the case throughout the week, the Sorbonne was heavily guarded by police. The UNEF, the only organisation to call for demonstrations, showed itself somewhat hesitant and indecisive, as three different times and meeting-places were given out in the course of the day. At midday a long procession led the police on a two or three hour dance round the centre of Paris, often at the double with the leaders imposing their own route by such devices as controlling the traffic themselves in such a way as to block the police. Fighting broke out when it finally returned to the Latin Quarter and found access to the Sorbonne barred. The first charge that day was made by the police, but tempers on both sides were so frayed that a clash was inevitable. The battle, which began at 15.30, lasted for nearly twelve hours, and was of a savagery unequalled in France (although not in Algeria) since the 1948 strikes.

About 10,000 students were involved in the demonstrations and strikes on Monday. Nearly three times that number, including several hundred university teachers, responded the following day to the joint call of the UNEF and the SNESup., and marched fifteen miles through Paris in the rain (and at least as many again were demonstrating in most of the provincial university towns). Two points are worth noting: the first is that the students marched by the National Assembly without so much as a glance at it, although it was in session; the second is that, once again using techniques developed by the Japanese Zengakuren, the students outmanoeuvred

37. The best 'blow-by-blow, day-by-day' account is still one of the first to appear, P. Andro, A. Dauvergon, L-M Lagoutte, *Le Mai de la Révolution*, Paris, Julliard, 1968.

the police to cross the Pont de la Concorde and so were able to march up the Champs-Elysées to the Arc de Triomphe, where they sang the Internationale. The police, who had received strict orders not to attack first, could do nothing, but in fact apart from that the route was negotiated by students and police during the march. At the end of the evening, when the procession returned to the Latin Quarter, despite the efforts of the leaders who had given the order to disperse, sporadic violence broke out and lasted until late in the night; all the marchers felt, after the discipline they had so far shown, that they had the right to return to their own area, but the police refused to let them pass. However, once fighting broke out, most students left, and during most of the three hours of disorders there were only two or three thousand students involved.

On Wednesday 8 May in the course of a speech in the National Assembly, the Minister of Education allowed a glimmer of hope to appear. A number of discreet negotiations took place on this and the following day, but the students remained firmly committed to their three prior conditions to any compromise: the re-opening of the Sorbonne, the withdrawal of the police from the Latin Quarter, and the freeing of all imprisoned students. But the Government was unable to concede then what Pompidou granted without a murmur on his return from Afghanistan on Saturday evening. In the meantime an increasing number of older schoolchildren, those who would soon be students, began to agitate. Strike pickets and delegations went from one *lycée* to another, and CALs sprang up everywhere, so that there were five thousand schoolboys and schoolgirls among the demonstrators on Friday evening. On the Wednesday evening the UNEF and the SNESup., again led a march of over twenty thousand demonstrators, but this time (why not the night before?) they were allowed to march round the Latin Quarter, and the leaders were able, not without some difficulty, to disperse them without incident.

The following day the Sorbonne remained closed,[38] and tension high. There were no demonstrations, but small groups of students and passers-by met and talked in the Latin Quarter. These spon-

38. The responsibility for this was entirely Alain Peyrfitte's. The Doyen can take the decision to suspend all lectures, courses, etc., in the university, but only the Minister can take the decision to close it completely. Thus, when at midday 9 May the Rector and Dean announced that certain lectures etc. would start again that afternoon, it is reasonable to suppose that the only thing that stopped this happening was a refusal by the Government to withdraw the police.

taneous discussion groups were to be one of the characteristics of May, but on this occasion they were remarkable, apart from the booing of Louis Aragon, the Communist poet and author, for the way in which accounts of their leadership were demanded of, and given by Jacques Sauvageot, Alain Geismar and Daniel Cohn-Bendit. Later in the evening some three thousand students left the surroundings of the Sorbonne to attend a meeting in the *Salle de la Mutualité* organised by the JCR. Various student leaders from abroad proclaimed their support for the revolt as did Ernest Mandel, the Belgian Trotskyite.

The last demonstration of this first phase, on 10 May, exactly a week after the first Paris riots, took place at the call of the CALs for the schoolchildren, and of the UNEF and the SNESup., for the students and teachers. At 19.30 some 10,000 demonstrators left the Place Denfert-Rochereau, and at 20.40, after a short detour, over 20,000 had gone up the Boulevard Saint Michel to the Luxembourg Gardens, the only route the police left open to them. There the order was given to disperse and occupy the area surrounding the Sorbonne. Soon after, at 21.15, the first barricade was built; by the end of the evening there were over thirty of them. Various desperate attempts were made to avoid a disaster, but the Government would not or could not make the necessary gesture. During the long wait some students left, but the majority, including many schoolchildren, remained. At 02.15 the order was given to the police to disperse the students, and the resulting pitched battle lasted for nearly three hours, and scattered rearguard actions continued until dawn. Long before, the police had completely encircled the area, so that it was extremely difficult for the first-aid volunteers to evacuate the wounded and for those students who wished to abandon the unequal battle to do so. Police behaviour was such that all who witnessed it were scandalised, and those living in the area, often at considerable risk to themselves, did all they could to help the students, throwing water over them from the windows, or giving succour to the wounded and exhausted; and some even did not complain on the morrow when they found their cars destroyed, admitting openly that the students had no alternative but to use them in self-defence.

That Friday night, '*la nuit des barricades*', the battle of Gay-Lussac (the street in which the heaviest fighting took place) was the students' finest hour. Afterwards they found themselves caught up in a series of situations which they had not foreseen, and with which they were not equipped to cope. The image they had created of themselves over that first week was tarnished, both by their enemies and some of their even more dangerous friends—the excitable neurotics that every revolt throws up, the *agents provocateurs*, the social outcasts from the working-class suburbs and the young unemployed (whom the students, and it is to their credit, were never to disown, considering them to be the victims of the same system as themselves), the *enragés* with no object but to create more chaos; and their good intentions, courage and integrity were not enough to prevent the fruits of their action turning somewhat sour. Even their great moral victory that night, dearly bought as it was, was not devoid of impurities and ambiguities. Five and a half hours, it is true, elapsed between the time the students occupied the area and the time the police charged, but who set the example of building barricades? Were they really, at the beginning, simply the manifestation of the students' resolution to stay put and a way of killing time? Who were the older men seen helping and advising the students in building them —sympathetic passers-by, Trotskyite professional revolutionaries, *agents provocateurs*, or, most probably at that stage, men connected with the fascist MJR? It is tempting to answer in the way most favourable to the students, as doubtless did many of the very middle-class inhabitants of the district. After all, the students were fighting for changes that were long overdue, and the great majority sincerely believed their cause to be a just one. But if the questions must remain open ones, no possible answer can change the essential fact: no conspiracy, no outside agency, could have succeeded in mobilising so many students and spurring them to such a desperate and courageous fight.[39]

39. The same questions do not arise in the case of the early demonstrations in the provinces, as although in the course of that week there were several thousand students on the streets in nearly every university town, it was only in Toulouse on 7 May that there was any serious violence.

What happened that week in the provinces was not always reported in the Paris press which depends very much on the correspondents of the local papers for its information; and where the local paper is biased towards the conservative right the demonstrations were systematically minimised. Such was the case of Dijon. Partly for that reason, and partly to show the evolution of opinion in a provincial town, a short account of the beginnings of the student revolt in Dijon is given in Appendix 1 (i).

DOCUMENT 10

Some student manifestoes

A

The Grenoble Charter of the UNEF, 1946

Preamble—The French student representatives, who legally convened the Congress of Grenoble on 24 April 1946, being aware of the historical value of that time when the French Union drew up the new Declaration of the rights of man and of the citizen,

on which is based the peaceful statute of nations,

in which the world of youth and labour can discover the basic elements of a social and economic revolution in the service of man, state their willingness to participate in a unanimous effort to rebuild,

being faithful to the traditional aims pursued by French youth when most acutely conscious of its mission, and faithful also to the example set by the best of them, who died when France was fighting for her freedom,

declare obsolete the institutions which govern them,

state their wish to take up a position, as so often in the course of our history, at the forefront of French youth, by freely outlining the following principles which form the basis of their tasks and their demands.

Article 1—The student is a young intellectual worker.

Rights and duties of the student as a young man

Article 2—As a young man, the student has a right to special social considerations in the physical, intellectual and moral field.

Article 3—As a young man, the student has a duty to be part of national and world youth.

Rights and duties of the student as a worker

Article 4—As a worker, the student has a right to work and to rest in the best conditions, enjoying material independence, personal as much as social, the whole being guaranteed by the free exercise of union rights.

Article 5—As a worker, the student has a duty to be as technically competent as possible.

Rights and duties of the student as an intellectual.

Article 6—As an intellectual, the student has a right to be able to search for truth and to be free to do so, which is the primary condition.

Article 7—As an intellectual, the student has a duty:

To seek, put forward and defend the truth, which implies a duty to ensure that culture is shared and advanced, and meaningfully to interpret history.

To defend liberty against all oppression, which is the intellectual's most sacred mission.

B

The 'credo' of the OAS and MJR

Although the following text dates from 1963, the author has been assured by a member of the MJR that it accurately reflects the goals and aims of that organisation.

What we are fighting for

Until victory is achieved the OAS will continue to fight:

1. For the complete destruction of the Gaullist regime, for the liquidation of its after-effects, for the execution of its leaders;

2. To set up a revolutionary regime which will re-instil a sense of struggle and self-sacrifice in our besotted people and which will above all enable France to rediscover her soul;

3. To build up a state which, while respecting essential liberties and exercising a system of law which is not over and above common law, will impose the interests of the whole against the ambitions of various factions and special interests, be they those of stateless finance or communist subversion;

4. For a transformation of the social order, so as to enable salaried workers to obtain the right, both at industrial and

professional levels, to share in profits and above all in the running of the economy;

5. For the constitution of a living Europe, belonging not to bankers and technocrats, but to universities, youth and armies;

6. For Eurafrica which will enable us to replace the axis of poverty that we have allowed to come into existence from East to West, with a North-South axis representing prosperity and culture;

7. For the creation of a militant Western bloc sure of itself and of the civilisation whose future lies in its hands, which will replace the defensive attitude in face of the communist threat by an aggressive attitude which alone will make eventual victory possible.

(Source: *Jeune Révolution*, 8 November 1963).

C

Occident

Young French people are tired:

Of being constantly given pamphlets in favour of the Vietcong assassins at the doors of their places of work, their faculties and their schools.

Of seeing the eternal traitors who only yesterday were supporting the Vietminh torturers and Arab terrorists in the name of 'PEACE', today becoming the hirelings of the Vietcong.

These people have tried the patience of French youth for too long and they know it. For more than fifteen days now, agents in the pay of Hanoi who come to distribute their calls to treason have regularly been put to flight by schoolboys and students united under the French nationalists.

The OCCIDENT movement spearheads this opposition. For several years now it has been fighting against the physical and moral terrorism used by the reds against French Youth in the name of their 'liberty'.

The OCCIDENT movement has been able, by virtue of its activities, its posters and its demonstrations, to get the upper hand in the street and make the marxists understand that their dictatorship has come to an end.

Join OCCIDENT and fight against reaction and the red front by fighting for a Nationalist popular Regime.

THE NATIONALIST YOUTH MOVEMENT.

(Leaflet distributed before May 1968)

DOCUMENT 11

Some views on Cohn-Bendit and the *mouvement du 22 mars*

FRANCOIS TRUFFAUT:

As far as I was concerned the 'Cinémathèque affair', as it is called, was a sort of prologue to events in May. I only realised this afterwards of course, in the light of May—but in fact the situation was somewhat the same, in miniature: 'intellectuals' who opposed the Government decision to get rid of Henri Langlois, (the founder and soul of the Cinémathèque) and who went out into the streets and got themselves clubbed. Government officials were doing the same thing with the Cinémathèque as they had done all over France: first they would subsidise, then they would infiltrate. I was clubbed for the first time in my life at the Palais de Chaillot demonstration, and I noticed that it was not as painful as all that. The truncheons were made of rubber, or some plastic material and once I even broke one. I had a very hot sensation in my head, but I was not bleeding. At the next demonstration, in the rue de Courcelles, the ordinary police had been replaced by the CRS. And the long riot truncheons appeared, the Charonne truncheons. This was on 19 March and it was then that I saw Daniel Cohn-Bendit for the first time, which is why, for me, the Cinémathèque represents a sort of prologue. In fact I think he came to two demonstrations out of three. To be quite honest I was not very favourably impressed. Several of us wanted to keep up an appearance of impartiality, we wanted to keep the fight 'apolitical', because we thought that if the affair became tainted with politics, Langlois would not have a hope of coming back as director of the Cinémathèque.

Then, when we saw this red-headed boy who had climbed up a lamp-post and who was calling us 'comrades', we all wondered who he was and what he was there for. Afterwards he got onto a window-ledge. I found him very methodical, very professional. He would wait for the crowd, and above all the young people from the 'Occident' movement, to be silent, because it was really to them that he was talking, and there was some danger of a confrontation. I think Cohn-Bendit had come to rue de Courcelles because he was interested in all forms of protest, then he became engrossed in what was going on, because he showed us things that we did not know how to do—but always calmly and by using the power of the spoken word. At the end of the demonstration we were quietly preparing to go our separate ways, but a boy had been arrested by the police, and it was at this juncture that Cohn-Bendit harangued us. He said: 'We shall not go away until our comrade has been freed'. I just thought that the poor boy was doubtless already in a police station somewhere.

As he was to do later on however, and on quite a different scale, in the streets of the Latin Quarter, Cohn-Bendit immediately decided to stay and secure his release, immediately decided that the only place to fight was there, on the spot. He said things such as: 'In Brittany the peasants waited six hours for one of their comrades to be freed. How long will the Parisians wait?' He was very cunning in fact. Because of him a few film directors did in fact go and talk to the police, and we did get the boy released—he was a schoolboy I think. I didn't even know one could do that sort of thing. When I asked who the red-headed boy was, who had taught us how to look after ourselves, I was told: 'he's a fellow from Nanterre.'

(Source: Philippe Labro et al., *op. cit.*, pp. 148–9)

The following extracts from interviews with students, and all other such extracts, are taken from material collected by William MacLean in the course of 27 interviews, based on a questionnaire, with students in Paris, Nantes, Strasbourg and Toulouse. William MacLean very kindly allowed the author to make his own selection, which is in no way 'scientific'. Any generalisation must await the publication of the interviewer's own analysis. To avoid overloading the text, a brief description of the students is given below, in the order in which they appear in this section and in following sections.

Law, Paris: interviewed 11 June 1968; 25, male, post-graduate; son of a travelling salesman, he envisages a political career with the FGDS; one of the more conservative students interviewed.

Cybernetics, Paris: interviewed 21 June 1968; 25, male, married, 2 children; he did not take part in any of the violent demonstrations and only joined the movement after 13 May, but felt very much at home in it.

Schoolboy, Paris: interviewed 15 June 1968; 20, claims several nationalities and comes from a disturbed family background; an exception not simply because he is a schoolboy, but in the wealth

102

of knowledge and figures with which he supported his arguments. He is an example of the more extremist activists.

Theology, Strasbourg: interviewed 13 July 1968; 26, male, of peasant stock he is a very strict Catholic, but politically is PSU; he accepts violence, and is a fervent revolutionary, considering purely university problems as secondary; his political awareness came while at university.

History, Nantes: interviewed 25 June 1968; 24, male, very much a west country man with thick peasant hands, but a piercing intelligence. He is not a revolutionary, but a realistic, down-to-earth union militant with a great sense of responsibility towards those he has left behind (his primary school peer group are all in the army, the police, or are small artisans).

Medicine, Paris: interviewed 9 June 1968; 23, female, married; a very correct middle-class girl who is, for example, shocked that a university faculty (Nanterre) could be built in the midst of slums; she is one of the many who, before May, had never considered either university or social problems outside those of her own faculty.

Political sociology, Paris: interviewed 16 July 1968; 26, male, a member of the MJR (see above Document 1B), he did not reject the epithet 'fascist': he was badly wounded in the Battle of Gay Lussac, and spent five weeks in hospital.

Law, Paris:

The supporters of the *mouvement du 22 mars* are anarchists; they walk around waving the black flag. I've nothing against the black flag, besides as far as I'm concerned a flag doesn't mean much . . . but I can see that it frightens people and that it doesn't have a very good reputation if you see what I mean. No, but they go a bit far. . . . They want to change society whatever the cost, but they have nothing to offer in exchange . . . So, precisely, I wanted to talk about the general aims of the movement. The main aim is political; they want to change society, but they don't have much to offer in its place. And that's the great movement. But I think even so the movement is interesting because *if* it has become so important, and *if* for example the UNEF, even . . . the *mouvement du 22 mars* is extremist, but then there is the UNEF which is a bit less so, although . . . it doesn't do badly! I think one can ask oneself:

why are we in this situation? And, well, I think its entirely the Government's fault.

Cybernetics, Paris:

At the beginning, before the events in May I knew of Cohn-Bendit and the *mouvement du 22 mars*, but personally I didn't approve of them at all, in fact I even thoroughly disapproved. Interrupting lectures . . . I hadn't seen the light then I suppose. And it's simply because of . . . I only judge from results you see . . . I totally disapprove of what happened at Nanterre, personally it bothers me a lot to see the walls of . . . to see the walls filthy. I don't like inscriptions on walls. But on the other hand, it's quite obvious that if there hadn't been the *mouvement du 22 mars*, Nanterre, Cohn-Bendit, and all the chaos, we would never have got anything. If 150 cars hadn't been burnt, we'd still have the old system, although it's not particularly pleasant to burn cars.

DOCUMENT 12

Some views on the origin and goals of the student movement.

Schoolboy, Paris:

I'll tell you something, I'm digressing a bit in telling you that the first time I took part in the student movement was in Berlin, last summer during the July–August demonstrations. I went to Berlin several times because I was in charge of trips for the Franco-German Bureau; or rather trips organised by the Franco-German Bureau; so I was directly in contact with people belonging to the SDS in Berlin, with the Commune, with Dutschke, Teufel and the others, and Dutschke said to us one evening: 'I know what I don't want, but I don't know what I do want.' And this is very true, because we're in the same situation; we can see what's missing and what's wrong, but I think what we want. . . . We can't draw up a programme at the moment, because there has to be a change in basic structures for that to become possible. So we can't really know what we want to have and what we want to do until we've broken down these structures. And a growing awareness took place, at different levels, amongst students—even amongst workers (for I've been to Billancourt quite a few times to talk to them, because I wanted there to be a link between my action, the students', as well as that of the workers), and what we want here and now, well we know what our immediate claims are obviously, since it was they that started the movement going. As to what we want in the long run: well a lot of us—I mean the people who are left-wing, to the left of the PSU if you prefer it, realised the truth of the fact that we just couldn't see the system evolving in any other way than in the perspective of a socialist system. Then we might be able to begin to discuss the different forms of socialism and the chances of building socialism into a system, into the present system. Shall we say that what we contest and what we want to do . . . and the problem that we are trying to make other people understand, well it's a bit complicated, but it means what it means, it's, it's the problem of the consumer civilisation. The consumer society, that's what we contest; we want to show people that they aren't made to live . . . well, rather that they aren't alive so that they can have a car, they aren't alive for the sake of material things. And if they think they're living for material things, then it's because they're intoxicated, and that in fact the real . . . man's real life is on a much higher sphere; it's in the realm of culture, at least I think it is, but then that's a personal opinion. It's in the realm of culture and I saw, during my last trip to Israel, which was a long one and I worked in a kibbutz for six months, I saw people who had nothing and who were incomparably happier than the people in this country who have everything, because they had . . . because culture was theirs and was at their disposal.

Theology, Strasbourg:

Because it was very new in Strasbourg, there were no demonstrations last year; at the last demonstration I went to, three years ago, there were two hundred people. I think it must have been in the second term—our first demonstration, at the time of the university halls of residence, in fact it started off as a meeting of sorts, not a street demonstration; there were some 800 people because three of four leaflets had been distributed. So I would say people were already beginning to be aware by the second term, a lot of students felt that something was wrong; then with the halls of residence affair, they saw that eight hundred of them could do anything they wanted, if really they were to join forces in aid of some cause; for example, still on the halls of residence topic, we said we wanted such and such a ruling, we wanted to participate, we wanted to be able to go into both boys and girls hostels; right, we were efficient, we got what we wanted and nobody said anything about it. I think that was . . . very important in Strasbourg; we realised that by joining forces we could get our way, so what followed was only logical because we saw that we could do the same thing for specifically university problems. And then of course since May, well the first demonstration too—what a surprise—there were at least 1500 of us, we never expected to be so many . . .

I would say that the average student was drawn into the movement without realising that he had been mobilised by the lack of job openings, or because his German course wasn't all that it might have been, but he had become engrossed in a movement whose leaders were thinking of anything but German courses . . . .

I didn't think May would happen quite so soon, but I was very glad that it did; but then that's what I was waiting for, what I was looking for, I found that . . . well . . . people weren't interested in political problems, they didn't realise what was happening, that they were passive and didn't react, so in fact that's what I'd been waiting for since I'd been in the movement.

History, Nantes:

We had our day of regional action here on 8 May I think, and what happened? It consisted of walking round the Duchess Ann Hotel, of going for a walk and that's all. In fact the unions are frightened of being swamped by the rank and file. When violence did break out, it was in fact for this very reason. And believe me it paid. In the case of Nantes this was particularly obvious on 13 May, because whereas the motions asked the Prefect to find offices for the Nantes branch of the UNEF, for our Paris comrades to be freed, for the Prefect's and the Rector's complaints to be withdrawn (since we'd done one or two things during the course of the year), for the restoration of the subsidy that had been abolished because of some of our activities during the year—people just went for an hour's walk, there was an enormous crowd for Nantes: 30,000 people; and there were demonstrations at St Nazaire as well. During the first part of the demonstration people just walked around; the representatives went to see the Prefect, who all but laughed in their faces . . . in fact he did laugh in their faces . . . He told them: that's not my responsibility, I shall have to refer to my superiors. Anyway it's always the same old story of nobody being willing to take the responsibility. Well after that people really got angry and 4 or 5,000 young people, against union instructions, went and shook the railings of the prefecture pretty violently and then went inside. At this juncture the police intervened. A few barricades. Nothing bad, huh! I mean nobody was hitting very hard, then. Finally there were discussions with the Prefect who, all of a sudden, gave back our subsidy, withdrew his complaint and the Rector's . . .

It's a fact that to begin with we were after the same things as at Nanterre. You know that challenge to everyday life at Nanterre or Antony (I'm thinking of the halls of residence) was fairly . . . spectacular let's say at Antony, and Antony was . . . shall we say roughly treated last year. Several times there was evidence of the police state they were denouncing, and in my opinion it was shown in a pretty clumsy way. That's one point. In Nantes we took practically the same . . . I don't think we're their disciples. I think

107

that what happened in Nantes . . . Because the team of people in charge laid down a pretty tough union line, and being at the same time connected with a fairly anarcho-unionist and situationist movement (it's a mixture, it's rather difficult to sort it all out), revealed by scandal, therefore a bit like Nanterre, what was illogical and contradictory about the university system, and even about the general system in which we live.

Medicine, Paris:

I've been at university for five years, you know, in the faculty of medicine and for five years people have been trying to outdo each other as regards reforms. One begins to get a bit tired of it all. People of my age are beginning to be part of adult life, while at the same time we aren't, while at the same time we're financially dependent, which is all the same rather . . . rather awkward. And then, there's this excitement almost; things are fermenting; and I think that, without one realising it, on top of it all there are these stories of . . . well yes, about technology, all that sort of thing, we were used to it, we allowed ourselves to be convinced, we . . . Then one loses one's sense of values. And . . . I think they acted as a detonator, in fact there's no doubt about it. All of a sudden people realised what we were living through. But we were living in such a stupid way—*we* first of all. We were just letting ourselves be completely alienated by all the stuff we were being told and . . . . In fact even now there are people who are very easily influenced by the chap who picks up the microphone; you can twist general assemblies just like that. It's because people aren't very sure of their convictions. And I think the . . . yes the *mouvement du 22 mars*, certainly exploded something, brought up to the surface something which undoubtedly had been latent for some time. Outside the university, for years and years there have been workers' and labourers' strikes, and they have been very tough strikes. There was some very tough striking at Redon for example, which was completely hushed up by the government, and the press in general. And . . . now everything has just exploded.

DOCUMENT 13

Statement made before the disciplinary committee of the university
of Paris,
Monday 6 May at 11.00

Gentlemen,

I challenge you,
I challenge the disciplinary council,
I challenge your tribunal.

Gentlemen, I am not challenging you as professors, my tutors,
whose job it is to impart to a student such as myself the knowledge
and culture which I need for the profession I intend to take up.

I CHALLENGE YOU, because you are gathered here today, acting
on the orders of a Government and State, which, by means of
selection and massive elimination has decided to turn out of the
University 2/3 of the students whom one of your colleagues, the
Rector CAPELLE, previously described as waste products.

I CHALLENGE YOU, because I find before me today not my
professors, but men who have agreed to carry out the work of the
CRS and to endorse the unprecedented decision to close the Sorbonne.

I CHALLENGE YOU, because whatever your verdict may be,
I wish to remain proud of my name and the sacrifices that my father,
a metal worker, made in order that I might continue my studies.
Like all workers, my father has to bear the burden of the governmental measures decided by the 5th Plan, which include the police-
style educational reforms that you accept.

In challenging you, Gentlemen, I realise that I am defending not
only the right to study and freedom in the university, but also your
positions as professors, your mission as teachers, your own dignity.
At the moment, Gentlemen my judges, I shall not reply to any of
your questions.

Michel POURNY

UNEF Militant
Member of the NATIONAL BUREAU of the FER

109

DOCUMENT 14

A Student's Account of the battle of Gay-Lussac

Political Sociology, Paris:

. . . I'd already taken part in a movement several times, because there wasn't really anything one could call a student movement in France, but I'd participated with students or other young people in non-violent activities of one sort or another, whose object was always to overthrow the regime and replace it with another one. This was the first time I'd been to a demonstration with a helmet, resolved to fight. It was the first time it had happened to me, although I'd already been to demonstrations, and violent ones too, but in the past I'd never decided to fight before going. Yet on this occasion, it was 5 or 6 May, I'd decided to fight physically against the regime.

I think . . . at the beginning the situation was becoming more and more tense. I went to the demonstration that evening, helmeted as usual and with a club which I hoped to be able to use, and then we went to the science faculty; there were quite a lot of us—tens of thousands of students—I reckon there must have been 20,000 or 30,000, perhaps even 40,000 young people, and they were all very purposeful; there were far fewer slogans, very little was said, even amongst ourselves, which was not the way it had been before; it was quite obvious that people wanted direct, violent action. When we got there, we took Boulevard Saint-Germain before going up Boulevard Saint-Michel; we couldn't go anywhere else—the CRS or riot police were blocking all the other exits, and when we got to the top of Boulevard Saint-Michel I was in the first row because . . . people with helmets had been put in the first row, and I was next to Sauvageot, who . . . hesitated for a moment, as if he wasn't quite sure what to do—in fact I don't think anybody knew exactly what we wanted at that time, and I dare say it was because of the fact that the UNEF had adopted a slightly more moderate position only a short time before, that Sauvageot simply turned to us and said—to the people in the first row—'We're going to blockade the quarter; do what you want, but blockade the quarter, keep it, it's an act of revolution.' The sort of words he'd never . . . they'd never heard before. Well, straight away, spontaneously, a few of us who were there took up the pickaxes we had with us and started to take up the paving stones, at the same time trying to convince the others near us that they ought to do likewise and pass the paving stones forward, so as to begin building barricades in order to blockade a quarter of Paris, a quarter of the capital of France. I stayed for half an hour and could see that everything was going well, from my point of view anyway, because there was definitely a revolutionary spirit developing amongst these students.

Quite by chance I met a friend of mine, who wasn't at all equipped for the demonstration. We took his car and went to his parents' house to find some stuff for him, and also to get a few bottles of wine and some fruit to give to the people behind the barricades who'd been working for several hours by then. We went back straight away with the firm intention of really blockading this street, and staying there as long as possible. It wasn't just a demonstration, or . . . a rebellious movement, it was an act of insurrection. I went on building barricades, carrying stones, paving stones, bits of wood to a lorry— anything which could be of use for a barricade . . . and . . . it was then I met Cohn-Bendit, who was there, going from group to group and who was . . . dressed just as usual, with nothing to protect himself; he was very, very calm, very sure of himself, he seemed like a fanatic finding his position reasonable all of a sudden, because he was in his element, because . . . he found life was just beginning to be normal and decent as far as he was concerned. We were carrying on taking up the paving stones in all the roads round about rue Gay-Lussac and the other roads in the area whose names I don't know, and then Cohn-Bendit arrived. He swore at us pretty roundly, and said, 'Look, the barricades are high enough, no provocation, there's no point going on with that, all I ask of you now is to . . . sit down, talk to each other, form political action committees' (action committee was quite a new word at the time, it was . . . I don't think it existed before—not the word anyway), and he said we should take each other's name and address, that it wouldn't be all over in one night, and so even if we were obliged to leave that night, we must be able to contact each other afterwards in order to start again on a stronger basis. I saw him . . . going from one barricade to another, we were in a sort of group. I was in the UNEF *service d'ordre*, perhaps only because I had a helmet. I think that constituted the UNEF *service d'ordre* at the time. And Cohn-Bendit was giving advice all round, he was very, very, very, calm, he was really very cool.

I think almost everybody in the street was helping in one way or another to build the barricades. There was one exception—I remember a young man who was perched on a car or a heap of something, haranguing the crowd and saying: 'Don't build barricades —if you do, the police will be obliged to get you out of the quarter, the Government's job is to re-establish law and order in the streets. It will be a massacre'. I think two or three people tried to reply, and then everybody left him because this was no time for words any more, it was straight action . . .

Well then, roughly, we went on building barricades, and then towards two or half past past two in the morning, we saw some red flares in the sky, no doubt fired by the CRS, or the police, which meant anyway that we had to get out, otherwise they would charge. As far as I know, up until then, no student, anywhere, had thrown a stone at the police, there were verbal insults but no violence. It appeared that the Government wanted us to leave this . . . our barricades. They began to throw an enormous number of tear-gas bombs, chloride bombs (the yellow ones) and offensive bombs . . .

Once again I was surprised at the determination shown by the young, by the students—there were a few workers there as well— who were breathing with difficulty, who could hardly see, who were crying and sometimes suffocating, but who nevertheless just stayed there. I was also surprised to see people who hadn't got a helmet like myself, or any of my equipment, but who stayed up in the front line regardless of the danger, who saw people being wounded all around them . . . who were then immediately carried away, towards the rear, usually by girls who were there with us, and there was always someone ready to take his place in the front line. I was astonished to see people not running away, resolved to occupy a street.

DOCUMENT 15

Some oddments

A

An appeal for help

APPEL AUX PARISIENS

IL Y A PEUT-ETRE DES 'GROUPUSCULES'
'ENRAGES DE L'ACTION'
MAIS IL Y A AUSSI DES
'MILLIONS D'ENRAGES DE L'IMMOBILITE'
QUI ACCEPTENT BEATEMENT DU PLUS PROFOND DE LEUR
FAUTEUIL CE QUE DIFFUSENT LES JOURNAUX, L'O.R.T.F.
OU MEME TOUT SIMPLEMENT CE QUE RACONTE LE VOISIN.

PARISIENS

NOUS NE VOUS DEMANDONS PAS D'AGIR
NOUS NE VOUS DEMANDONS PAS DE NOUS DEFENDRE
NOUS DISONS SIMPLEMENT QU'IL EST DE
VOTRE DEVOIR
D'ETRE LA, DANS LA RUE OU MEME A VOS FENETRES
D'ETRE LA, PASSIFS SI VOUS NE VOULEZ PAS AGIR, MAIS
D'ETRE LA,

PRESENTS
CAR
LA FORCE DES YEUX QUI REGARDENT
EST UNE
FORCE DE JUSTICE

LA MATRAQUE
N'OSERA PAS ENTRER EN DANSE SI VOUS LA REGARDEZ
AVEC DES

MILLIONS D'YEUX

B

A 'revolutionary' song

Nearly all the students sang the Internationale a great deal of the time. This is one of the other songs some of them presumably sang (to the tune of the Carmagnole and Ça Ira).

M'sieur Grappin avait résolu (bis)
De nous faire tomber sur le cul (bis)
Mais son coup a foiré
Malgré ses policiers

113

Refrain:
Valsons la grappignole
C'est la misère
ou la colère
Valsons la grappignole
C'est la colère à Nanterre
Ah, ça ira, ça ira, ça ira
Morin Lefebvre on les emmerde
Ah, ça ira, ça ira, ça ira
Et le touraine
On s'le paiera
Et si on s'le paie pas
On lui cass'ra la gueule
Et si on s'le paie pas
Sa gueule on lui cass'ra.

Bourricaud s'il fait des dégats   (bis)
Ce n'est pas avec ses gros bras   (bis)
c'est la sociologie
qui pète quand il chie
                    Au refrain
Ricoeur n'crach'pas sur les bonnes soeurs   (bis)
Mais il préfère les pasteurs   (bis)
C'est tous les jours dimanche
Le bondieu dans la manche
                    Au refrain
Maisonneuve écrit dans l'Aurore   (bis)
C'est pas un singe c'est un porc   (bis)
Doazan n'aime pas Fourier
C'est qu'il est constipé
                    Au refrain
Les staliniens de l'UEC   (bis)
Voudraient baiser les ouvriers   (bis)
Ils n'ont qu'leurs permanents
A s'foutre sous la dent
                    Au refrain
Les étudiants sont des pantins   (bis)
Moi j'en chie vingt tous les matins (bis)
Déja leurs lendemains
Chantent comme des catins
                    Au refrain—Final
Valsons la grappignole
Flics en civil, murs de béton
Valsons la grappignole
Profils d'études, programmations.

114

C

The young Gaullists

ETUDIANTS...

Le 11 Novembre 1940, vos ainés manifestaient à l'Arc de Triomphe et les Allemands les fusillaient. En 1968, des agitateurs étrangers insultent la France.

"Le drapeau français est fait pour être déchiré et transformé en drapeau rouge... "

COHN-BENDIT, Amsterdam le 22 Mai,
dépêche AFP

CE N'EST PAS VOTRE LUTTE MONTREZ-LE ! Rejoignez les Jeunes des C.D.R.

Secrétariat Permanence :

5, Rue de Solférino, 75 - PARIS 7ᵉ Tel. 705-90-27

CHAPTER THREE

THE OCCUPATION OF THE FACULTIES AND LYCEES

'The randier I am, the more revolutionary I become,
The more revolutionary I am, the randier I become.'

'Be sensible; bite off more than you can chew!'[1]

THESE two slogans written during May, the one on the walls of the Sorbonne, the other on those at Censier, symbolise two aspects of the students' and schoolboys' revolt. On the one hand there was a sort of gigantic happening in the course of which Frenchmen started doing some most extraordinary things, like talking to complete strangers in the street. On the other hand, there was a universal demand for radical reform of secondary and higher education in France. Starting from very much less than what exists in many other countries, the reformers ended up by demanding considerably more; but these demands were worked out, reasoned, formulated and presented in a way which provoked the sometimes unwilling admiration of those who were set in authority over the authors of them. Although these two phenomena, the happening and the reform projects, were in many ways distinct—they were not always to be found in the same places nor were the same people necessarily involved—they were both basically motivated by the same desire for individual and corporate responsibility on the part of those to whom up to now French society has systematically refused it.

Unless it be considered revolutionary to behave in the Sorbonne as though one was in Polynesia, it is obvious that the young man

1. These are both very free translations by the author of the following: 'Plus je fais l'amour, plus j'ai envie de faire la Révolution, Plus je fais la révolution, plus j'ai envie de faire l'amour', and: 'Soyez réalistes: demandez l'impossible.' Julien Besançon, ed. *Les Murs ont la parole*, Paris, Tchou, 1968, contains these and hundreds of other examples of the 'verbal revolution'.

who wrote the first slogan was not a revolutionary in any meaningful sense of the term. Political revolutionaries tend to have rather more puritan attitudes, whereas what was expressed there was much closer to the attitude symbolised by '*le repos du guerrier*', the release of tension after action. What is significant is that the release found such easy and open expression. It is even possible that, as the student movement was overtaken by bigger and more important events, there were a certain number of students who no longer had any clear idea of what to do with the 'student power' they had achieved, who turned to a 'hippy' style of life as an end in itself ('make love not war' was on the walls as well). But whether or not by the end of May, as one commentator has stated,[2] couples were actually copulating openly in the corridors, there was no segregation in the 'dormitories' and opportunities were not lacking. At the time of the Algerian War student activism was often a means of sublimation, particularly for girls; sex, if practised, was more for hygiene than for pleasure. In May their younger sisters tended to go to the other extreme. Sex was not only expected of them; they had come to expect it of themselves, and they went to it with a will which suggested that they had gone somewhere the other side of freedom. Lack of proper contraceptive information meant that this has certainly increased, if only marginally, the number of unwanted pregnancies in France.[3] But in a sense it was typical of many of the more extravagant aspects of the student movement. Where normal safety-valves do not exist, and the lid blows off, the forces that break out tend to go to extremes.

For this casting down of social barriers and taboos was not of course confined to sex. Following the example of the students, large numbers of people discovered not so much the freedom of speech, which in a formal sense has always existed, as the freedom of public discussion with total strangers. Interminable debates on all manner of subjects took place, sometimes in the open, on street-

2. Epistémon, op. cit., p. 57, but it must be said that neither the author nor anyone else he has spoken to encountered this.
3. There were also some other undesirable side-effects. A certain number of older men started a white-slave traffic among some of the very young girls. Whether or not, as one version has it, this was the work of government agents setting out to discredit the students, it is certain that the publicly branded 'undesirable elements', *les Katangais* (cf. p. 200) had no hand in it, since they co-operated in rescuing some of the victims. The same sources may also have been responsible for the hashish and LSD, neither of which are as common among French students as they are in some student circles elsewhere.

corners or in the markets, sometimes in the shelter of a university lecture hall. Students and schoolboys took part in general assemblies and commissions which not infrequently continued all night. By dint of talking endlessly about the implications of what was happening many began for the first time to formulate their own ideas about the nature of the society they lived in, and their place in it. It is true that few of these discussion groups were democratic in any formal way, and questionable decisions were sometimes taken. But there was in general very little of the bullying and intimidation of the authorities and other students that undoubtedly occurred at Nanterre. Those who attended some of these meetings were struck by the tolerance which prevailed. If a minority opinion was voiced and shouted down, there would always follow an effective appeal for calm and a reminder that everyone had the right to his say. Votes were certainly taken in dubious circumstances, such as in the course of spontaneous meetings to which there had been no general summons or after an all-night sitting when only the least sleepy remained. But this was not, as some have thought, a deliberate policy, modelled on the Chinese principle of direct democracy. It was rather an indication of the students' revolt against any and all authority; for traditional democratic voting procedure requires a structure and with it a formal authority which the students consistently rejected (many of the smaller meetings had no chairman).[4]

At the same time there was something more than a little bourgeois about this aspect of the student revolt (French students are essentially a bourgeois phenomenon). From being an austere temple of learning (it was built at the end of the nineteenth century as a temple *to* French culture) the Sorbonne became a sort of gigantic theatre, a kind of 'Round House', where total freedom was allowed to everybody to live as they pleased and to express themselves in their own way, where the quadrangle resembled a garden fête except that charity stalls were replaced by political ones and the Israeli propagandist rubbed shoulders with the El Fath one, and where in short a miniature unstructured libertarian society grew up, had its moment of grandeur, and finally died a rather sordid death. But this

4. It also underlines the spontaneous character of the student movement, and the fact that, although there were spokesmen, there were no effective leaders once the movement had left the streets. For a democratic structure can only be existed if there exists already a recognised authority or structure of some sort—cf. chapter 6, where it is shown how the workers always turned to the union delegates to set up their strike committees.

kind of total rejection of normal social values is only possible for those who start off with a secure base in the society they reject. The 'beat' and 'hippy' movements of the last two decades have recruited their followers almost exclusively among the middle classes; in a sense they represent just the kind of safety-valve which French society does not tolerate. The difference between those movements and what happened in the Sorbonne is that in Britain and America the bourgeois young revolt against the kind of choices offered, the kind of responsibility which will have to be assumed. In France, however, both the choices and the responsibility are minimal; the pattern of life, even the bourgeois one, is much more predetermined, down to its minor details. But in all cases those who revolt in this kind of way set out from a privileged position.

Nevertheless what happened in the Sorbonne revealed real needs, both moral and material, which go beyond class distinctions. There is no reason why the right to a say in one's own destiny, whether it be sexual, social, economic, political or educational, should be the prerogative of any one class, and in France the vicious circle which starts by assuming irresponsibility and ends up by creating it applies not only to children but also to the workers. May 1968 revealed to many the full implications of this for the first time, and the joyous freedom of the Sorbonne ('This is the tenth day of happiness' ran another slogan) was just one way in which this recognition was expressed. But perhaps the most striking result of the occupation of the Sorbonne was in a rather different sphere. From the very first days a remarkable young pre-primary teacher organised a day and night nursery which was open at all hours to anyone and everyone, and the number of young parents who both used it and helped to run it, efficiently and hygienically, showed to what an extent such an institution was needed. Day nurseries of course exist in France, but they are few, expensive, have fixed hours (they will only take children all day), and are to be found in residential areas and not near to work-places. The Sorbonne experiment showed that a system which has the exact opposite of all these characteristics can work very well; the example was followed during May and June in most university towns, and there has since been talk of generalising it by setting up nurseries near factories.

The situation in the Sorbonne was, as has been suggested, symbolic but it was not typical. Partly because it is itself a sacred symbol, partly because the most bitter fighting took place around it and for it, the Sorbonne was desecrated in a particularly extremist manner.[5] The provincial faculties were on the whole much more reserved: there were fewer posters, leaflets and wall slogans. And of course, although there were often just as many demonstrations, relatively few degenerated into riots, so that the excitement and tension were somewhat less. Finally, as everywhere, to live in the provinces is not the same thing as to live in the capital city. Social norms are more rigid, deviations more severely sanctioned, and total anonymity is virtually impossible.

But everywhere there was the same zeal for reform, although the number of students actively involved in preparing them varied from faculty to faculty. Some final texts were voted by quorums of over 50%. In general, however, it is probably fair to say that some 30% of all students were actively involved in the movement in one way or another. A small minority of these, rightly thinking that a root-and-branch reform of the educational system was linked to profound changes in society as a whole but perhaps ill-informed of the size and difficulties of the task they were undertaking, abandoned the university for political activism. Even allowing for these and for the few cranks and people with suddenly discovered and rather suspect revolutionary vocations, that still leaves an impressive number who, despite transport difficulties, came in every day to participate in the working out of a blue-print for a new and better university. The remainder either stayed at home or went off to the country, either because they were resolutely hostile to what was going on, or because they were genuinely unable to make up their minds and preferred to work for their exams in the meantime, or because, like their fathers under Pétain, they preferred to see which way the wind was blowing before committing themselves (a typically French attitude for which the French have a word, *attentisme*).

With minor variations the occupation of the faculties occurred in more or less the following way. The buildings were occupied in an atmosphere of euphoric excitement, and after a few preliminary scuffles the presence of the teaching and administrative staff was in general tolerated, and the participation of professors in discussion-groups welcomed. Obviously only those who sympathised with the

5. A somewhat similar situation developed at Nanterre, although for almost diametrically opposite reasons. Once Paris and the Latin Quarter had become the centre of events, Nanterre was revealed in all its barrenness for what it really was, a cultural wilderness.

movement either met together or with the students, but in some cases, particularly in the early days, the number of young lecturers was proportionally greater than that of the students. Innumerable commissions were set up to deal with a wide range of subjects, from practical matters like relations with the press and other faculties, to the ideological content of university education, the way it is taught, teacher-student relations, the university and society, etc.

At the same time it became obvious that some central coordinating committee was necessary, and student councils were elected. These were not intended to be permanent, and although few went to the extreme of the Sorbonne where, in theory if not in practice, a vote of confidence was taken every day, usually some mechanism was devised whereby the council could be revoked at a moment's notice. Although this rarely happened, difficulties arose very early on. For once the first excitement had died down it became apparent that the students were divided into two camps, the moderate reformers and the radical ones. The moderates maintained that the first thing to do was to work out a modified examination system so that exams could still be held, more or less as usual, in June. The radicals argued that there was a unique opportunity to put forward proposals for structural reforms, that this would be impossible if exams were in everyone's mind, and that the only thing to do was to put them off until the beginning of the new academic year. Discussions were bitter, and it looked at one moment as though the whole movement was going to fall apart over this question. Finally, however, with the help of outside events which showed that it was unlikely that the country as a whole would be back to normal at the time that exams would be held, the radicals won the day and practically every examination, including the *baccalauréat*, was put off at least until after the end of the term and in most cases until September or October.

The result was a quite extraordinary effort, both in terms of quantity and quality. Nearly every institution of higher learning produced its own reform proposals, including arts schools, the various faculties, many of the *grandes écoles* such as the *Polytechnique*, the *Ecole Nationale d'Administration* (the very traditional, conservative and highly competitive school for future civil servants), and the *Centre National de Recherche Scientifique*. The Paris faculties of law and medicine brought out veritable 'white papers' which merited, and in general received, careful attention. It is difficult—

121

and it would be invidious—to single out any for detailed analysis, but there were a certain number of points common to most of the proposals which can be resumed as follows.[6]

The first series of proposals concerned the running of the establishments. The students had achieved power, but they could not hope to keep it entirely to themselves. Various types of 'legislative' and 'executive' committees were proposed, on which students would be represented on an equal basis with the professors and the administration. The most vexed question was whether or not the students would have the right of veto on these committees. Those who argued for such a right did so not so much in the name of 'student power', whatever some of their more flamboyant spokesmen may have said, but simply to ensure that the new system would be respected and made to work (the students after all were thinking more of those who would come after them than of themselves). However, in the majority of cases the more reasonable view prevailed, and there was no veto; but such a solution depends on the good will of all concerned, and only the future will tell whether the radicals were not in fact justified.

The way in which the majority of students were taught, as well as what they were taught, was also to be changed. The idea that there exists one block of knowledge to be transmitted across a great gulf to a whole lot of isolated individuals was to be abandoned. There was to be no more gulf, and the students would work much more in groups; some even went so far as to suggest that part at least of the exams could be passed collectively. If there were not enough professors to ensure a closer and more seminal contact between teachers and taught, senior students could guide the work of junior ones. Thus there would be a permanent reciprocal relationship between learning and teaching.

A second series of proposals aimed at destroying the monopoly of the Ministry of Education over the whole field of higher education. This entailed the granting of administrative and financial independence to the different establishments. Many different ideas as to how this was to be done were put forward, not all of them very practical. Although all suggested that there should be a number of independent units, there was much less agreement when it came to the questions of how many such units there should be, their size

6. An account of the general atmosphere, although not of the reform proposals, in the Paris faculty of medicine and the Institute of Political Science can be found in chapter 6 of Seale and McConville, op. cit.

and composition. Concerning the budgets of these units, one of the most daring proposals was that something similar to the University Grants Commission should be created in order to distribute the funds available.

If to these points is added the demand for freedom of political and union expression within the university precincts, it is possible to form an idea of the reasonableness of most of the proposals. Except in a few cases such as at Strasbourg, Caen and Rouen, where a combination of extremely radical students and extremely reactionary professors meant that no agreement could be reached, in the great majority of faculties the new statutes and reforms were voted by a majority of students (including some of those who had been hostile to the movement in the beginning) but a minority of professors—although in one or two cases a sufficient measure of agreement was reached for the Doyen to begin implementing them before the end of the term. To an outside observer the proposals seem moderate. In the context of the French educational system they appear to be revolutionary; too much personal prestige, too many sacred traditions are at stake. But the serious and reasoned quality of most of the texts shows that the students are not necessarily as incapable of exercising the corporate responsibility they claim as many of their elders and betters believe. In May, however, all the shackles were thrown off. Will the result be the same when, as must inevitably happen, some of the shackles are put back on, and the whole weight of a Frenchman's early education begins to make itself felt again?

For during the whole of this turbulent period practically nothing was heard of the primary schools and, compared with the faculties, relatively little of the *lycées*. Yet, although few people took their revolt very seriously at the time, the *lycéens* showed very clearly the truth which the most perspicacious of the students had grasped, namely that the student revolt had no meaning if it was simply to be confined to the sphere of higher education. The extent of the *lycéens'* movement varied enormously; in quiet country towns with no university there was very little agitation. But where there were demonstrating students to give a lead, CALs were formed and, in Paris and a few other towns, the school premises were occupied. The revolt began primarily out of solidarity with the students (there was practically no agitation in the CEGs for example). But agitation in the *lycées* was nothing new; protest against the strict discipline[7] and rigorously enforced regulations had been growing over the past few years. If the students provided the immediate pretext, the deeper causes were to be found within the *lycée* itself.

As at the Sorbonne, where incidentally many schoolboys and girls spent a good deal of their time, the atmosphere in the occupied *lycées* was, at least to begin with, fairly chaotic. The most politically active joined the students who were trying to make contact with the workers, or invited workers and trade union representatives to discussions in the *lycées*. Apart from the many who stayed at home to work, others were less sure of what to do; they had their own grievances, but even less chance than the students of forcing through reforms on their own, and so they tended to follow the lead given by the latter. Much in fact depended upon the teachers. Where there were young ones who were sympathetic to the movement, strike committees and pupils' councils were formed. The example spread, and by the end of May there were several *lycées* which were being run, administratively speaking, very efficiently by the children. And, as in the faculties, there were endless discussions among the pupils themselves, and between them and their teachers and, on occasions, their parents.

What emerged from these was in many ways remarkably similar to what the students were demanding: the right to be consulted on matters directly concerning them, the right to some form of political and social information and expression, and the right to be taught in a way that takes account of their own intelligence and initiative. And so projects for the election of delegates to the various administrative and disciplinary councils were elaborated, as well as for a cultural centre in each *lycée* in which meetings, lectures (by people outside the *lycée*) and other activities could be held—in which also newspapers and periodicals could be available. Finally, again as in the case of the students, concrete proposals for different teaching methods were put forward, including the possibility of collective study groups.

The dominant theme was the desire to be treated, if not as adults,

7. This is strict enough in the ordinary *lycée;* it is even more so in the few *lycées techniques* which, despised by the bourgeoisie, prepare for a practical engineering *baccalauréat*. The discipline is so strict (chalk circles round the drawing-boards, outside which the pupil may not move) that it seems like a deliberate conditioning for the factory in which the pupils will eventually have to work, even if it is as middle-grade technical engineers. CALs were set up in them and in some places, such as Marseilles, played a very active role, even though their members were not destined to become university students themselves.

at least as potential ones, and to be given some measure of control over, and responsibility for, their own lives. The opposition to this was, however, greater even than in the case of the students; the hostility of the majority of teachers, and indeed of parents, was very marked. Nevertheless, a significant number of people (teachers, parents, and above all the children themselves) became aware that the traditional *lycée* was neither the most perfect nor the only model available. Many teachers were impressed by the maturity and intelligence of their pupils, and some of those who had been most disabused acquired a new hope and faith in their mission. But perhaps the most permanent and, in the long run, decisive result of the ferment in the *lycées* will prove to be the growth and strength of the pupils' own organisation, the CALs. In the occupied *lycées* the majority of pupils became members, and even if they become subject to the French tendency to factiousness, they will continue to provide an organisational framework which by its very existence throws doubt on the accepted notion of the pupil's role. And that is something with which the traditionalists will have to reckon.

Those who lived through the student revolt of May 1968 will remember it as long as they live. Apart from its more violent aspects, it produced something that might almost be called a new art form. Besides the traditional mountains of leaflets, some of them gems in themselves, and revolutionary newspapers, of which the most successful, *Action*, looks like becoming a permanent weekly, the walls of Paris were covered with slogans and poems. Sometimes these developed into conversation pieces, as passers-by amended them or added other slogans of their own. Paris talked to itself both literally and through its walls, as it never does under normal circumstances. But what will be rembered above all are the hundreds of posters produced by the students of the *Ecole des Beaux Arts*, which transformed itself into an *Atelier Populaire*. Many of these posters, in a striking and often beautiful way, portrayed the hopes and fears, the struggle and idealism, of an extraordinary generation. The movement may not have had the leaders it deserved; it certainly had the artists.

DOCUMENT 16

Students in the occupied faculties

Cybernetics, Paris:

It's . . . it's a revolution, there's no question about it. It's a revolution, but it hasn't . . . it hasn't any aims if you follow me, it's a . . . it's purely an opposition movement. It's based on the fact that it rejects a certain number of things, but we haven't . . . well it's obvious that some of its aims are very philosophical, the well-being of man, etc., but it's empty really, there's nothing concrete at the bottom. We don't have this or that precise claim to make. It's simply a negative movement. But—that's very important. Well . . . I don't mean . . . it's not derogatory to say that it's destructive. Now we can build, but we want to build on new foundations. There's a very simple example. There used to be an association of alumni which relayed information. We didn't like a certain number of things about this association. There were two solutions; one could make this association do what one wanted, do things decently. But we didn't choose that solution, we just ignored the association and created another one. Why? Because the new one . . . will have been produced by the May movement. We don't want to patch up old institutions in order to get what we want, we want something new.

There are a certain number of general objectives, but nothing very specific. Well, you can't hope for a programme. Yesterday for example in the Assembly, we were electing the members of the final representative committee. Well, a good many people who have been coming here for the last month and a half were standing as candidates. Most of the people in the lecture hall asked them 'What is your programme?' But these people had not understood what the movement was all about. It was not a question of saying 'I'm going to do this, I'm going to do that.' It's not a question of what one's programme is. It's a question of finding people who are going to perpetuate the movement . . . eh . . . in one direction. It's a question of democratising universities . . . well, personally, that's what interests me the most, the fact that there are . . . that there aren't enough workers' sons and especially sons of agricultural workers. But you can see that . . . these are general tendencies, and there is no precise aim. You can't ask people to have a programme.

I think the whole of the French university system will have to be reorganised, because it's based on principles which are false. The faculty principle. What are faculties? They group a certain number of subjects for purely geographical reasons, whereas these divisions should be based on subjects, not on geography. This would mean that all the cybernetics departments in France would come together in a national cybernetics faculty, if you follow me, that mathematics all over France would be brought together in the same way. So the present error, that is to say this geographical grouping, has to be replaced by a grouping based on subjects. Because what does . . . do these geographical divisions result in? The geographical divisions nearest to the centre prosper the most because of the Napoleonic system of centralisation, and good planning is impossible because money is allocated to the various faculties, whereas if planning is to succeed—well—it's not a question of . . . of . . . it doesn't mean that we're making a political choice when we say that there has to be planning, it's simply a logical option, the very fact that one directs—research work has to be directed—if it is to be directed, then each subject must be grouped on a national basis, and then money could be shared out, because I think in fact that it's a problem of money, a problem of professors, a problem of premises.

I was a member of a representative committee on cybernetics which was dissolved yesterday; at the same time we elected a final committee, but I was not a candidate. This committee was made up of twelve students, six teachers, four monitors and two representatives from the administrative staff. That means that the students have a majority in relation to other groups, but there is parity in the sense that the students only have half the members—although in fact there is no real parity since the teachers and administrators are in the minority. Its role is administrative; in fact all the decisions made by the Director of the Institute in the past are now made by the representative committee. Which means to say all the administrative functions, appointments—of new teachers, etc., teaching, programme and many other activities. It has a great deal more power than the former Director, since its opposition role gives it the authority to change those professors who are not doing their job properly. There is a general assembly, which is rather disappointing, but there is one from time to time. In fact I dealt with outside relations in the representative committee, I mean relations with industry, with other subjects and relations with other schools of cybernetics.

127

Law, Paris:

I'm not really in a position to talk about . . . the faculty of science or arts, but there are a lot of things which ought to be changed at the faculty of law, particularly professorial prerogatives, chairs . . . It's that, this system of chairs. It's an abomination, this system. When you think that a professor is the *titular* holder of his chair, that he can *choose his own* assistants, that he can keep the chair *as long as* he wants, until he retires, and that he can even *put off* his retirement until quite an advanced age, well you can see what the results are—catastrophic. You get professors who just shouldn't be there any more. Who lecture . . . it's almost shameful to give lectures like that.

Theology, Strasbourg:

The main thing I want to insist on is that the university problem can't be discussed without touching on a whole lot more. There were three commissions at the summer university we had here. Well, the first of them dealt with university problems, but the second one worked on the problems of French society . . . we . . . well we looked at the functions of parties and unions in France, we examined industry, self-management, then Yugoslav and Soviet experiences, and finally participation as seen by de Gaulle and Capitant; and the third commission was on developing countries, I mean the relationship between our struggles and the objectives of these countries. I reckon that's vital.

History, Nantes:

This is how it happened; the dons put up some proposals. Which the students rejected out of hand.

The students worked out a project. Which the dons rejected out of hand. It was necessary to find some common ground, and that is how the text reorganising the faculty was produced.

At the moment there is a committee which is working on general problems, teaching methods and teaching content, on which are working people from nearly all departments who are questioning their disciplines from the point of view of the student. On the dons' side, there is the same thing—an inter-disciplinary committee which is at work. In fact their results are quite positive . . . yes, quite positive.

128

To the extent that, for example, the dons remain within the old structure . . .; they say that for the faculty to function properly—well, the number of lecturers and the number of buildings would have to be doubled; in that case 70 extra lecturers are needed—and the Ministry has proposed 7 for next year. You see the problem. As for the students, they reckon that the maximum teacher/student ratio should be one to 25; and that work should be done essentially in groups, both for research and pedagogic reasons . . .

Medicine, Paris:

No, no. To begin with the professors came to have a look; during the first week they came to see what was happening. Some of them were horrified. One said: right, now, you've had your little game and we'll get back to normal routine. In fact a lot of them were like that. But then there were others waiting for the wind to change, to know exactly what we wanted. And then there were others who came . . . a psychiatrist for example came to say: there's not enough psychiatry . . . and somebody else would come to tell us: there isn't enough physiology, there isn't enough chemistry. Which meant that for the first week we were a bit submerged by all these professors coming to see what was in the movement for them, with their own claims, their own regrets, the whole lot, so finally we just decided to get rid of them during . . . I can't remember now if it was for ten days or fifteen days. They couldn't come to the commissions, and we were going to work out what we wanted, and then afterwards, for technical points, even . . . well anyway when we really needed them, but only to get the reform in the faculty of medicine going, then they could come once we had decided what we wanted.

*   *   *

At the beginning I wasn't at all keen on the hospital-university reform . . . well, reform in general. I was only in favour of a reform in the faculty of medicine. As far as I was concerned the fellows at the Sorbonne were a lot of jokers and little. . . . And then I began to think about it. . . . And I went to the Odéon a lot because, amongst other reasons, my husband was in charge of the First Aid centre there; so I was often at the Odéon, I listened a lot, I found out a lot and finally it didn't take me long to become convinced that we would never get the university reforms we wanted under the present regime.

So the first step was to get rid of the present Government. And then it was at about this time that the labour strikes started. And there I made a decision in supporting them . . . I voted in favour of the motion saying that students had a common cause with the working classes because, as a student, striking against lectures, exams and everything, I was giving myself the right to occupy the Faculty; that being the case, I can't see why I should oppose workers' rights to occupy their own places of work. So from that point of view their cause was my cause.

Future Engineers in Lyon

It is the engineer who ensures order in the factory, who is obliged by the imperatives of profit to organise worker exploitation in order that the concern be competitive, production be profit-earning, and the factory grow . . . And that completes the whole infernal process: work in order to be able to continue working, sleep in order to be able to work the next day, and go to the cinema, make love, dance, in order to forget that one works.

And the engineer takes on workers, declares them redundant, increases the work quota. He develops worker co-operation in the functioning of the factory so that the workers are not aware of being hoodwinked. And then the university justifies the work the engineer does in case he should be tempted to realise that his role is that of a cop: technical and scientific progress; Humanism which enables him to believe that he is not a member of the priveleged classes, interested only in profit, but that he works for the common good; professional conscience, and the ethics of work (in this respect the unanimous criticism made by professors, students and the administration against the 'idle' and the 'sluggards' is significant).

So, are we once again going to see all these people who say that they belong to the left and 'support the workers' continue to demand a technocratic modification of their teaching system in order to preserve their privileges, and, worried about the validity of their diplomas, to be satisfied that they are well paid while at the same time denying the existence of the class struggle (which frightens them) and trying to get the workers to take part in their own exploitation.

(Leaflet distributed by some students of the *Institut national des sciences appliquées* in Lyon, 21 May 1968.)

DOCUMENT 17

Some Reform Proposals

A

A Moderate Approach

THE ORGANISATION OF TEACHING

The commission considers that lectures and seminars should be closely linked. It discussed them each separately however. A student-teacher body, formed each year and for each period under examination, would be responsible, in the light of criticism of the previous year above all, for planning the subject matter of education and for defining the way it should be organised within the following framework.

(a) Lectures.

Three points of view were raised:

1. A small minority is in favour of simply maintaining lectures in their present form.

2. A minority feels that they should be replaced by a free polycopy of the lecture, which the professor could supplement with a few explanatory comments.

3. The majority were in favour of a fundamental change in the form of lectures. Two possibilities emerged:

(i) At the beginning of the term the lecturer would set down the main points of a given problem (chronological references, leading ideas). The professor could then suggest which of the ideas put forward in the lecture might be examined in greater detail in the seminar. In this way students could begin research work under the supervision of assistant teachers, who would themselves be under the authority of a professor who would come and discuss the work in the seminars.

(ii) The problem being studied is narrowed down to its essentials during the first part of the term in the different seminars. The teachers then confer amongst themselves in order to know exactly what questions have been raised and to acquaint themselves with any recent information on the topic. The teacher who is best qualified to talk on the subject devotes the end of the term to explaining it in detail to all the students and to answering questions raised in the seminars.

(b) Seminars.

1. Each term the students and their assistants draw up a list of specifications concerning the subject on the programme. These specifications comprise the various types of exercise to be done during the term (for example: talks, book reviews, bibliography cards, rapid oral expression exercises, reports, essays, etc.) and indicate the number of exercises the student is willing to do and the teacher willing to correct. If this were applied, it would be possible to mark each student continuously and 'know his ability to study history'.

It ought to make it possible to do away with the end of term exam, although a minority of the commission pronounced themselves in favour of keeping the final exam as a further reference.

2. At all events, dialogue between students and assistant teachers is essential. At the beginning of the second term, an undirected course lasting one week might serve to further free expression among students in the group, concerning all the problems which interest them.

3. By the end of the first year and the beginning of the second, seminars would allow students to undertake personal, uninterrupted research work: by this we mean that, while the student would, from year to year, be introduced to new periods of history, he would at the same time be able to go more deeply into a definite problem concerning a definite period; this obviously means that the assistant teacher who helped the student at the beginning must continue to supervise his research work.

4. Some think the seminars could be divided into university work groups which would prepare the following work session with various talks, which would then be the subject of a debate under the assistant's direction. There ought not to be more than half a dozen students in a university work group.

(Source: *Mouvement social 64*, July–September 1968, *La Sorbonne par elle-même*, pp. 353–4.)

B

A more Radical Approach

A general assembly of students, practitioners, research workers and teachers:

1. Rejects the present technical and ideological organisation of the so-called social sciences.

2. Disputes the traditional divisions between these sciences: sociology, psychology, psychiatry, social psychology, psycho-analysis, linguistics, ethnology, economics, psychotherapy, pedagogy, etc.

3. Denounces these divisions as being historically based, contemporaneous with the capitalist organisation of society, which is an organisation embodied in the defunct university system, in the form and content of the teaching given thereas well as in the methods used by the practitioners it secreted and threw on the market.

4. States that a split exists at all levels (practice, theory, training), between critical social sciences and orthopedic social sciences (that is at those which aim at adaptation and adjustment inside the system under attack).

5. Declares that critical social science can only come into being if:
—each of the present disciplines is broken down;
—there is confrontation with the critical part of each of the other disciplines;
—there is confrontation between practitioners at their places of work, where several disciplines would be practised.
Therefore announces: the creation of the Critical University of Social Sciences.

6. This university does away with the separation between the place of work and the seat of learning:
—every student must at the same time be a practitioner;
—every practitioner must at the same time be a student;
—every teacher and every research worker must also be a practitioner.

7. In its own field (social sciences), this university is the only 'place' for research and the training of social workers.

8. The first task of the Critical University will be to work out a new enumeration of the disciplines, the very definition of which will have to be rethought.

9. During the course of this work, the following details will be fixed:

(a) the organisation of the Critical University of Social Sciences;
(b) the training methods to be used;
(c) the content of the teaching;
(d) its interior organisation and its links with places of work and with secondary education.

(Source: *Ibid.*, pp. 362–3.)

C

The Schoolchildren

LET US FIGHT:

1. For the creation of a schoolboy 'Union'.
2. For the revision of programmes which are overloaded and not adapted to working life.
3. To solve the universities' and techs' selection problem.
4. For a new type of exam.
   Quadripartite management of establishments:
      Administration, teaching staff, parents, pupils.
5. To secure job openings following success or failure in the technical and ordinary '*bacs*'.
6. For better psycho-pedagogic training of teaching staff.
7. To alter the character of lessons.
8. For a more appropriate syllabus.
9. For pupils' rights to be represented at teachers' meetings.
10. For the inclusion of civic training in lectures.

(Leaflet distributed by the pupils of the *lycée La Sauvagère* in Lyon.)

THE PUPILS OF THE LYCEE AMPERE
PLACE DE LA BOURSE (Lyon)

THE LYCEE COMMITTEE wants the administration officially to:

recognise the elected committee

allow it the use of some rooms

reserve part of the notice board for its needs

allow people from outside the *lycée* to be invited to rooms reserved to pupils

admit pupil participation in the internal and disciplinary councils of the *lycée*

Furthermore, the Committee wants pupil-teacher commissions to be set up to examine the following problems:

pedagogy and teaching

programmes

timetables

teaching methods

exams

careers

guidance

teacher–pupil relations

THE COMMITTEE

Monday 20 May

The pedagogic commission drew up a detailed study the content, analysis and solutions of which are remarkably clear. With such a report we can unfortunately only give an account of the main ideas.

1. All professors must have psycho-pedagogic training.

2. Secondary education must make every attempt to produce a common effort from pupils and teachers, in order to create closer links between school life and everything concerned with school life.

3. This means that pupils would prepare the lessons themselves and then work would be done in small groups belonging to mixed classes of not more than 25 pupils, which would, if possible, be supervised by assistant teachers.

4. Audio-visual equipment is essential for pupils and teachers, and a psychologist should also be attached to the school.

5. The creation of a cultural centre open to everybody would give body and soul to a school where there are very few signs of life.

———

The commission on administration produced a worthwhile study to do with the problems of pupil participation in decision-making in the school, autodiscipline, budgetary decisions, freedom of information, freedom of expression, the right to oppose and to propose, management by pupils of a cultural centre and the creation of general assemblies which would be composed of teachers—pupils —parents—administration, on a local, academic and national level.

(Source: Final report by the pupils of the *lycée* Jean-Baptiste Say in Paris.)

PART TWO

THE WORKERS' REVOLT

'Dommage! Il me semble que nous sommes passés si près de quelque chose de nouveau.'

Anonymous twenty-year-old worker, quoted in *Le Monde*,
2–3 June 1968.

E*

INTRODUCTION

THE French industrial revolution started later, took longer, and even now is less complete than in most other Western industrialised countries. Some of the factors which go towards explaining this have already been touched upon; the result is that the French economy was, and to a remarkably large extent remains, dominated by the small family firm (see table at the end of this Introduction). The point about the 'two hundred families', of whom so much was made in the decade before World War II, is not so much that they controlled the levers of the economy, but that they were the tip of an iceberg. The hundreds of thousands of other firms were also family ones, run by a *patron* to whom the workers were expected to touch their forelocks, and who regarded his firm uniquely as his private property, the symbol of his status and the means by which this status could be maintained, an extension of his personality and authority, exactly as his forbears (real or imagined) had regarded their land. Even today it is not uncommon in the provinces to find small and medium-sized firms whose managerial staff is recruited entirely through relations and marriage alliances, to whom the term 'market research' refers to something the wife or the maid does once a week, and who employ the familiar and degrading *tu* to men who are expected to reply with *vous* and *Monsieur*.

This situation came into being partly because in the early days the State provided much of the necessary initial capital, which by somewhat limiting the need for the private accumulation of capital, slightly mitigated the evils of nineteenth century industrialisation. It was able to continue because of the largely self-sufficient nature of the French economy (exporting has never had to be a prime consideration), protected from foreign competition by high tariff barriers. Thus the Great Depression hit France considerably later than most other countries and, although its symptoms were slightly less chronic, they lasted much longer, so that France had not really recovered by the time World War II came. True the French post-war economic recovery has changed a good many things, as John Ardagh so ably shows,[1] but the French are only just beginning to realise what an open economy really means and it is still the case that in selling the brand image counts for more than quality or

1. Op. cit., *passim*.

cost. Moreover, cultural idiosyncrasies remain, such as the obsession with secrecy, the horror of face-to-face negotiations, the inability to work as a team and the refusal to delegate or assume the slightest responsibility, which have been touched on in Part I and which in part explain why some of the younger managerial executives joined the workers' revolt.[2]

But cultural characteristics, no more than any other social institutions, are not entirely impervious to economic and social transformation. One of the reasons why they have appeared to be so in France, apart from the educational system, is that the French Patronat, with a remarkable awareness of the implications of the class struggle, formed themselves from very early days, and particularly after World War I, into an efficient and effective pressure group.[3] United in their determination to resist any attack on their own authority or the principle of free enterprise, the *patrons* were less so when it came to a question of means. This became particularly obvious when the Patronat's negotiators had their mandate revoked after the Matignon Agreements in 1936; the majority of the patrons, frightened out of their lives (and this fear has been transmitted to their successors), could still not afford the wage agreements which staved off worse disaster. And so after the war, besides the *Conseil National du Patronat Français*, there was formed the *Confédération Générale des Petites et Moyennes Entreprises* (the *Centre des Jeunes Patrons* also appeared on the scene, but while its more progressive influence has been far from negligible, its impact has not yet been decisive).

However, despite these divergences the policy of the Patronat has remained essentially the same: to make whatever apparent sacrifices are necessary in order to avoid conceding anything important, and where this policy fails, to sabotage unscrupulously any laws or agreements which threaten the status quo. Wage increases are accorded, under pressure, but they are immediately passed on to the consumer in the form of ever more artificially inflated prices, and in a sense the growth firms in the more industrialised areas

2. These characteristics have been remarked upon by every sociological observer of the French scene; cf. in particular Daniel Lerner's contribution to H. D. Lasswell *et al.*, *The comparative study of elites: an introduction and bibliography*, Stanford University Press, 1952, and his more personal account of his interviewing experiences which appeared in *Encounter* 8 (3), March 1957.

3. The best account of the French Patronat is still to be found in Henry W. Ehrmann, *Organised Business in France*, Princeton University Press, 1957.

subsidise the other firms. For there is a difference of as much as 70% between the average wage in the poorest region (the Limousin) and the Paris equivalent. Nevertheless, the basic take-home wage is still abysmally low, since over 20% of workers earn less than 6000 francs a year (c. £10 a week), and 39% less than 8000 francs a year (c. £13 10s 0d a week).[4]

Further, the Patronat have succeeded in imposing the department as the level at which wage negotiations take place for any one sector of industry (e.g. metalworkers, including both automobile and steel workers, and building workers). This avoids the inconvenience of national agreements, as in Sweden or Britain, that it is difficult to escape implementing them; it also avoids the obvious danger of plant agreements, such as are common in the United States, of dividing the Patronat against itself. It is significant that very few followed Renault's courageous initiative in signing a plant agreement in 1954, and of those that did fewer and fewer renewed them.

But the fundamental objection to plant agreements is that they look far too much like some form of 'participation'. For it is obviously unrealistic to expect employer and union to negotiate seriously if the latter cannot look at the books. Even if the former resorted to cooking up yet another set of crooked ones (there is already one for tax purposes), the very principle is something that the Patronat will never willingly admit. Various attempts, some dating back to the nineteenth century, have been made to inaugurate some form of participation, but they all shared the fate of the Loi Chéron of 1919, which only a handful of firms, most of whom were in any case on the verge of bankruptcy, made any attempt to apply. After World War II a law was passed setting up joint worker-management committees in every firm, with the express proviso that the workers' delegates should not have union status; a glance

---

4. Institut National de la Statistique et des Etudes Economiques, *Etudes et Conjoncture*, July 1968. The percentages are of course greater in the provinces than in Paris, and it is not uncommon in the lower income ranges for family allowances to exceed the weekly wage packet. It is true that a certain number of bonuses may be added, but there are usually strings attached (e.g. no unauthorised absenteeism—i.e. strikes). The Patronat object that they have to pay the highest social welfare contributions in Europe, up to 40% of the wage paid, but as with individual contributions there is a ceiling, which obviously favours the higher income groups—as does the fact that France has the highest rate of indirect taxation and one of the lowest of direct ones. All this could easily be remedied by the Government, if the Patronat were willing to co-operate.

at Document 20 will show what happened to that timid experiment. Recent Gaullist moves towards imposing some form of profit-sharing have ended up with enough loop-holes to take the sting out of them, although they do provide one reason why some sections of the Patronat are distinctly anti-Gaullist (another reason is connected with the economic implications of the President's foreign policy).

As for the general economic situation, in the spring of 1968 it was causing anxiety to the Government, employers and workers. A balance of payments problem had begun to appear for the first time for several years, production was stagnant, investment at a minimum, and the Bourse even less active than usual (at the best of times it plays nothing like the same role as the London or New York stock exchanges, as Frenchmen tend to consider it only as a source of quick profits, and look to the State, property or their mattresses to safeguard their long-term savings), so that at the beginning of the year the Government was forced to take some measures to encourage consumer spending. The imminent end of protectionism within the Common Market had caused a veritable panic among employers; in 1966 there were more mergers than in the whole of the previous decade, and there were as many as 60 in 1967 alone (still fewer than in Britain, however). And, for the workers, there was unemployment. For although official statistics on the subject are notoriously inaccurate, it is generally agreed that the figure of 500,000 was reached before the strike broke out. The most alarming aspect of this, although in view of the demographic situation not the most surprising, was the number of young people affected. It was still easy to find work at apprentice rates, but once they reached the age of eighteen a great many could not find any job at all, or at best one well below their qualifications.[5]

It is against this background that must be set the extraordinary and unofficial general strike that followed the student revolt in May 1968. It was unofficial because none of the unions ordered it, and they did not even foresee it because they were out of touch with the workers. Some of the reasons why this was so, and why the

5. Unfortunately there are no reliable statistics concerning the percentage of school-leavers and young people among the unemployed, so that an accurate estimate of the extent of structural unemployment in France is not possible. For what it is worth, Labro *et al.*, op. cit., p. 8, quote an estimate of 250,000 young unemployed by the *Union Nationale des Associations Familiales*, and Seale and McConville, op. cit., p. 154, state, without giving their source, that 29% of the population of the Burgundy region under 25 years old was unemployed.

unions have never been able to present a united front to the Patronat are examined in Chapter 1. As in Part 1, chapter 2 recalls what happened and tries to show what were the main forces at work, while chapter 3 is an attempt to assess some of the workers' motives, aspirations and reactions at grass-roots level.

DOCUMENT 18

Industry in France

Size of firms and number of wage-earners by region, 1966.

Column A: number of industrial firms (excluding commerce and service industries).
Column B: number of such firms employing no wage-earners.
Column C: number of such firms employing 1 or 2 wage-earners.
Column D: number of such firms employing 3 to 5 wage-earners.
Column E: number of such firms employing 6 to 9 wage-earners.
Column F: number of such firms employing 10 to 49 wage-earners.
Column G: number of such firms employing 50 to 199 wage-earners.
Column H: number of such firms employing 200 to 999 wage-earners.
Column I: number of such firms employing 1000 or more wage-earners.
Column J: number of such firms for whom statistics are not available.
Column K: Percentage of firms, among those employing at least one wage-earner, employing fifty or more.
Column L: number of industrial wage-earners.

144

Source: INSEE.
Note: The biggest single difference, reflected in the percentages, is between columns C, D, E, F, on the one hand, and G, H, I, on the other. It is perhaps a coincidence that firms employing 50 or more wage-earners are legally obliged to have workers' delegates and worker-management committees. What is certain is that one-third of industrial wage-earners work in firms where such institutions do not exist. All those regions where there are more than 5% of firms employing 50 or more workers (column K) are to be found to the east and north of a line running from Le Havre to Marseilles.

	A	B	C	D	E	F	G	H	I	J	K	L
Alsace	17,155	6,342	4,779	2,114	1,194	1,884	625	193	22	2	7·7	232,095
Aquitaine	43,064	20,841	12,529	3,989	1,908	2,929	683	164	13	8	3·9	249,113
Auvergne	22,501	9,774	7,597	2,201	985	1,527	328	72	16	1	3·2	150,052
Burgundy	23,172	9,402	8,447	2,271	954	1,489	448	132	12	17	4·3	178,852
Brittany	36,240	17,016	12,087	2,950	1,138	2,353	557	109	11	19	3·5	198,342
Central Region	31,918	12,666	10,510	3,612	1,675	2,465	741	170	12	67	4·8	251,396
Champagne	16,608	6,287	5,060	1,927	933	1,631	569	191	10	—	5·3	200,428
Franche Comté	15,400	6,147	5,006	1,644	772	1,282	418	113	21	6	5·9	177,969
Languedoc	25,871	11,962	8,189	2,417	1,108	1,715	386	55	1	38	3·2	122,518
Limousin	14,863	7,330	4,638	1,352	535	737	227	41	3	—	3·6	70,694
Lorraine	22,326	8,821	6,477	2,495	1,189	2,252	760	300	32	1	8·1	373,024
Midi Pyrénées	39,915	19,794	11,747	3,584	1,726	2,420	518	108	17	78	3·2	207,817
Northern Region	36,785	15,205	9,800	3,620	2,070	3,887	1,556	509	60	4	9·8	607,875
Lower Normandy	16,914	7,393	5,742	1,570	709	1,082	338	70	6	4	4·3	120,024
Upper Normandy	16,190	5,913	5,034	1,956	919	1,583	566	196	18	5	7·7	215,062
Loire	36,847	14,973	12,681	3,920	1,667	2,574	818	196	18	—	4·7	292,194
Picardy	18,280	6,632	5,812	2,091	1,047	1,832	655	191	19	1	7·4	233,589
Poitou Charente	25,775	11,170	9,235	2,396	1,060	1,436	383	83	6	6	3·2	133,318
Côte d'Azur—Corsica	52,596	20,368	17,431	5,909	3,139	4,479	1,061	187	12	10	0·6	353,351
Paris Region	138,863	39,287	44,793	18,981	11,253	17,914	3,909	1,139	132	1,455	5·2	1,707,478
Rhône—Alps	77,842	31,578	22,956	8,422	4,576	7,797	1,939	519	49	6	5·4	755,960
France: Total	729,125	288,901	230,550	79,421	40,557	65,268	7,485	4,738	481	1,724	5·1	6,831,151
Number of industrial wage-earners employed by each category of firm			301,267	298,015	295,227	1,401,701	1,645,445	1,815,237	1,074,259		*66·4	6,831,151

* Percentage of industrial wage-earners working for firms employing fifty or more wage-earners.

145

DOCUMENT 19

The 'credo' of the CNPF[1]

1. The economy must be in the service of man, in order that by doing his job he may improve his standard of living, gain promotion, the chance to improve himself and the means to provide a better future for his children.

2. Invaluable means of improving man's condition are provided by the possibility of setting up and developing businesses in complete freedom, while at the same time respecting natural economic laws. Their production guarantees an improvement in the standard of living. Their work offers vast and fruitful scope for man to realise his potential.

3. A real improvement in the standard of living, made possible by industrial production, can be seen both in the lowering of prices of important consumer goods and in the progressive rise in salaries paid to workers of all grades. These two means of expressing a general improvement in the standard of living must be balanced by healthy competition between concerns both in and outside the country.

4. Profit is one of the driving forces behind economic growth, and it guarantees the future by virtue of the investments and expansion for which it is responsible. It is the counterpart of risks taken, the reward for good management, and is profitable to the community, just as loss and bankruptcy penalise poor management and are harmful to the community. By increasing creative enterprises profit does not by any means amputate salaries, but rather is essential to an increase in employment and an improvement in the standard of living of wage earners; Marxist economies are in the process of rediscovering this basic truth.

5. Progress is born of movement and the need to emulate; of a perpetual, free and dynamic changing of positions between all those who contribute to the creation and circulation of wealth. Any measure tending to entrench these relative positions will only remove the flexibility which the economy needs, and will therefore impede social progress.

6. True and free prices are essential to all economic and social life which is aiming at progress. While there can be no real progress

1. For a different view see Document 31.

without stable currency, there can no more be a stable currency without free and true prices.

7. When inflation threatens a currency's stability, experience shows that it can never be fought efficiently and for any length of time by artificial means: freezing, taxation, artificial support and subsidies only aggravate the disease by hiding it and prolonging it.

8. The State assumes considerable responsibilities when safeguarding the currency and the competitive potential of the national economy: it must at all times regulate its own spending in relation to the economic situation of the country, not as an isolated entity, but in relation to competing countries. The more—to excess in fact—the State has intervened in the economic and social field, the greater will be its responsibility.

9. Foreign competition and the development of international trade are needed to stimulate producers and offer a wider choice of stock to consumers. But competition cannot be healthy, nor free-trade beneficial, unless loyal commercial practices are respected, and unless conditions governing production and distribution are in harmony in all fields;

10. The right to work is one of the major objectives of economic life. However a change of business, profession or even home, may be seen to be essential to the efficiency of a person's work, his own future and national production. Real security of employment for everybody can only be ensured by perfecting the personal, professional and family conditions which are needed if these changes are to take place, by improving basic professional training and conditions of reclassification and readaptation. Heads of business and their professional organisations should give constant thought to these problems;

11. The basic risks of existence should be socially safeguarded. They must be guaranteed by systems adapted to the specific nature of each risk. Individual or collective iniative must not be replaced in an excessive way by legal obligation, which is already considerable. It is desirable that the present situation should evolve, while respecting vested rights, towards a system which would make possible an increase in the share of direct wages in a company's wage burden;

12. As far as business management goes, power cannot be divided; experience shows that any other formula leads to paralysis. It is the fact that there is a man responsible at the head of the company which best allows authority to act in a humane way, and is the best

guarantee that the necessary dialogue between wage-earners and employers will take place;

13. In the economic and social field the State and the other publicly owned bodies are responsible for public services and for the general infrastructure. It is up to the State to apply a ruling as to the way in which each person, without prejudicing anybody else, may exercise his rights and duties, his initiative and responsibilities. It must see that healthy competition is maintained, explain and facilitate economic options, without however planning and directing everything. It is not its job to interfere in the management of private companies, nor to confront them with artificial competition by means of public or semi-public companies;

14. If the economy is to develop, it must be fed to a certain extent by private savings. For this to be the case it is essential that whatever the State deducts should not prevent companies from sharing profits with shareholders, who, after all, take a proportion of the risks. Rates of interest, like prices, should be genuine and free in order to ensure, without intervention or other expedients, that an equilibrium is maintained between savings and necessary investment.

January 19, 1965.

DOCUMENT 20

Worker-Management Committees

A

What they are

Function. These committees have two legally defined functions, one economic, the other social.

(*a*) They are kept informed of financial, technical, and economic decisions of the management. The latter have to convey to the worker-management committee from time to time such results as have been obtained and any new projects. The committee is also entitled to give an opinion on those measures envisaged by the head of the company which are likely to affect conditions of work and employment.

(*b*) Worker-management committees are in theory able to co-operate with the management on the improvement of working and living conditions of the staff. Lastly, they participate in the running of social activities, for which they are sometimes directly responsible; their rights vary according to the legal status of such works.

Composition. Worker-management committees are compulsory in firms having at least fifty wage-earners. Members are elected for a period of two years by those workers who have been in the company's pay for at least six months.

The size of a committee depends on the number of wage-earners: it varies between one titular and one deputy representative for fifty wage-earners and eleven titular and eleven deputy representatives for more than ten thousand wage-earners.

Twenty hours a month, paid in the same way as normal working time, are allowed to the titular representatives for the exercise of their functions.

The committees meet at least once a month, under the chairmanship of the head of the company or his representative, who thus becomes a member of the committee. Delegates of representative trade unions in the firm also attend meetings, but in a purely advisory capacity.

The committees choose their secretary from among the titular representatives, and the general functioning of the institution often depends on him.

Lastly, the committees may set up working-committees to deal with a wide range of subjects. Non-elected members of the staff may also sit on these sub-committees.

(Source: Hubert Lesire Ogrel, *Le syndicat dans l'entreprise*, Paris, Seuil, 1967, p. 25).

B

How they actually work

Out of twenty-five thousand French firms employing more than fifty people, there are fewer than nine thousand worker-management committees, and only a third of these are effectively active. They often enjoy real success in the field of social benefits (but would not the latter have existed without the law?). On the other hand, the failure on the economic side is only too obvious. Right from the start this was due as much to obstacles raised by employers as to the attitude of the CGT, which had a very large majority everywhere after the Liberation, and whom one could hardly expect to have any experience of class collaboration.

After the trade union split in 1947 a great many worker-management committees turned into lists for rivalry within the workers' movement, which itself was just not ready to make proper use of its prerogatives.

The committee was too often reduced to organising the canteen, holiday camps, or Christmas trees, and soon the worthwhile militants, who might have made something of them, lost interest. This was all the more the case since a great many employers were rapidly recovering ground won by the unions. In short, the law was not put into practice. Public authorities showed no interest and work inspectors turned a blind eye to the many infringements to which it was subject.

(Source: *Le Monde*, 22–23 March 1965).

C

The employers' underhand tactics

When the management of the Julian Redois company in Machecoul (Loire Atlantique) answer a request for elections: 'We consider that our workers and employees are all delegates; for at any given moment they can discuss their problems with us, either individually or in a group, and we have always understood each other perfectly', we are faced with the same refusal of all forms of collective demonstration. When the most incredible attempts are made to change election results, or prevent any office being performed in the normal way, it is always the management's sovereign authority that is found to be at the bottom of it all. If there is one sphere where examples abound, then this is it. We shall quote some of the most striking ones amongst those that we have come across in the course of several years' findings.

The firing of candidates as soon as the list was made known was a frequent practice, to such an extent that a special law was needed, the decrees of 7 January 1959, in order to give legal protection to candidates. This has led to a considerable improvement in the situation, although firings are still not unknown.

The following are some of the obstacles put in the way of the electoral process: refusal to present a list because it is not acceptable to the management (the firm of Croppet at Le Rosemont in the Doubs department); bad practical organisation: at the Kelton watch factory in Besançon the management only allow voting to take place for half an hour, after work, and without taking into account the fact that the staff coaches are due to leave; elsewhere (in Saint-Brieuc) it is necessary to squeeze through a narrow corridor in order to get to the polling booth; at the Citroën factory there is an average of 1000 people enrolled at each booth, these being open for four hours, while the assembly lines are still running.

At the Panhard factory they have found a way of minutely and scientifically disorganising the vote: each detail taken by itself seems insignificant, but together they make normal voting practically impossible. At the Ivry factory in 1966 there were five notices announcing the elections for 7000 workers, against fifty in previous years; the numbering of the polling booths was completely changed without any warning, the electoral colleges named in reverse order, and electoral lists were put up only in the booths. Since it is forbidden to move around inside the factory, there is no way of knowing where to go to vote. No list of candidates was posted up anywhere, etc. Because of this the percentage of voters dropped from 68·8% in 1964 to 38·6% in 1966, which enabled an employers' newspaper to write that workers in this particular company were not interested in their representative bodies. . . . In another factory the notice about elections is printed in letters about three times smaller than the one next door offering a 'trip on a pleasure boat'.

Elsewhere, the time and place for voting is typed on copying paper which makes it practically illegible. There are other examples: not enough voting slips for a given list, or handing out envelopes containing blank votes; refusal to allow polling booths to be supervised by a representative of each list; sometimes the votes are counted in the privacy of the manager's office.

(Source: Hubert Lesire Ogrel, *op. cit.*, p. 59–60).

CHAPTER FOUR

TRADE UNIONS, WORKERS AND
INDUSTRIAL UNREST

'The great majority of workers no longer take the union militant
as their model'.
Andrieux and Lignon, *L'Ouvrier d'aujourd'hui*, Paris, Rivière,
1960.

ALTHOUGH only a small minority of people pay union dues there
is a union organisation of one sort or another for practically every
sector of the economy. Many of these, like the main workers' unions,
are federations, such as the *Fédération de l'Education Nationale*, the
Confédération Générale des Cadres, the *Centre National du Patronat
Français*, and the *Fédération Nationale des Syndicats des Exploitants
Agricoles*. Besides these, a certain number of branches, such as the
Paris transport workers or the metalworkers, have their own
independent trade unions, usually characterised by the word '*autonome*' in the title. These may be an inheritance from a distant past,
or they may have been formed, often with employers' encouragement, in opposition to one or other of the main workers' federations,
the *Confédération Générale du Travail*, the *Confédération Française
Démocratique du Travail* or *Force Ouvrière*. But whatever their
origin they complicate the industrial scene, not only by multiplying
the number of unions involved in any negotiations, but also by the
fact that they are not necessarily more representative of their
particular branch than the big federations. For example, the CFDT
has its own teachers' union, and there are plenty of metalworkers
who are members of one or other of the federations. But not even
these can claim to be representative of the workers in any meaningful
sense of the term. Of the fourteen million or so industrial workers[1]
probably not more than 20% are paid-up members, although half
as many again may say they are members and indeed pay dues from
time to time. The CGT can probably claim something over one
and a half million, the CFDT 7–800,000 and the FO 300,000.

1. The usual estimate is nearer thirteen million, but there are over two million
immigrant workers in France (mostly Algerians and Portuguese), and statistics
concerning these are not very reliable.

153

The smallness of their membership is one reason why French trade unions, compared with their British or American counterparts, have not been able to force either the Patronat or the Government to accept them as responsible negotiating partners; on a different level a shop-steward does not have a right to offices on the premises, nor can he do union work in the firm's time. Their inability to achieve a strong bargaining position is in part due to the existence of several rival federations; this weakness is enhanced by the Communist control of the CGT,[2] a fact which, rightly or wrongly, is often used to justify a profound distrust of all trade unionists, and in particular CGT ones. But even if other factors had been equal, it is doubtful whether the unions would ever have opted for the American solution, which they explicitly reject. The trouble is that they have never evolved any other strategy to deal with the problems posed by a consumer society from which many (although by no means all) of the most glaring injustices have been removed. Like much of the French Left they keep harking back to a past when, at least in retrospect, the issues were more clear-cut and the struggle more meaningful. With no clear strategy to support them, their tactics have become increasingly *ad hoc* and ineffective, so it is not altogether surprising that many workers were becoming increasingly dissatisfied with the unions. What is surprising is that the unions were apparently unaware of this growing restiveness.

Ample evidence for this is provided by some recent strikes, but before considering one or two examples it is worth taking a slightly longer look at how this situation arose.

If the French trade unions are today far less integrated into the social and economic framework than their American counterparts, their origins in the nineteenth century were somewhat less turbulent. Unless one counts the uprisings of 1848 and 1871 there is little to compare, for example, with the bloody violence that accompanied the Pullman labour dispute. But the French labour movement has always had considerable difficulty in getting itself accepted, if not in fact—in 1902 there were 614,000 union members—at least in

2. This does not mean that all workers who vote Communist, or even all those who are card-carriers, are members of the CGT; nor does it mean that all members of the CGT vote Communist. But a sufficient number of important union posts, particularly at the top, are regularly held by Communists to justify the term Communist-controlled; and in fact there are rarely, if ever, policy differences between the CGT and the CP.

law. Even today, although the right to strike is written into the preamble of the 1946 Constitution (which also became the preamble of the 1958 one), the law does not recognise the existence of a trade union inside a firm.

The trouble started with the French Revolution and the idea that there should be no intermediary between the citizen and the State. In 1791 an Act was passed forbidding all associations designed to further the economic interests of a particular group, whether it be of employers or employees. In fact, the employers soon found it comparatively easy to circumvent, but it was not until 1864 that the workers obtained the right to act in common, although they still might not associate. This right was accorded by an Act of 1884, upon which all subsequent legislation connected with trade unions is based. It is still heavily inspired by the ambiguous notion of freedom inherent in the 1791 Act. The right to strike (although with certain limitations, such as five days' notice, which date from 1963) is granted, although the right to picket is not. The 'union shop' as well as the 'closed shop' is expressly forbidden, and every worker has the right to join the union of his choice. The proliferation of unions which might be expected to result from this is limited by the concept, introduced in 1919, of 'the most representative unions', to which are accorded certain rights and privileges. In fact, however, the Government has the power, which it uses, to decide unilaterally which unions are most representative. Thus, although the unions are officially represented on certain public bodies, in the eyes of the law they still remain what they were in the nineteenth century, essentially private associations with few rights but many obligations not to infringe the rights of others (the right to work, the 'private property' that is the firm's, etc.). The law thereby reinforces the tendency of the French patron to consider a strike as being first and foremost a blow to his authority;[3] this tendency is perhaps slightly less marked than it was ten or fifteen years ago (although the spate of retaliatory lock-outs in 1967 casts doubt on this), but it is still inconceivable that in France a well-organised strike be considered

3. And his first reaction is to resort to force. During the May strikes, Citroën, which with Michelin is the only large firm still to be run on the authoritarian lines of half a century ago, immediately asked for a court order to remove the pickets. In normal circumstances such a request is granted, as it was the year before for Rhodiacéta (see below) where, however, it was not enforced as it happened to coincide with the general election campaign. Citroën, however, did not even obtain a court order, although whether this eminently sensible decision will change the jurisprudence in the matter is open to doubt.

as 'clearing the air' and allowing labour relations to start off again on a better footing.

Another brake on the extension of the power and influence of the unions is linked to the uneven character of French industrialisation. The corollary of the prevalence of the scattered, small, family firm was the lack of a large industrial proletariat. Like the French farmer who is still holding up the rationalisation of agriculture by his preference for a far from affluent but sure and independent livelihood derived from mixed farming, many of those who did leave the land were able to find jobs in which, even though their wages were minimal, their status was nearer to that of an artisan or craftsman than to the proletarian condition of the miner or the worker on the assembly-line. The fact that it was not until the introduction of the value-added tax on 1 January 1968 that the mass of small artisans and shopkeepers were forced to face up to economic realities only underlines the following paradox: in the country which, probably to a greater extent than any other non-Communist country, has been aware of the reality of the class struggle and has argued vehemently about it, there has been a less complete, if not less rigid, polarisation of the classes than in those countries where industrialisation has progressed further and, at least in the twentieth century, more peacefully.

The effect of this situation on the unions was twofold. On the one hand, as it is obviously easier to recruit in heavily industrialised areas, it reduced their strength at a time when French industry was much less concentrated than it is now, particularly as the Amiens Congress of 1906 decided that the federation should be based on industry and not on trade. The arrival on the scene of several federations after World War I further complicated the problem by making head-counting an unduly important consideration. On the other hand, like the Communist Party which has beeen forced to defend such un-Marxist anachronisms as the small family farm in order to keep its rural vote, so the unions were often forced to support the claims of groups whose interests did not necessarily coincide with those of the working-class as a whole, let alone the bourgeois economy.

To these structural considerations must be added a certain number of political factors which, although their importance is often exaggerated, have undoubtedly influenced union growth and behaviour. The first, and for nearly twenty-five years the only, union federation, the CGT, was formed in 1895. For some time the action of the unions complemented that of the various political socialist movements, but when the socialist Millerand in 1899 accepted office in a non-socialist government, the doubts of the unionists concerning the efficacy of political action in a bourgeois democracy increased. At the Amiens Congress of 1906 the anarcho-syndicalist tendency triumphed and a clean break was made with all political parties. This reflected the conviction that parliamentary democracy was merely a means of duping the workers whose sole effective revolutionary weapon was the general strike. It also reflected what was already becoming a definite cultural phenomenon, the inherent belief of a great many Frenchmen that political parties, and by extension the vote, do not constitute an effective means of improving their lot.[4]

By 1918 the CGT could claim 1,800,000 members, but there were also in existence a certain number of relatively small unions which joined together in 1919 to form the antecedent of the CFDT, the *Confédération Française des Travailleurs Chrétiens*. This Catholic movement was of course motivated by opposition to the anti-clericalism of the period, but it was also strongly opposed to the militant anti-patriotic internationalism of the CGT as well as to its doctrine of the general strike. It was in fact an extremely moderate union federation, concentrating its action on family and social welfare and preaching 'collaboration between the classes'. But the Patronat, blind as always to its own long-term interests, refused to cooperate with it, and the federation was forced to adopt increasingly uncooperative positions. In 1936, when its numbers had perhaps reached half a million, many of its members acted in concert with the other federations independently of the official CFTC policy.

For from 1921 onwards there was a third federation on the scene. One year after a fraction of the Socialist Party broke away to form the French Communist Party, a fraction of the CGT left to form the CGT Unitaire. While the latter remained resolutely revolutionary in attitude if not always in practice, the main body concentrated on extending its influence and building up an organisational structure both in France and abroad; and although this policy had no effect on the Patronat, the Government on occasions showed itself some-what more comprehensive. Whenever the Communist and Socialist Parties allied themselves, the two federations united only to separate

4. See above, pp. 46–7 on the political socialisation of the French. As the passage there quoted shows, this distrust of political parties does not necessarily make the unions' task any easier.

again when the political alliance fell apart. This happened during the brief period of the Popular Front and again, for a scarcely longer period, after World War II. In December 1947 however, for the first time it was the Communist majority that remained and the Socialist minority who, encouraged by the Americans,[5] left to form the CGT–FO. Although at the factory level the FO has produced some dynamic militants, nationally it has had very little influence, being for the most part content to follow the wavering Socialist Party line. But the CGT, after cooperating with the post-war Government, even to the extent of working with the first Planning Commission, adopted an attitude of open and unremitting hostility as soon as the Cold War reached France with the expulsion of the Communists from the Government in 1947. This attitude, which was directed as much against the other unions as against the Patronat and the Government, began to change only during the last few years when the Communist Party started its attempt to win recognition as a respectable and democratic political party. Overtures were made to the CFDT and in 1966 the two federations came to a tactical agreement, but in practice it never amounted to a great deal and by the beginning of 1968 the agreement was, to all intents and purposes, a dead letter.

The CFTC emerged from the war years marked, as were many progressive Catholics, by the events of 1936 and by the Resistance. By 1945 it had affirmed not only the necessity of State intervention in the economy and in social disputes, but also its independence of any outside control, whether it be by a political party or by the Church. The left-wing tendencies of a whole generation of young Catholics were reflected in movements like that of the worker-priests, the increased activities of youth organisations such as the *Jeunesse Agricole Chrétienne* and the *Jeunesse Ouvrière Chrétienne* as well as in the militancy and growing influence of young members of the CFTC. This influence was particularly noticeable in the industrial areas hitherto relatively untouched by the CFTC and where the term 'chrétienne' in the union's name was more of a

5. It had long been suspected that many of the organisations dependent on the Socialist Party, if not the SFIO itself, were financed by the CIA. This was confirmed in 1967 by the declarations of Mr Thomas W. Braden who had worked closely with Allen Dulles at the head of the CIA (cf. *New York Times* 8 May 1967). The break-away of the FO, as well as the SFIO newspaper *Le Populaire*, was financed by the American Federation of Labour through the intermediary of the International Ladies' Garments Union; when the AFL required money for this and similar purposes in Europe, the CIA gave it.

hindrance than a help. For many, however, it was not easy to abandon what had been, and for them remained, the union's *raison d'être*, and it was not until the 1964 Conference that the decision was taken by a 70% majority to substitute 'démocratique' for 'chrétienne' and so to create the CFDT.[6] The minority have continued to call themselves the CFTC, and the Gaullist Government, which depends on the Catholic vote, insisted on recognising them as a 'representative organisation' along with the new CFDT.

The freshly-baptised federation was of course forced to define more clearly its goals, and its policy statements now abound with terms such as 'economic democracy' and 'democratic planning' which suggest, in their different ways, that it is coming closer to an acceptance of the facts of industrial society than any other section of the French Left. For the Left, both Communist and Socialist, has all too often concurred with the Right in attributing the outward signs of an affluent society to the malignant influence of the American way of life on a sacrosanct French culture, and has tended, by persisting in a somewhat eschatological analysis of modern capitalism, to define the goals of the class struggle in terms of political power rather than of economic influence. Thus the CFDT, by opting to work within the existing system whatever the Government, was able to move towards a policy that combined wage-claims for the left-overs of the industrial mutation with structural reforms designed to give greater responsibility and control both to the workers themselves at the factory level and to their representatives at the national level. When May 1968 arrived and with it the general strike, which the CFDT had no more foreseen than the CGT, the strategy and tactics implied by this policy were far from having been worked out. The position of the CFDT did mean, however, that once the CGT had decided to limit and control the movement

6. This had become practically inevitable with the election in 1961 of Eugène Descamps, one of the post-war generation of militants, to the post of secretary-general. This change of leadership presents a striking contrast to the other movements of the French Left. Léon Jouhaux, who was at the head of the CGT after the 1921 split, was still there in 1947 to head the newly-formed FO: Benoît Frachon, who was secretary-general of the CGTU in 1936, was only 'kicked upstairs' to the sinecure of President approximately thirty years later. This phenomenon, which is equally true of political parties of the Left, cannot be explained solely in terms of bureaucratic tendencies or the iron law of oligarchy; the French Left has always relied heavily on personified symbols, but these can become outdated—see below, p. 191 on Frachon's reception by the Renault workers.

rather than to push it towards a general uprising, it appeared as a more 'revolutionary' force than its Communist-controlled rival and thereby gained an enormous, although possibly only temporary, tactical advantage.

It is on the tactical level that the weakness of the French unions has always been most evident, and this can be illustrated by pointing out that whereas in English the word 'strike' usually designates a work-stoppage of unlimited duration, in French the equivalent notion is expressed by the phrase *'une grève illimitée'*, since *'grève'* by itself usually refers to a stoppage of anything from a quarter of an hour to a day, the exact duration being fixed in advance by the unions.[7] The average length of a French strike has always been remarkably short, and this is still true today even though there is a general tendency in all countries towards shorter strikes. The reasons for this are closely linked both to the weakness and rivalry of the unions and to the inability of employers, whether a *patron* or the State, to see in a strike anything but a direct challenge to their authority (and not, for example, a bargaining counter). In fact, a strike in France is most often a swift, and occasionally violent, explosion of anger or frustration, and frequently the best use the unions can make of it is to force a reluctant employer to negotiate; it is rarely, if ever, used to exert pressure while negotiations are going on. At the same time wildcat strikes are practically unknown since local union sections are not subject to any central or federal discipline; and if ever a strike does start 'spontaneously' it is immediately 'covered' by one or other of the unions in the not unreasonable hope that a successful conclusion to it will bring them new members. Again, and perhaps most important, the unions often hesitate to call for large-scale strikes because they cannot be certain that they will be loyally followed.

One or two examples from recent history will serve to illustrate these points. The great general strike of 1936 did not have its origins in any union call to action; it arose not out of any dissatisfaction with the unions, but as a spontaneous desire to express the hope and joy occasioned by the electoral victory of the Popular Front coalition. The unions benefited enormously from it, both in membership and

7. For example, in 1965 there were 1,674 strikes or stoppages. Of these well over half lasted one day or less, and nearly two-thirds of this majority was composed of strikes lasting half a day or less. Further, there were 281 stoppages of one hour or less—cf. *Revue française du travail*, July–Sept. 1966.

prestige, as it was they who negotiated with the Patronat and the Socialist Prime Minister, Léon Blum, the famous Matignon Agreements by which the workers obtained, besides much that turned out to be ephemeral, their first paid holidays (two weeks) and the conviction that they had won an enormous victory; but it is highly improbable that the unions could have called the strike themselves.

Again, after the war in 1948, the CGT took the precaution of holding a referendum before calling for a miners' strike in the North. The strike turned out to be long, bitter and bloody (at one point the whole area was in a state of seige), but the miners held out, partly because they had voted on it, partly because their social and economic conditions warranted it, and partly because they had the support of the local population. The last factor is particularly important. In 1962 another miners' strike, this time in Decazeville in the Aveyron and organised by the CFTC, owed its success to a large extent to the support and solidarity of the whole region. In the next year, 1963, in Grenoble, when the workers of Neyrpic, a firm dealing in turbines and hydraulic research, went on strike over a question of the breaking of signed wage-agreements and general management, they found that they had the support not only of the law faculty and the Grenoble students but also of many of their own engineers and executive staff.

The unions are not unaware that the success of a strike very often depends on factors outside their immediate control, and this is probably one of the reasons why the CGT, which can always count on its Communist members, launched a series of overtly political strikes and demonstrations during the period when the Communist Party was in the wilderness. The most singular occurred in 1952 with the demonstration protesting against the presence of General Ridgway in France, the most spectacular in 1962 when seven people died while protesting against OAS activities. But in the long run they probably did more to weaken than to strengthen the workers' movement particularly when, with the Gaullist régime firmly established and political parties reduced to a secondary role, their interests could be effectively promoted in Parliament.

All this does not mean that the unions' efforts have been either negligible or ineffective. The French worker has shared in the prosperity consequent upon France's post-war economic recovery, although to a lesser extent than other categories of the population. He has four weeks' annual holiday, social security, and a start has been made in the institutionalisation of collective bargaining with its greater guarantees of employment. But the picture is not nearly as bright as it might be. Large areas of poverty remain, the real income of even the better paid workers does not compare as favourably with that of neighbouring countries as Government statistics would suggest, the social security system is far from perfect, there has been less redistribution of income than in Britain, and longer hours with less congenial home, transport and work conditions.[8]

It should by now be clear that this situation is by no means entirely the fault of the unions. In addition to the other factors already mentioned, in recent years the unions have had to put up with increasing hostility, contempt, and snubbing on the part of the Patronat and the Government. This can range from minor pin-pricks to open flouting of the *Code du Travail* which, even when it is respected, is often interpreted so literally and abusively as to render many of its clauses meaningless.[9] Employers resort more and more to lock-outs and continue to exercise a very strict veto, on the pretext that nothing controversial is allowed, over what is put up on union notice-boards, while the Government recognises the unrepresentative CFTC and ignores or by-passes any board or committee on which union representatives sit.[10] With their action

8. For some further details, see below, pp. 191 et. seq.

9. There are of course a few notable exceptions, some of which are mentioned by John Ardagh, op. cit., pp. 34 and 56. But very few escaped the holocaust of May. Paternalism, even when enlightened, always demands something in return, and there comes a moment when this is no longer acceptable.

10. Jacques Capdevielle kindly volunteered the following account of an incident which occurred in Lyon on 8 January when M. Chirac, Secretary of State for Employment, attended a meeting of the *Commission du Développement Economique Régional*, on which the unions are represented. The incident, a minor one which received little or no publicity at the time, is nevertheless typical of the Government's contemptuous attitude (an attitude all the more surprising in view of the purely advisory nature of the CODER's vote) and does much to explain the traditional profound distrust of the unions towards anything which smacks of 'participation'.

'In the morning when the participants arrived at the Prefecture, they learnt that the agenda, which had initially been limited to employment problems, had been extended to the whole of the regional economic situation. At 12.30, before the end of the session, the CGT and the CFDT delegates asked for a vote on the advisory opinion on employment to be carried forward to the next session, which normally takes place at 15.00. Whereas the Secretary of State and the other members of the CODER were the guests of the Prefect, the delegates lunched in a nearby restaurant in order to draw up a text which would satisfy the other organisations (particularly the agricultural ones) and enable a unanimous vote on the advisory opinion to be taken. When the CGT and the CFDT delegates

and their influence increasingly circumscribed, the unions have resorted more and more in the last few years to a sort of guerrilla tactics, with minor stoppages, token strikes and the occasional demonstration designed to affirm their existence without risking an all-out battle which, in the present circumstances, they could not be sure of winning and which might, as far as the CGT is concerned, compromise the return to respectability of the Communist Party.

These tactics have provoked an increasing sense of frustration among the workers. The unions were not always unaware of this and the CGT in particular on more than one occasion took in hand an unorthodox movement and killed it. A glaring example of this is the strike against redundancy in the declining iron and steel industry of Lorraine. There had already been trouble in 1963 and it broke out again in the spring of 1967. The CGT took control, called the strike, organised it, and broke it after three weeks; one more week and the industry would have been in serious difficulties,[11] but the CGT preferred to negotiate an agreement that consisted of little more than vague promises. Redundancy firing continued afterwards as before, and in much the same conditions, and the spirit of many of the workers was sufficiently broken for them not to take part in the general strike a year later.

But the extent and depth of the restiveness, as illustrated by the extracts of interviews at the end of the chapter, went largely unnoticed. Whether local union officials were over-worked or simply thinking and acting on a different level, basic communication between the masses and the unions was not functioning, as a glance at the union conferences would show. Nevertheless, the signs were there, and it is worth having a brief look at one or two of them. The strike at Rhodiacéta in the spring of 1967 was in many ways a classic one, but the way in which it flared up again nine months later showed not only the obstinacy of the employers in not keeping their promises, but also the inability of the unions to grasp and act upon the real problems. The events of Le Mans, in the autumn of the same year, show how a series of disconnected strikes and

came back into the conference room at 14.45 they learnt that the vote on the advisory opinion had already taken place during their absence, since the session had begun a quarter of an hour earlier than the normal time-table. Faced with these tactics . . . the delegates of the two unions left the room. At the subsequent reception the Secretary of State listened at some length to the FO delegates, before replying briefly to those of the two larger unions. . . .'

11. Cf. *Le Monde*, 23 April 1967.

demonstrations turned, without any apparent reason, into a short but violent revolt.

Rhodiacéta,[12] a subsidiary of the chemical giant, Rhône-Poulenc, is a firm manufacturing synthetic fibres; it has a factory in Besançon, three in the Lyon district, and one further down the Rhône valley at Roussillon. Fifteen years ago it bought up the relevant American and British patents and with the aid of artificially high prices made handsome profits in which the workers, who were reckoned to be among the best off in the area, to some extent shared. However, little or no provision had been made for the day when the patent rights would expire, and as this happened to coincide with the opening of the Common Market frontiers prices dropped by 40–50%, which necessitated an agonising reappraisal. The resulting reorganisation was carried out without consulting or even informing those most directly concerned, and involved, among other inconveniences, a certain amount of short-time working (as often as not disguised so as not to have to break into the unemployment fund).

The reorganisation also involved an increase in the number of shift-workers, so that by the end of 1966 these amounted to 5,000 workers, or 40% of the employees of Rhodiacéta. The system generally adopted was that of four teams working two days on the morning shift, two on the afternoon, two on the night, followed by two days off. Although shift workers benefit from higher wages and a few extra days holiday in addition to the regular two days off, they lead a very irregular life (only twenty minutes is allowed for meals when they are on duty) and are completely cut off from normal social life, not to mention their families.[13] Combined with the results of the agonising reappraisal this produced an explosive situation, and at Besançon the shift-workers had already downed tools every Sunday from 15 November 1966 to 25 February 1967.

As usual this tactic did not produce any results, and on 25 February the morning shift at Besançon, acting independently of the unions, not only refused to start work but occupied the factory canteen, thereby starting an 'unlimited' strike that lasted in general for a month (slightly longer in the case of one or two of the other factories). The CFDT immediately took charge and sent delegations

12. Much of the following material is drawn from an article by François Galle, 'Conflit social à Rhodiacéta', in *Projet*, 24, April 1968.
13. Shift-working is not, of course, something new; what is comparatively recent is the workers' claim to civilised living conditions and a normal social life.

164

to bring out the other factories, but in Lyon the CGT was more powerful and a 24-hour strike was declared each day and picket-lines set up, but the factories were not occupied as in Besançon. The strike was described by some observers, basing their view on the claims put forward and the determination and efficiency with which it was conducted, as resembling an American strike. There was certainly determination and efficiency, helped by support from the local population (for example, the students and the Catholic Workers' Action in Besançon, other strikes in Lyon), but the employers' tactics were far more French than American, as witness the non-payment of wages due for February, appeal to the courts against the pickets, and refusal to negotiate until they were removed. Moreover, the deep-felt grievances of the shift-workers, who had developed a real phobia of the factory, were scarcely touched upon.

From the beginning the CFDT, followed by the CGT, emphasised the need for guarantees of employment and income, which was not unreasonable in view of the fact that the employers' tactics could be taken to mean that the future of Rhodiacéta was far from assured. Towards the end, for political reasons connected with the general election (5 and 12 March), the CGT added a wage-claim. Under pressure from Paris the employers eventually agreed to negotiate and agreement was reached with the unions, although at one point the latter were reduced to issuing statements implying that it was only the obstinacy of the strikers which prevented them signing even earlier. And indeed, although important guarantees were obtained together with a 5% wage increase and the inclusion of certain bonuses in the regular wage-packet, the unions had consider-able difficulty in persuading the workers to go back to work. For the only mention of the shift-workers' grievances was a promise that they would be discussed later.

This promise was not kept, and there was continual trouble throughout the year. The employers took no action, preferring to wait till December when they announced a series of redundancy measures and a reduction of bonuses, family allowances, etc. Wildcat strikes again broke out (partially covered by the unions to avoid legal sanctions), and the employers replied by a lock-out, described as 'technical unemployment'; this time, as there was no impending election, the CRS were present to stop pickets and enforce the lock-out. After the return to work 92 shift-workers were fired, of whom nearly 80 were union militants or members. This round went to the employers, but it left a very bitter taste.

The example of Rhodiacéta shows up not only the bitter, resentful hostility that any strike provokes in the French Patronat, but also the reluctance of the unions, even if they were aware of the explosive nature of the situation, to stake everything on a full-scale battle with the object of obtaining an outright victory and the satisfaction of genuine grievances. It is of course difficult to assert now that such a strategy would have been successful, but the extent to which the movement spread in the region (e.g. to the big lorry firm, Berliet, where the violence and material damage caused by a group of young workers provoked a lock-out which, coming just after the election, was enforced by the CRS; and to a smaller firm, Cellophane, in Saint-Maurice-de Beynost, where the long strike was notable for the viciousness of the employers' reaction against immigrant Portuguese union militants) suggests that the chances were at least fairly good.

The explosions of violence that occurred in Le Mans in the autumn of 1967 are much more difficult to analyse and explain. At the annual Conference of the CFDT in November, the delegate from Le Mans got thunderous applause when he said: 'Comrades, the workers of Le Mans fought, they fought well', but no-one was any the wiser as to the whys and wherefores of it. Although it passed relatively unnoticed at the time, the sudden upsurge of anger and frustration, especially by the young, can be seen, with the advantage of hindsight, as an indication of what was to happen in May 1969.

The West, one of the most underdeveloped parts of France, has been in a state of chronic unrest for some years. In several towns a series of demonstrations of agricultural workers on 2 October had turned into bloody battles with the police, the young playing a leading role. The CGT and the CFDT had called on all workers to make the week of 7 to 14 October an Action Week; on the whole this was not very successful, except in the West and particularly in Le Mans where there were a certain number of scuffles between police and demonstrators. The departmental representatives of the two federations decided to pursue their action and, after another demonstration on 20 October, called for a strike and demonstrations in Le Mans on 26 October. The Prefect had banned all demonstrations in the centre of the town, but up to 15,000 strikers went to five assembly points on the outskirts. In the early morning Renault workers (and others, since at one point they were estimated at 5 or 6,000, which is about double the number employed by Renault) set up a barricade and, armed with slings, kept up a battle against the tear-gas of the police for two hours, after which they returned to work. In the afternoon other strikers succeeded in forcing a police barrier, and from then until late into the night Le Mans was the scene of savage street-fighting; twenty CRS were wounded, and probably at least as many demonstrators. Large numbers of women were noticed at the assembly points, and young workers and students were particularly prominent in the fighting.

Why so much violence? The unions had called for the demonstrations to protest against the social security decrees and rising unemployment. On the first count, despite the fact that they affected the workers more than anyone,[14] the unions had not previously been able to mobilise opinion, so it is unlikely that they were an important factor here. The second was probably much more so, especially as it affected above all the young, as in all the West. It has already been shown to what extent existing unemployment in France hits the young, and this is particularly true of the West, which boasts the highest proportion of children completing secondary education. The result is that very often they have to accept jobs well below their qualifications. Employers are not slow to take advantage of this situation and in many of the smaller firms pay and working conditions are abysmally bad.

Unfortunately it would need a proper survey accurately to determine the causes of the outburst, but it is likely that some at least of the factors mentioned would figure in it. In any case, there is no doubt that the workers and students (i.e. the future unemployed) of Le Mans were very angry, as were the workers of Rhodiacéta. And they were not the only ones. Other examples could be cited, of which the most recent would be the strike at Saviem, the Renault lorry branch in Caen, which dragged on, interrupted by spasmodic worker-student violence, for a couple of months before the uprising of May. Whether this justifies saying that the uprising would have occurred with or without the students is unimportant; the fact remains that the students were there to light the fuse and, as events were to confirm, the powder was very dry.

14. Earlier in the year M. Pompidou had bullied the National Assembly into giving him special powers to reorganise, among other things, the social security system. The resulting decrees, published in August when everyone was on holiday, entailed a decrease of worker control over the running of the system and an increase of 50% in the percentage of medical expenses that is not reimbursed.

The Amiens Charter of the CGT, 1905

The confederal congress of Amiens confirms article 2 which creates the CGT.

'The CGT, which is outside any political grouping, unites all workers conscious of the struggle to be waged if salaried workers and employers are to disappear as such'.

The congress considers that this declaration recognises the existence of an economic class struggle between the workers and all forms of exploitation and oppression, both material and moral, which the capitalists employ against the working classes.

The congress follows up this theoretical affirmation in greater detail on the following points:

In the claims that it makes every day, trade-unionism is attempting to coordinate workers' efforts, is aiming to improve their well-being by obtaining immediate improvements, such as a decrease in the working day; an increase in wages, etc. . . .

But this task only represents one side of the work of trade-unionism; it is preparing complete emancipation, which can only be achieved if the capitalists are dispossessed; the general strike should be the means of action, and it considers that while unions today are resistance groups, in the future they will be responsible for production and distribution, the basis of social reorganisation.

The congress declares that this twofold task, since it is both daily and for the future, stems from the situation of the salaried workers, which weighs on the working class and makes it the duty of every working man, whatever his opinions or political or philosophical tendencies, to belong to that most essential grouping, the union.

Consequently the congress confirms that, outside the corporative body, the union member is entirely free to take part in the activities of whatever form of opposition most closely resembles his own philosophical or political concepts, but in return he is asked not to expound in the union opinions that he may profess outside it.

The congress decides that, as far as organisations are concerned, if trade-unionism is to be really effective, economic action must be directed against employers, and that, as union groupings, confederal organisations will not concern themselves with parties or sects which may, on the side, pursue social change in complete freedom.

DOCUMENT 22

Length and frequency of strikes

Length of industrial disputes 1965

One hour or less	281
One hour to half a day	307
Half a day to one day	314
One day to one week	408
One to two weeks	166
Two weeks to one month	153
One to two months	27
Longer than two months	18
Total	1,674

(Source: *Revue française du travail*, July–September 1966).

Average length of strikes for 1960:

France	1	day
West Germany	2·2	days
Italy	2·5	days
Norway	3·7	days
U.S.A.	14·7	days

(Source: J-D. Reynaud, op cit.)

F*

Strikes in France 1953–1965

	1953	1954	1955	1956	1957	1958	1959	1960	1961	1962	1963	1964	1965
Number of disputes	1,761	1,479	2,672	2,440	2,623	954	1,512	1,494	1,963	1,884	2,382	2,281	1,674
Number of strikers (in thousands)	1,784	1,269	792	666	2,161	858	581	839	1,270	833	1,148	1,048	688
Number of working days lost (in thousands)	9,722	1,440	3,079	1,423	4,121	1,138	1,938	1,070	2,601	1,901	5,994	2,497	980

Source: Revue française du travail, July–September 1966.

DOCUMENT 23

Trade Union hierarchy

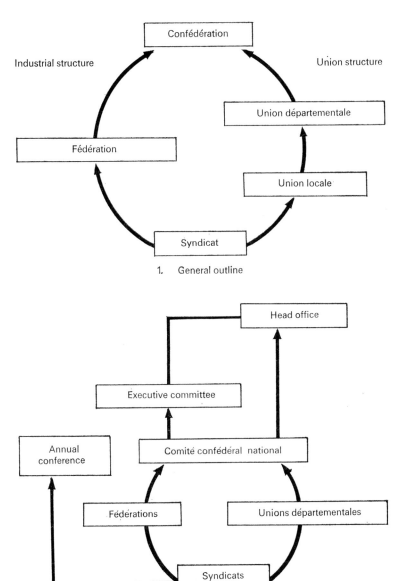

1. General outline

2. The Power structure

DOCUMENT 24

Three union militants

The following texts are extracts from interviews obtained by Jacques Capdevielle and René Mouriaux with local union militants in Grenoble and Lyon from November 1967 to March 1968. They illustrate many of the themes of the preceding chapter: the difficulty of being a militant, the gap that separates the rank and file from the union hierarchy, the ineffectualness of much industrial action and the consequent deception and increasing bitterness among the rank and file.

I handed over my job as a collector [of union funds] a bit—a month—ago; but then, I've become a general collector. S. does the collecting in his workshop. I've put a collector in my place now in the workshop, whereas he does the electricity workshop. As far as collecting inside our place goes for example, there's one big problem, that's the outside work. On the factory level there are no complications—the boss, the foreman, people like that, don't get in the way of our collecting. But outside work, that's a problem. Outside work is pretty changeable. You get a job going on in one place for 3 months; in another place there's a job that's going to last a year. The trouble is that in that case you can't find a representative or somebody responsible for that particular job. I'll give you an example; as soon as there's a collector, or someone who stirs things up a bit on some site, the management uses some excuse or other to take him away and shove him on some other site. He's going to take 6 months to readapt, and by then the whole thing's forgotten. Then there are holidays and so on. . . . I mean that by taking someone away from one place, or if you give him a dirty job, it enables you . . . I mean, he gets discouraged, he doesn't worry about it any more if he hasn't got any responsibility, he just does the collecting from time to time. Then the site foreman. . . . But as far as the workshops are concerned, you can say that until now there's never been any trouble there. As regards collecting, anyway. . .

[The gap between the rank and file and the union hierarchy starts] straight away, immediately. Between us and the headquarters in Grenoble. They get instructions from Paris, and that's all. That's it. In fact we were at a meeting a month ago. Before it started we were given the petition thing, to get petitions drawn up, without finding out if we agreed. The thing was ready before. Well, me, I shouted a bit, some others shouted too. There was R. and L. So for them it was the petition. Whether we agreed or not, they had been told to get a petition drawn up for social security; these petitions had to be drawn up whether we liked it or not. . . .

I don't believe in localised strikes any more. We went on strike again at our place. Why did we strike? To get a pay rise, for example; always supposing that the boss lets us have one. Right, what does that change? Does it solve any problems? The problem hasn't been solved; in 6 months you've got to start again. The social security problem, schools, things like that, the unemployment problem, nothing will be solved. And the blokes are coming out less and less for these small strikes. They can see they don't change anything. Anyway . . . perhaps the pay slip looks a bit better, but all the big problems, all the fundamental problems are still there. We're still fighting for the same thing. What the blokes want is for one problem to be taken after another, and each solved once and for all. For that they'll all come out. You warn them 6 months ahead. 'Right, this is what we're going to do; we're going to attack this problem, and we won't allow it not to be really gone into in detail.' That would work.

(From a recorded interview with a CGT militant—not a member of the CP and whose sympathies lie rather with the PSU—working for a building material and construction company in Grenoble: 11 November 1967.)

After that of course there are the habits you get into, the fact that in our federation we're, how shall I put it, we've . . . that we're still a bit too attached . . . in relation to '45, to institutions . . . Perhaps we could have changed since, I don't know if you see what I mean. So obviously, that gets in the way a lot, it holds us up. That's my opinion, that's what I think. And . . . I don't know . . . me . . . we're too inclined to listen to what the federation says. But the rank and file of the SNCF in Grenoble, I don't know what it's like elsewhere, but . . . the rank and file in Grenoble just . . . has no existence. Okay, the union works when it's a question of deciding minor things, practical work to be done, but when it's a question of something important . . . it can only . . . of course, it can only . . .

It can't apply any pressure, because . . . This also stems from the structure of the SNCF, I think, but also, to a great extent, from the impression we have, well, that a lot of mates have, of just being guided, well, of being shown the way, etc. So I don't know. I reckon it's bad. I try to say so each time I can. They say I'm an anarchist. Perhaps. I don't think I'm anarchist because I try to organise, whereas as a rule the anarchists don't go in for organising.

(From a recorded interview with a CGT militant working on the railways in Grenoble: 16 January 1968.)

We still work the way we did 10 or 20 years ago. There's no file. There should be a file for every movement, in order to carry on. . . . You start a movement without any very clear idea. You haven't got anything planned in advance. You embark on something, you're asking for such and such a thing. The management manoeuvres you into its way of thinking. At the moment the strike for bonuses has lasted off and on for a year. The management isn't stupid. It suggested meetings, and drew up a file, once in possession of all the facts. Then it was in a position to judge. Depending on the different branches, it tries to break up the movement in such a way that the blokes are no longer united. It will apply certain resolutions, and the union will have a job to do anything about it. Certain advantages are obtained, but it will be much more difficult to get to grips with the real problems because you'll have lost the support of 30–40% of the blokes. If there's another movement tomorrow, the whole affair must be analysed. We go into battle without having anything established, without a line—even if we've got to change it on the way—there is one, but it's much too superficial. That, I am against. The militants aren't changed often enough. They've been fighting for 10 years. There's no point wasting your time with analysis, they say. When the blokes get hot-headed, we'll go and see what we can do. The young ones analyse what they see a bit more than the older blokes. There's the lack of time, that's an enormous handicap. The blokes are working, the meetings are held during the lunch break. To start something moving, it's a job getting hold of the chaps, even during the lunch break. You don't get many blokes. In the evening, it's difficult; the blokes come in coaches. . . . As a result we're not organised. . . .

It's easier when you've got some young ones—the mentality of the older ones dominates attitudes to the work to be done in the movement. The young ones are more pugnacious, they're not afraid of the foreman. You can send the young ones to a school more easily. You've got to keep after the blokes; we don't educate them enough. The older blokes saw '36, they've seen others like us. You've got to get yourself accepted. It's difficult to ask them to keep records—with the numbers of union members, the causes of fluctuations in membership—the same thing goes for votes at elections. The older ones don't want minutes to be kept of meetings. The young ones realise that each section must have a structure. We've got no records, or very few, which we can use. The older members are a bit cut off; they don't accept certain things, they hang on to their old ways.

(From a recorded interview with a CGT militant working in a large factory in Lyon: 25 March 1968.)

CHAPTER FIVE

WORKERS AND STUDENTS:
AN UNEASY ALLIANCE

1 The General Strike: up to the Grenelle Agreements.

'For ten years now demographers and sociologists have repeatedly prophesied the coming of the wave of youth. Well, the wave has reached us, and is beginning to break.'

Pierre Viansson-Ponté in *Le Monde*, 15 May.

DURING the week-end that followed the Gay-Lussac battle it was still possible to believe that the token general strike called for Monday 13 May would simply mark the successful climax of ten days of student riots. The students, of whom the great mass had had neither the time nor the opportunity to formulate concrete proposals for educational reform, might be thought to have every reason to be satisfied. Had not the Prime Minister given in to every single one of their conditions? Moreover, by Monday evening all the arrested demonstrators had been released, and the police withdrawn from the Latin Quarter. True, the Sorbonne was immediately occupied,[1] but it is conceivable that if the rest of France had remained on the sidelines their problems could have been solved, or at least de-fused, by the opening of genuine discussions with the principal student and teacher unions and movements.[2] As it was, however, four of the most powerful trade unions,[3] possibly in response to the students' appeals for help during the night of Friday and Saturday, but more probably to take advantage of the

1. The arts and social sciences annexe of the Sorbonne at Censier had been occupied since 11 May, as also had the law faculty at Rennes and parts of the Universities of Strasbourg and Bordeaux.
2. This hypothesis may seem very implausible in the light of later events, but it did not appear so at the time. It also serves to underline the point that if certain social, economic, and political factors made some kind of explosion highly probable at some time or other, at no time during the month of May was it inevitable that events should take the turn they did—see below, p. 187 on the censure motion in the National Assembly.
3. The CGT, CFDT, FO, and the FEN.

coincidence of dates,[4] to show their strength and their hostility by protesting against the particularly brutal nature of police repression, called for a general strike. The undisguised joy of the political activists among the students was increased when, on the day of the strike, between 500,000 and 800,000[5] Parisian students and workers, converging from the Gare de l'Est and the Place de la République, joined forces to march together up the Boulevard Saint Michel to the Place Denfert-Rochereau. And to crown it all, after considerable argument it was finally settled that the three main leaders and spokesmen of the students should be in the front rank with the union leaders, including Georges Séguy of the CGT. The longed-for alliance between students and workers was at last realised.

However, if one looks more closely at what happened in Paris and in the provinces on 13 May, it is possible to see that the seeds of the coming unrest were well and truly sown. To begin with the Paris march, many of the slogans, far from being concerned simply with police brutality, were politically militant in character ('Ten years is enough!', 'De Gaulle, resign!' etc.). Further, despite the banners proclaiming student, teacher and worker solidarity, the student-worker alliance was extremely fragile, at least as far as their respective organisations were concerned.[6] On the other hand, not only was there a certain amount of fraternising between young workers and students, but when, after the official dispersal order, some four or five thousand young marchers continued, first towards the Elysée but later, when reason had prevailed, to the Champ de Mars, the militant students among them found their numbers considerably swollen by workers. Finally, it is usual in a march of this sort to find political leaders and public figures up at the front with the leaders of the march. On this occasion, only union and student leaders were at the front while such prominent people as

4. The putsch that brought de Gaulle to power, part real, part threatened, part imagined, occurred on 13 May 1958.

5. Over and above a certain level, accurate crowd arithmetic is impossible. The one thing that can be stated with certainty is that the 'official' figure given by the ORFT news (171,000) was very wide of the mark.

6. The mutual distrust, already apparent, degenerated later, as will be seen, into open hostility. It was only with the greatest reluctance that Georges Séguy consented to march in the same line as Daniel Cohn-Bendit. Just before the latter was declared *persona non grata* in France, Georges Séguy replied to a journalist's question with the words: 'Cohn-Bendit? Never heard of him.' At the time, and in its context, this answer was interpreted, perhaps not unjustifiably, as expressing not merely contempt but also racialism: cf. p. 88.

MM. Mitterand, Mendès-France, Mollet and Waldeck Rochet[7] were lost in the crowd half-way along the huge column. Thus when the students in their march across Paris nearly a week earlier had blatantly ignored the National Assembly, they were reflecting a widespread opinion that the present crisis, however interpreted, was not one which parliamentary deputies, whether of the majority or of the opposition, were capable of resolving.

No less significant, if less fully reported by both contemporary and later commentators, was what happened that day in the provinces. The strike was, properly speaking, far from 'general'. Considering that the reasons for the strike had nothing to do either with wage-increases or with the class-struggle, but everything to do with a situation which to most people in the provinces had up to then appeared as specifically Parisian, this is not surprising. In general, those who came out on strike were to be found among the most poorly paid workers, in depressed areas or in centres of recent industrial unrest. Thus while the industrial complex in the East and North-East was relatively unaffected, the greatest number of strikers were to be found in Toulouse, Lyon, Grenoble, Nancy, the mining areas of the North and, to a lesser extent, in the West.

But perhaps more important than the strike itself were the demonstrations and marches. In several towns, such as Toulouse, Lyon and Marseilles, where in each case the number of marchers was between 30,000 and 50,000,[8] more people took part than at any time since the Liberation. In many cases also, the slogans were of a similarly political character to those shouted during the Paris march. Besides these, two other aspects take on a special significance in view of what followed. At Rhodiacéta, both in Besançon and Lyon, everybody went on strike. In both branches the management retaliated by announcing a lock-out for the following day, but in each case was obliged to annul the decision under pressure from the demonstrating strikers who, in Lyon, went as far as to invade the factory premises.[9] Secondly, in a number of smaller towns the demonstrators, or at least part of them, marched

7. Respectively, President of the FGDS, ex-Prime Minister and parliamentary deputy who had accepted the PSU whip, secretary-general of the SFIO, secretary-general of the French Communist Party.

8. Estimates from *Le Monde* and the local press.

9. Also interesting in view of what followed is the fact that the students who accompanied workers to the factory did not go in but remained outside the gates.

on the prefecture.[10] In many places, such as Besançon, Saint-Brieuc and Caen, there were no incidents, but at Le Mans 300 young people split off from the 20,000 marchers and took the prefecture by storm, forcing the gates, destroying the cars in the courtyard and stoning the windows. A similar but unsuccessful attempt in Clermont-Ferrand was repulsed after a pitched battle with the police. In Nantes, again after an impressive meeting and march of some 15,000 to 20,000 people between 1,500 and 2,000 students, some of them armed with clubs, marched on the Préfecture to present their grievances. After a brief clash during which barricades were set up, a delegation went to the Prefect and obtained all that they asked for.[11]

In Paris the overall impression was that 13 May had gone off much better than might have been expected. The unions, and in particular the CGT, had shown—as they were to do again and again—how well they could control their troops and that, while ready to provoke the Government, they were not willing to go adventuring any further. In the provinces the situation was rather different. Accustomed as they were to localised strikes and small demonstrations, the size of the marches and the violence that accompanied them in some places brought home to many, perhaps for the first time, that the tumultuous events of which Paris had been the scene during the past ten days concerned them directly. Possibly as a result of that, the initiative was now to pass, if only temporarily, from Paris to the provinces.

That which the students of Nantes had not been able to obtain by other means, they obtained by violence. In those parts of the world where legitimacy and consent have virtually ousted force and terror as the principles according to which rulers obtain and keep the obedience of their subjects, violence becomes an increasingly potent and efficient weapon in the hands of the dissenter. This lesson, which frightens even the most progressive liberals, was again brought home to Frenchmen in a particularly striking manner by M. Pompidou's total surrender to the Paris student demands

10. More important than the Town Hall, the prefecture is the seat of the Prefect, who is the departmental representative of the central Paris administration.

11. Their demands all arose out of the incidents which occurred on 14 February, as a result of which both the Prefect and the Rector of the Academy had started legal actions, and the grant to the Student Association was withdrawn—see above, p. 74.

on 11 May. On 13 May the workers of Rhodiacéta at Lyon applied the lesson. On 14 May at Château-Bougon, near Nantes, the workers of Sud-Aviation also applied it. The State-run aircraft firm which built the Caravelle and is now working on the Concorde had for some time been the scene of a conflict between the management which wanted to reduce working hours and the workers who were prepared to accept this only if it involved no loss of purchasing power. At three o'clock, after yet another meeting with the management had failed to produce any results, a handful of young union delegates invaded the executive offices and made the managing director and one or two other executives prisoners in their own offices. A strike committee was formed, picket lines set up, and of the 2,800 workers who had only a few days earlier vetoed a proposal of the CGT and the FO for a total strike in favour of a series of half-hour token strikes, 2,000 spent the night of Tuesday-Wednesday in the factory.[12]

On the following day, Wednesday 15 May, there were one or two isolated strikes, such as those which took place in the shipyards of Bordeaux and among certain sections of the air navigation staff, but they bore little or no relation to the events of the last couple of days, the latter strike in particular having been planned at least a week earlier. But the one which finally set off the chain reaction was at the Renault factory in Cléon, near Rouen, where in a manner remarkably similar to that of the young workers of Sud-Aviation 200 young militants, acting without the stimulus of a lingering open dispute and quite independently of the unions, brought all the 5000 workers out on strike. They demanded the granting of permanent contracts to the 700 workers on short-term ones,[13] a minimum wage of 1,000 francs a month (c. £20 a week), a forty-hour week, and an extension of union rights. The manager refused to leave, thereby making himself prisoner, and a proposed meeting with the board of directors was refused by Renault head office the following day.

The strike began in Cléon in the afternoon. The same afternoon the Renault workers at the Flins factory, near Mantes, stopped

12. *Le Monde*, 16 May, complemented by *Action*, 11 June.
13. Three- to six-month contracts are common practice where immigrant workers, particularly Algerians and Portuguese, are concerned. To offset fluctuations in demand Renault had recently extended the system to some French workers. Yet the nationalised car firm had been in many respects a pioneer in the field of industrial relations—see above, p. 141.

180

work for two hours in sympathy. The next day the majority of the 11,000 workers voted to strike, and by two o'clock the red flag was flying over the occupied factory. By midnight the other Renault factories, at Boulogne-Billancourt just outside Paris (30,000 workers), Sandouville near Le Havre (4,500 workers), Le Mans (3,000 workers) and Orléans (800 workers), were all occupied. On Friday 17 May it was the turn of Rhodiacéta and Berliet in Lyon, and from then on the movement spread like wildfire. On Saturday the number of strikers was being estimated in terms of hundreds of thousands; by Monday 20 May it was a case of millions, and France, with no transport,[14] no postal communications and no industrial power, was to all intents and purposes paralysed. The unofficial but generally accepted figure of ten million, out of a working population of nearly 14 million, was probably reached by Thursday 23 May (Ascension Day and a national holiday). The only sector then relatively untouched was the iron and steel industry of Lorraine.[15]

How did this situation come about? Wildfire indeed is not an exaggerated metaphor. At Flins, from the very first day, workers rushed around the countryside to carry the news and bring other factories out on strike. As the movement gained momentum, older militants caught the enthusiasm. Union rivalries were briefly forgotten, only to be remembered when it came to the internal organisation of the strike. Here the CGT, with more militants at its disposal, had an advantage. Once the decision to occupy a factory had been taken it was more often the CGT which had men to spare to send to other factories in the area, in the not unreasonable hope that the union which started the strike would gain most new members. At times they occupied the switchboard and prevented any communication between the CFTD militants and their departmental office.[16] Rarely however, at least in the early stages, did this leave any bitterness. Too big a thing was happening, and there was too much to be done.

In their headquarters in Paris the unions, at first suprised and

14. Food continued to be brought to the towns by road. The fact that there was at no time any shortage underlines the fact that in France, as elsewhere, the railways are grossly underused.

15. See above, p. 163. Firms which are run by Americans or on American lines also tended to be spared, such as IBM and Simca (although in the latter case American-style management seems to be combined with typically French discipline).

16. Such an incident is known to have occurred in Grenoble; it is reasonable to suppose that it was not unique.

more than a little perplexed, had little difficulty in taking the strikes in hand, at least to all outward appearances. The union delegates on the various workers' committees had more knowledge of the functioning of the factory and the union militants greater experience in the organising of strike committees, picket-lines, etc., as well as in the formulating of grievances. But all this was at the local level. At no time did the unions send out a call for a general strike. In France more perhaps than elsewhere, and for the unions more than for the political parties, a general strike remains the ultimate revolutionary weapon of the workers, and to have brought it into play at this stage would have enabled the Government to mobilise from the start all the counter-revolutionary forces. As it was, by encouraging, as they did after the first few days, a general strike without actually proclaiming it, by provoking the regime without openly challenging it, the unions left the Government with nothing at which it could effectively hit back.[17] On this much the CGT and the CFDT were agreed, at least at this stage. But this tactic also implied keeping the strike within the limits which they had defined for it, and it was at this point that it became increasingly apparent that there were important differences of opinion, most noticeable in the type of claims advanced and in the attitudes towards the students, both between the CGT and the CFDT and within the CGT itself. These will be dealt with in greater detail later on and in the next chapter.[18]

As the movement spread from the students to the industrial workers, so it spread from the workers to other sectors of the community. In general, the eyes of the agricultural workers were fixed on Brussels, where there was to be an inter-Common Market demonstration on 27 May, rather than on Paris. By nature conservative and somewhat cut off from the rest of society, the majority

17. Thus M. Pompidou's television broadcast on the evening of 16 May, and the Cabinet meeting he presided over on 17 May, both devoted to the problem of 'keeping order', were simply propaganda devices. Any action on his part at that stage would only have precipitated a much more serious situation.

18. It should be clear from the foregoing that no explanation of the strikes based on any form of conspiracy theory will hold water. Apart from the fact that it is difficult to see who the conspirators could have been (the student activists did not have a worker audience before May and no organisation during May, while the unions and the Communist Party, the only people with an organisation capable of being used for revolutionary ends, were blatantly caught napping), it is unlikely that a plot would have developed in the same way as the strikes did, i.e. as a chain reaction starting from a single fuse.

of them were content to follow the cynical example of their leaders at the head of the FNSEA. In a statement published on 17 May the latter announced, in terms which allowed no misunderstanding, that they were willing to refrain from opening a 'third front' with the students and workers, but that the government would have to pay a heavy price for this support, particularly in Brussels.[19] This threat was accompanied by the announcement of a 'day of warning', which was to consist of a series of localised demonstrations on Friday 24 May. However by no means all of the agricultural workers felt that the student and worker movement was simply an isolated event which could be used to their advantage. This was particularly true in the Nantes area, in the Loire-Atlantique, where the 13 May demonstrations had comprised agricultural workers along with students and workers. In various parts of the North-West of France local federations of the FNSEA affirmed in different ways and to varying degrees their solidarity with the movement, independent demonstrations took place, and road blocks were set up;[20] on 24 May, the 'day of warning', about 200,000 demonstrated throughout the country. This was fewer than had been expected, but in several widely scattered places, such as Périgueux, Quimper and above all Nantes,[21] the demonstrations took a violent turn. The influence of the young farmers' organisation, the CNJA, had a lot to do with the increased social and political awareness of a small but important section of the farming community, and it was not uncommon to see CNJA banners alongside union and student ones during the demonstrations.[22]

Unrest was known to exist among the farming community, and the only surprise was that it did not take more radical forms. What was much more unexpected was the action of the cadres. In a few firms some of them followed the workers in going on strike, and in

19. The price was duly paid. The agreement reached in Brussels on 29 May enabled the target date of 1 July to be kept, at least symbolically, but did absolutely nothing towards solving the milk marketing problems of the Common Market.

20. E.g. in Quimper, Périgueux, Saint Brieuc, Guingamp, Loudéac, etc.

21. In Nantes, a five-hour pitched battle took place between police and demonstrators. It is claimed that a certain number of the ring-leaders came from Paris, and this may well be true. The fact remains that several attempts at mediation nearly resulted in a lynching. A final attempt, by a man who had just resigned from the CGT, was not merely successful in stopping the fighting, but led to the strange sight of bitter enemies of a moment before fraternising with one another, and talking over their common problems, including the moral ones of policemen: cf. also pps. 207–10.

22. See below, Appendix 1 (iii).

Paris regular meetings were held in a room set apart for them at the Sorbonne. Further, on the night of Tuesday 21 May two different groups occupied the offices of the CNPF and of their own union, the CGC. These 'operations' were carried out not only by representatives of all the unions, with the exception of the CGT, but also by members of the political club, *Technique et Démocratie*.[23] There were in addition a certain number who claimed that the necessary renovation of French society could only be carried out by action performed independently of the traditional political and trade union organisations. Although these incidents were relatively minor, their repercussions on public opinion were considerable: that the undergraduates of yesterday should show their sympathy with the undergraduates of to-day was one thing; quite another was the fact that those responsible for the transmission of authority in industry should begin openly to contest that very authority.

The centre of gravity of the movement had clearly shifted away from the students. If this shift was accurately reflected in the newspaper headlines, the opinions and commentaries published by the same papers were still devoted, to a greater extent than was warranted by events, to the students and the educational system in general.[24] The latter sector became completely paralysed on 20 May when the primary and secondary teachers' unions called for a strike and open discussions with their pupils. Most schools were closed down; a few in Paris and the big towns were occupied day and night, and so remained open. But the whole French University, in the Napoleonic sense, had become one vast discussion group.[25]

23. See below, ch. 8. Although they never went as far as a general strike, there were also a certain number of stoppages, meetings, wage-claims etc., in some advertising agencies.

24. This is largely explained by the fact that the commentators for the most part knew far more about the educational system than they did about the industrial one (when the general strike was discussed in the press, it was usually in political terms, which suited both the Government and the CGT). It is true nevertheless that the total destruction and rebuilding of an educational system which, however archaic and creaking, was still ideologically adapted to existing French society, had enormous revolutionary potential—but of course it could never be carried out by the students alone.

25. As had the Odéon National Theatre, whose Director was Jean-Louis Barrault. It was occupied on the night of 16 May by an independent group of students and others, led by Jean-Jacques Lebel, the organiser of 'happenings'. The UNEF and the SNESup. both disavowed the occupation, but the *mouvement du 22 mars* felt compelled to approve it, and indeed swiftly took over the control of the theatre from Lebel.

However, the principal concern of the minority of political activists among the students remained the establishing of contact with the workers. At the union level they had a certain limited success. On 20 May the UNEF and the CFDT held a joint press conference in which they underlined the mutual independence of structural reforms in education and in industry. But a few days later the CGT publicly cancelled a meeting with the UNEF, and although they tried to minimise this later by emphasising their sympathy with the mass of students, the hopes raised by the Paris march of 13 May were dashed for good.[26]

At the individual level, the students' success was equally limited, but perhaps more far-reaching. Workers came to meet and talk with students at the Sorbonne from the first day of its occupation, and at Censier, the activists' headquarters, political discussions of a very high level, in which a fair sprinkling of workers, young and old, participated, were frequently interrupted by calls for students to go to factories in the Paris area, and even in Brittany, which were either on the point of striking or had already struck. The workers, and particularly the union pickets, were often extremely suspicious, if not outright hostile, but surprisingly often communication was established. Thus very early on some students from Nantes spent a night with the pickets of Sud-Aviation. In Paris the most spectacular attempts were the solidarity marches to the Renault workers in Boulogne-Billancourt, and some contact was made across the picket lines. But it was only in Besançon that the contact was in any way institutionalised. There the strike committee of the Rhodiacéta factory and the university Action Committee came to a formal agreement by which representatives of each had the right to go and address meetings in the other's territory. Despite the reservations of local CGT militants this agreement was kept, and it provides a striking example of one of the principal characteristics of the whole movement, the breaking down of what had hitherto been regarded as watertight barriers.

26. The apparent reason for the rupture was the refusal of the CGT to disapprove the government's action in declaring Daniel Cohn-Bendit *persona non grata* in France on 22 May, and it is possible that the identity of interests on this question between the government and the Communists was coincidental. However, the CGT had already made known its desire to negotiate at the national level (see below, p. 190), and if the negotiations were to be conducted on the straightforward basis of wage-claims, it was in the interests of everybody, the Government, the Patronat and the unions, that the students be kept very firmly on the sidelines.

During this period the Government was, to say the least, ineffective, if not totally inactive. The least ineffective, as well as the least inactive, was the Prime Minister, Georges Pompidou. In the special debate on education in the National Assembly on Tuesday 14 May he made an excellent parliamentary speech in which he showed himself to be both aware of the profound need for reform and willing to have students collaborate with the Government in the working out of the details. However, instead of inviting the leaders of the student movement to confer immediately with the Government, M. Pompidou went out of his way to draw a distinction between the UNEF and the other organisations. Two days later, when the strike movement was well under way, he made a first attempt to discredit the entire student movement when he appeared on television immediately after Geismar, Sauvageot, and Cohn-Bendit.[27] 10,000 reservists of the Gendarmerie Nationale were called up, and there were rumours, unfounded if not uninspired, of troop movements. Throughout the week-end there were numerous ministerial conferences, at which were regularly present the Minister of the Interior and the Minister of the Armed Forces. On Sunday 19 May, de Gaulle, who had cut short his visit to Rumania by a few hours, presided over a small Cabinet meeting at the end of which both the Minister of Information and the Prime Minister publicly repeated the President's summary of the situation: '*La réforme, oui*; *la chienlit, non!*'[28] This ill-considered remark was not made simply for lack of anything better to say; it was aimed directly at the students (although this had to be spelt out to the unions in a series of telephone calls), and was part of a policy designed to isolate them.[29]

27. For a similar interpretation cf. *Le Monde*, 18 May.

28. *La chienlit* has no exact equivalent in English. Literally, it means 'shitting in one's bed' (*chier*, to shit, *les chiottes*, shit-house, etc.) but it also means 'masquerade', 'carnival'. De Gaulle is reported to have used the word twice before, although not in print and not in an official capacity, when referring to the Fourth Republic, and the extreme right-wing weekly, *Minute*, had recently used it to describe Cohn-Bendit's activities at Nanterre. On all these occasions it was obviously the figurative meaning that was intended, but few Frenchmen are familiar with the word, and those who heard it for the first time on this occasion could not fail to take it for an expression of sovereign contempt.

29. The failure of the students and workers to join hands in any massive way doubtless inspired this policy. It was confirmed by the fact that on 17 May the planned student march on the ORTF was cancelled, largely because of the opposition of the CGT who considered it a provocation. On the same day, and a quarter of an hour after it was due to open, the CGT cancelled a large Youth Rally which they had planned and sponsored on the outskirts of Paris.

This policy, the only remotely positive one the Government had at the time, was sustained throughout the following week. An alternative was offered by the debate in the National Assembly on the censure motion tabled a week earlier by the Communists and the Federation. It was the last opportunity for the elected representatives of the country, in a debate that was exceptionally given full coverage by radio and television,[30] to show that they had even the slightest understanding of what it was that was shaking France to its foundations and, by so doing, conceivably to alter the course of events. As it was, the motion gained even fewer votes than the previous one in April,[31] and the debate, apart from one or two rare speeches and the courageous actions of two left-wing Gaullists,[32] was quite undistinguished. One incident, however, stands out. On the second day of the debate, Wednesday 22 May in a sharp exchange with Pierre Cot, an independent deputy who accepts the Communist whip and is by far the best speaker in the Assembly, the Prime Minister claimed to have proof that among the students there were 'ringleaders controlled from abroad'. The reference was clearly to Cohn-Bendit, and later in the same day it was officially announced that he would not be allowed back into France. *Le Monde* commented that the Government had again failed to measure the results of its actions; in fact it had probably measured them fairly accurately.

On the Wednesday, Thursday and Friday, there were three student demonstrations in Paris each one more violent than the last. The immediate causes, sometimes obscure, were different in each case, but it is reasonable to suppose that not one of them would have occurred had not the Government, with the full support of the Communist Party,[33] decided to ban Cohn-Bendit. The first one, on 22 May, called by the student organisations at the last minute when they heard the news, gathered only a few thousand and went

30. The greater part of the ORTF personnel had been on strike since 20 May, although essential news coverage was assured, independently by the radio, less so by television. For a fuller discussion see Appendix 2.

31. Only those in favour of a censure motion vote, and an absolute majority (244) is required for its adoption, which entails the dissolution of the Assembly. On this occasion 233 votes were mustered as against 236 on 25 April when the main subject was the news coverage of the ORTF.

32. René Capitant, law professor, now Minister of Justice, who, having announced that he would vote for the motion, preferred simply to resign his seat: and Edgar Pisani, who had resigned as Minister of Agriculture in 1967. He made the best speech of the debate, voted the motion, and resigned his seat.

33. Cf. *L'Humanité*, 24 May.

off without incident until the dispersal order; from then until the small hours the usuall small groups of fascists and anarchists continued stone-throwing battles with the police. On 23 May there were a few peaceful demonstrations in the provinces, in particular in Lyon, Bordeaux, and Caen, involving not more than a thousand students in each case.[34] In Paris a large-scale riot grew out of nothing: a small scuffle in the Place Saint-Michel, the police invaded the Latin Quarter, the students swarm to defend the Sorbonne, and resort to burning barricades, Molotov cocktails and slings. No organisation had called for a demonstration, and indeed both sides were agreed that it was the fault of *agents provocateurs*. The only new elements were that since the demonstration of the day before police were massed on the Pont Saint Michel and that a certain number of older well-dressed men were noticed among the students. More of these were noticed the following day and some of them were recognised by journalists as having belonged to the presidential bodyguard during the 1965 presidential election campaign.[35] It would seem therefore that, if *agents provocateurs* there were, they were not drawn solely from among the students.

24 May, the day fixed by de Gaulle before his departure for Rumania on 14 May for his television broadcast to the nation, was the agricultural workers' 'day of warning', and what happened in towns like Nantes has already been described. The student organisations the day before announced a big rally, after four converging marches, at the Gare de Lyon for 19.00. The CGT, alone of the unions, had also announced two marches, one on the left bank and one on the right, for the afternoon. The ostensible reason for this was to put pressure on the Government and the Patronat to negotiate; the real reason was to offer a counter-attraction so that as few workers as possible would join the students. By 19.30 it was obvious that the space in front of the Gare de Lyon was not big enough (there were at least as many students and schoolboys as the 20,000 workers who followed the CGT marches) and a move was made in the direction of the Bastille, one of the usual places for holding rallies. But the police barred the way, and the student leaders began negotiating with them about the best route they could take. The police, who probably realised that the only hope for a peaceful

34. It is interesting to note that the Rector of the University of Caen, who is a civil servant, replied to the students that, speaking unofficially, he saw no reason why Cohn-Bendit should not be allowed to return to France.
35. P. Andro, A. Dauvergne, L.-M. Lagoutte, op. cit., p. 138.

end to the demonstration was to let the students march through Paris as they had done on 7 and 8 May, were ready to come to an agreement, but they had first to obtain the approval of a 'higher authority'.[36] After a quarter of an hour's wait a negative reply came back, and from then on the police did nothing to help the student leaders and organisers avert what turned out to be the most bloody battle so far. The students, with a certain tactical intelligence, scattered into smaller groups and resorted to urban guerrilla tactics throughout a large area of Paris, but in so doing they played into the Government's hands. For, even if the cost in human terms was extremely high,[37] the desired result was achieved: the students, as a political force, were finally discredited in the eyes of a large and influential section of public opinion. Although on 24 and 25 May a large number of demonstrations took place in the provinces without any serious incident occurring (e.g. students and workers marched together at Caen, Limoges, Grenoble and Toulouse; in each case the police kept well in the background), the accidental death of a police officer[38] in the heavy rioting in Lyon reinforced the isolation of the students.

In the meantime de Gaulle had made his first lamentable television broadcast in which his only concrete proposal was for a referendum-plebiscite; for once the *Conseil d'Etat* found the courage to declare it unconstitutional. However, the disastrous effects of this speech were in part mitigated by the Government announcement that they were willing to preside over discussions between the Patronat and the unions during the week-end. The timing of this announcement suggested that the Government had given in to pressure from the unions, thus underlining the 'serious' character of the CGT marches

36. According to *Le Monde*, 26–27 May, the negative reply was given '*en haut lieu*'. This phrase is regularly used when off-the-record information exists that a decision was taken outside the normal hierarchy. In this case it would mean that the decision was not taken by the Minister of the Interior but by the Prime Minister or, more probably, by the President of the Republic or a member of his private Cabinet at the Elysée.

37. Police brutality on this occasion was so blatant and so excessive that even *France-Soir* not only noticed it but headlined the fact. One young ex-student died, so the official announcement ran, as a result of a knife wound. It was only after the general election was over that the true cause of his death, a grenade splinter, was made known.

38. Police Commissioner Lacroix is said to have suffered from a weak heart and to have died from shock. This unofficial version is probably the correct one in view of the fact that he was knocked down (and not run over) by a lorry going slowly enough to come to a halt against a street lamp without seriously damaging it.

as opposed to the irresponsible student rioting. In fact, the Government, the Patronat and the CGT had come to an agreement on this tactic somewhat earlier.

On 25 May André Barjonet, one of the economic advisors of the CGT and their representative on the national Social and Economic Council, announced his resignation from the CGT and the Communist Party. His example was followed by a few local officials in the provinces, and was the first open sign of an increasing unease in the ranks of both the CGT and the CP. One of André Barjonet's complaints concerned the attitude of the union towards the students, about which little need be said. The other and more important reason for his resignation was his belief that the CGT, far from trying to understand the movement and channel it towards lasting structural social and economic changes, was doing all it could to put a brake on the movement in order the better to control it. In a published interview[39] he gives a striking example of this. On the morning of Monday 20 May Georges Séguy made a speech to the workers of Renault at Boulogne-Billancourt in which he stressed the fact that there was no question of the strike becoming insurrectional, and that the main emphasis would be put on wage-claims. Immediately afterwards a member of the Patronat, speaking on behalf of M. Huvelin, President of the CNPF, telephoned to the CGT for confirmation. This confirmation was given the following day, and the subsequent telephone calls to the Prime Minister's office can easily be imagined. In any case, as from Tuesday 21 May the CGT knew that the Patronat wanted to negotiate, and the Patronat knew that the CGT would limit discussions to wage-claims. Needless to say, none of this was made public, least of all to the strikers. This incident illustrates the degree of collusion that existed between the Government, the Patronat, and the CGT. The subsequent refusal of the strikers to accept the Grenelle Agreements underlines the extent to which the CGT had lost the ability accurately to assess the mood of its troops.

2. From Revolt to Repression.

'Everything is still possible'.
André Barjonet, Charlety Stadium rally, Monday, 27 May.

The Renault factory in the Paris suburb of Boulogne-Billancourt sprawls over both banks of the Seine. In the middle, on the Ile

39. Philippe Labro et al., op. cit., p. 168.

190

Séguin, is a vast hangar containing the assembly-line of the successful little Renault 4. This was the strike headquarters. The works managers' offices, on a raised platform from which the hangar could be surveyed, had been turned into union offices and the balcony in front of them covered with slogans and microphones. On Monday 27 May it was possible to see makeshift beds behind the cranes. Posters and slogans covered the walls and in three or four different languages expressed solidarity with immigrants, the young, and even students. One particularly prominent poster read: 'Today 5% of workers' children go to university, we want that to change'.

The Grenelle Agreements, negotiated throughout the week-end by the Prime Minister, the Patronat, and the unions, were signed at 07.30; half an hour later 12–15,000 workers, nearly half the factory total, were assembled in the hanger to listen to the bleary-eyed negotiators of the CGT, the CFDT and FO. The mood of the workers was clear. Benoît Frachon, the ageing President of the CGT, whose task was to prepare the ground for an announcement of an historic victory by a eulogy of the working-class struggle which took him back to World War I, spoke first and got a very cool reception. By the time Séguy's turn came to spell out the victory he was forced to declare, what was almost certainly untrue, that he had not signed anything; it was obvious that the workers were going to reject the Agreements, and the final vote was in fact a mere formality. A similar performance was to have taken place at the Paris Citroën factory, Quai de Javel, but the negotiators' courage failed them. Berliet in Lyon, and Sud-Aviation in Marseilles also came to the same decision that morning, and practically all the other strikers, informed either by telephone or by transistor radio, followed suit.

At first sight this universal rejection seems surprising, for the Agreements provided for a 35% increase in the minimum wage (*Salaire Minimum Interprofessionel Garanti* and its agricultural equivalent, the SMAG) from c.420 francs a month—c. £8.10.0 a week—to c.580 francs a month—just under £12 a week; a general wage increase of 10% (7% immediately and 3% in October); and, although no agreement was reached on a sliding-scale, regular bi-lateral meetings on wages and prices. The principle of a shorter working week was also agreed upon; first steps in this direction were to be taken during 1968, and further ones before the end of the Fifth Plan in 1970. Minor alterations were made to the social security decrees (the percentage of medical expenses not reimbursed was reduced from 30% to 25%—before the decrees it had been

20 %), and strike wages were to be paid at the rate of 50 %. Moreover the Government undertook, after further consultations, to introduce a Bill giving the unions greater rights and protection in the firm. These concessions were substantial. If account is taken of those who were on the old minimum wage—or even, as was sometimes the case in small country firms, below it—those whose wages were between the old and the new, and those whose wages were just above the new, the raising of the minimum wage affected over seven million workers in industry and commerce, which in a country whose capital city is rated by UNESCO to be more expensive than New York, is nothing short of scandalous. Although a certain number of clauses did not amount to much more than promises, the basic principles were clearly stated, and it is probably only a question of time before they will be implemented.

It is true that the Agreements went much further towards satisfying the CGTs wage claims than the CFDTs demands for structural reforms, and in that sense they marked the culmination of a tacitly agreed strategy rather than a radical innovation. In calling a strike the primary consideration of the CGT has often been to be able to justify it *a posteriori* to the workers, and wage claims, even if only partially satisfied, enable them to do this very well.[40] In return, and the economic situation permitting, the Government as well as the Patronat were happy enough to accord a minimum of wage increases in order to avoid such delicate subjects as the place and degree of authority and responsibility in the firm. As the Agreements granted what the CGT had been demanding for years it was natural that all parties should consider that that would be enough. Even the CFDT, although to some extent out-manoeuvred, had some reason to think that important foundations had been laid. Why then were they all mistaken?

Much of the explanation lies in a false analogy, encouraged by the press, with 1936 and the Matignon Agreements. It was in fact a little too easy to remember that a spontaneous general sit-in strike was settled by an agreement reached between the Patronat and the unions under the aegis of the Prime Minister, and to overlook some of the essential differences between the situation then and that

40. This has also been the traditional strategy of the American Unions as their slogan 'More!' suggests. The CGT, however, unlike the American Unions, is neither sufficiently powerful nor sufficiently well-organised to be able to demand, and obtain, the right to consult the firm's books in order to meet the employers' economic arguments against the granting of wage increases: cf.ch. 4.

thirty-two years later. In the first place, the 1936 strikes broke out immediately after the victory of a Popular Front electoral alliance (and before the formation of a government); thus the strikers had some reason to believe, even if events were to prove them wrong, that promises would be kept and that the first preoccupation of the Government would be the betterment of the workers' lot. Secondly, what was accorded, and preserved, by the Matignon Agreements constituted a real breakthrough, a qualitative and not merely quantitative improvement in the workers' situation; the classic picture of the young working couple going off for their first ever holiday in 1936 on a tandem bicycle is not only part of left-wing folklore—it also accurately represents a certain reality. But it is difficult to imagine any such picture resulting from the 1968 Grenelle Agreements. Finally, to go on strike in 1936 involved considerable sacrifices and often real hardship; this was much less the case in 1968 when even before the Agreements were concluded wages already outstanding were paid and many firms advanced up to 50%, and in a few cases much more,[41] towards the payment of strike days.

And so, in general, the strike went on. The workers of a certain number of small firms, for which the Grenelle Agreements marked the extreme limit of what they could afford or even sounded their death knell, went back although often lack of supplies meant that there was little or no work to be done. This was particularly true in country districts and in the declining industries of the East and North, but these were in any case the very areas least affected by the strike. More typical is the case of the miners. The nationalised industries depending directly on a Ministry (mines, gas and electricity, railways, the Post Office, etc.), were not affected by the Grenelle Agreements and separate negotiations took place between their union representatives and the Ministries concerned. The first agreement to be reached was with the miners, on 28 May, but it was not until the following Saturday, 2 June, that a few men went back to work in the mines of Lorraine, and it was not until 5 June that the situation in the mines was back to normal.

But this does not mean that the strike was continued with the same enthusiasm everywhere. The majority of workers certainly thought that greater material gains could be obtained, but those who thought in terms of structural reforms were in the minority, and there

41. A certain number of firms whose hostility to de Gaulle was greater even than their hostility to the strikers advanced 75% or more.

were probably a good many, particularly in areas where the threat of unemployment was most acute, who would have been happy to go back to work quite quickly. However, the combination of class solidarity, strengthened by the fact that the Government had already used the CRS to evacuate one or two key postal centres, and union pressure (the Government in every other respect having thrown in the sponge, the unions had little option) meant that the workers' front remained united for at least a week after the Grenelle Agreements, and even then, as will be seen, did not crack all at once. In the meantime, there was a very real prospect of revolution, and to many the only question that remained was whether it would be a peaceful or a bloody one.

From Monday 27 May until Friday 31 May there was a power vacuum in France. After the workers' rejection of the Grenelle Agreements the Government was no longer in control of the situation, and this fact was made abundantly clear by its belated and apparently reluctantly taken decision not to prevent the Charlety Stadium rally from taking place that same afternoon.[42] In any case, unrest among the police was such that it is by no means certain that orders would have been obeyed.[43] And that was to be the central problem throughout that week. For France was not only economically paralysed; it was administratively paralysed as well, since the greater part of the civil service was on strike. Many town halls, including those of large towns like Toulouse and Le Havre, had been occupied by the employees, and the strike now spread to the departmental prefectures. The North was most affected by this, but so were other towns such as Poitiers and Besançon, where the Prefect of the Doubs department and two or three senior officials—with, so it is said, their passports in their pockets—were all that remained in a

42. The UNEF, the FEN and the PSU, with the approval of the CFDT (the CGT organised a dozen small meetings all over Paris to keep its members away) led a march of, at its height, some 35,000 people to a rally in the Charlety Stadium on the Monday evening. A great success for the students, as not only did it show once again that they were capable of organising a peaceful demonstration when not hampered by deliberate provocation, but it was also adorned by the presence of André Barjonet and Pierre Mendès-France (who however did not address the meeting); its political import was greatly exaggerated both at the time and later. Even if unjustified, the impression was given that the rally had been used as political propaganda for Mendès-France and the PSU, and both were to suffer for this in the election.
43. Cf. Appendix 3.

building that was virtually in a state of seige, and was to remain so for some time, protected only by local detachments of the mobile gendarmerie. In Nantes a central strike committee had been set up and the town practically isolated; all in-going and out-going traffic had to submit to a control by the strikers. The example was followed, although only for a few hours at a time, in Caen and Clermont-Ferrand.

In short, the tension was acute, fighting could have broken out at any moment, and revolution was not simply the slogan of a minority but an unspoken question-mark in the minds of many. Communications between Paris and the provinces, even by telephone, were difficult and in many cases impossible, and the situation resembled nothing so much as that which de Gaulle had known at the moment of the Liberation when it was a continual battle to gain control of the prefectures, not from the Germans, but from the Resistance. However, instead of standing firm as they did then, many Gaullists began to panic, and there is some reason to believe that a number of files were burnt, diplomatic illnesses caught, and pressing engagements discovered in Brussels. Those who were less cowardly turned in on themselves, searching for a scapegoat. The resignation of Alain Peyrfitte, Minister of Education, was accepted, and there was a move, inspired and led by Georges Pompidou himself, to force de Gaulle's resignation.

The Opposition, hamstrung by its lack of unity and torn between the desire to take advantage of the obvious power vacuum and the realisation that any unconstitutional government would neither last very long nor do the Left any good in the long run, was reduced to considering, in a perfectly constitutional way, the possibility of a majority of 'noes' in the unconstitutional referendum planned for 16 June. François Mitterand, Pierre Mendès-France and Eugène Descamps, Secretary-General of the CFDT, all made announcements whose purport was the same: an appeal to Mendès-France, who was in fact the only French politician endowed with a charisma remotely comparable to that of de Gaulle, to head a provisional government. The Communist Party, despite an acute awareness of its own best interests, was also compelled to draw similar conclusions from the existence of the power vacuum, but, unwilling to accept Mendès-France, contented itself with calling for *'un gouvernement populaire et d'union démocratique'*. With better tactical sense than its non-Communist allies, it realised that the only hope lay in an immediate and voluntary resignation of the Government—hence the giant (half a million) but tightly controlled demonstration organised by the CGT in Paris on Wednesday 29 May, and the demonstrations, similar in number and size to those of 13 May, that took place in the provinces. The Government did not in fact fall of its own accord, and the Communist Party may have lacked revolutionary fervour, but the impression of force and cohesion that it gave, at least during those few crucial days, was in striking contrast with the squalid flounderings of the disunited non-Communist Left in whom nobody had much faith.

If de Gaulle ever thought of accepting M. Pompidou's suggestion that he should abandon politics, he never gave any sign of it. Although at the time his movements were shrouded in mystery, it is now reasonably certain that he used the 'hot' line to make sure of Moscow's neutrality, and obtained the necessary assurances from certain army generals both in Paris and in the French base at Baden-Baden. The subsequent, long-overdue amnesty of all political prisoners and exiles suggests that these discussions were accompanied by some rather sordid bargaining. However that may be, when de Gaulle finally returned to Paris and ended the suspense which he himself had done so much to create, he had recovered his old assurance and his voice had regained some of the old magic and authority. In a four-minute broadcast (not televised because of the strike at the ORTF) in the afternoon of Thursday 30 May, that assurance and authority were transmitted to his supporters: he and M. Pompidou would remain at their posts, the National Assembly was dissolved, the referendum postponed, and a general election would be held; to ensure the orderly running of the campaign the Prefects were invested with the title of Commissioners of the Republic as at the Liberation, and Frenchmen were invited to take part in 'civic action' to counter the 'threat of dictatorship' by 'totalitarian communism'.

As the Opposition spokesmen immediately emphasised, the call to 'civic action' was not without its ambiguities and dangers. If it was simply an appeal for counter-demonstrations, it was quite legitimate, but the tenor of de Gaulle's speech, which divided Frenchmen firmly and irrevocably into sheep and goats, and the term 'civic action' which recalled the Gaullists' private para-military organisation, the *Service d'Action Civique*, led many to fear the worst. However, the demonstration which took place on the Champs-Elysées immediately after the speech showed that the worst would not be necessary. Planned and organised during the brief interregnum when de Gaulle appeared to be sulking in his tent by those two high priests of Gaullist underground team-work, Roger Frey and Alexandre Sanguinetti, the demonstration surpassed all expectations. Even if allowance is made for the lorry-loads brought in from the countryside and for those who did the walk from the Concorde to the Arc de Triomphe twice, nearly half a million people demonstrated in favour of de Gaulle. Those who shouted 'Cohn-Bendit to Dachau' were the exceptions; the majority were middle-aged people, many of them women, who had probably never even thought of demonstrating in their lives and would probably not have done so then had they not just heard the accents of someone who was prepared to use whatever means were necessary to impose order on a situation that was becoming increasingly anarchic. Both in appearance and motivation it was a 'bourgeois' demonstration, but it was a very successful one and it marked the turning-point in this unusual story.

Appearances to the contrary notwithstanding, the decisive factor was not the giant Paris demonstration and the numerous smaller ones that were organised in the provinces the following day by the hastily formed (or rather re-formed, since the Gaullist infrastructure had always been there) Committees for the Defence of the Republic.[44] Nor was it the various measures taken over the week-end, such as the formation of a new Pompidou Government from which most of those most closely associated with the riots and strikes—the Prime Minister excepted—were absent; the Army manoeuvres round Paris and the stationing of armoured detachments on the southern motorway; the release of tension by the release of petrol for the annual Whitsun massacre (68 road-deaths), the CRS having expelled the strikers from the petrol warehouses. Nor was it the logical and expected decision of the Communist Party and the CGT to accept the fact that the battle would now be fought out in electoral terms; any other decision would have provoked a blood-bath and, probably, a military dictatorship.

What was in fact decisive was the passage in de Gaulle's broadcast where he identified the enemy as 'totalitarian communism'. For whereas up to this point a very large number of Frenchmen had expressed themselves, either in word or in action, in a way that left

44. Except in Lyon, where the crowd was estimated at 60,000, the demonstrations rarely drew more than 5,000, but there was hardly a provincial town of any importance in which there was not a demonstration on either the Friday or the Saturday.

little room for doubt about their hostility to the existing order, the rest of France, with minor exceptions like the extreme right-wing movement *Occident*, had remained silent. Some, perhaps many, had remained silent in the beginning out of sympathy for the students, doubt, or aversion for police methods; others were avowedly hostile, but few dared speak out openly in defence of a crumbling educational order and an indecisive Government. When the student movement turned into a general strike the number of those in the second category, those who had no spokesman, swelled considerably to the detriment of the first. They had no spokesman for much the same reason that the Government found it so difficult to act: they did not understand what was happening and there was no easily identifiable enemy to serve as a pretext for mobilising all the conservative strength of the country. De Gaulle, by a skilful use of innuendo which left it to the listener to make the formal and unjustifiable identification of 'the party which is a totalitarian enterprise' or 'totalitarian communism' with the staid French Communist Party, provided the necessary rallying-point. The identification of the enemy and the call to action were enough to turn the tide.[45]

The rest of the story is in many respects sordid and squalid. The Government set an example of repression (arbitrary arrests and expulsions, the sacking of militants in the ORTF and the nationalised industries) which the employers were not slow to follow, but although unpleasant to watch it was comparatively mild. Three deaths, of one schoolboy and two workers, as a direct result of police action in June was not as bad as had been feared. The restraint was due to the great surge of public support which enabled the Government, followed by the employers, to adopt a policy of inactivity (*laisser pourrir*) towards the remaining strikers. This involved not negotiating and letting the strikes peter out through lack of money and, above all, lack of hope in the face of an increasingly hostile, and badly frightened, public opinion. When the strikes did not show signs of petering out as expected, every means was used of bringing pressure

45. Besides rallying the conservative right, de Gaulle's speech may also have had another result which the speaker had certainly not foreseen. For it is possible that large numbers of non-student intellectuals and white-collar workers who had joined the movement associated the 'totalitarianism' of the CP with the 'bureaucratic totalitarianism' against which they were revolting—and so came to the conclusion that no political solution was possible on the Left. For a pertinent comparison of the cultural models of intellectuals and workers, see R. Sainsaulieu and D. Kergoat, 'Milieu de travail et modèle d'action' in *Analyse et Prévision* 6 (6), December 1968.

to bear on the workers, from rigged ballots on the question of returning to work[46] to intimidation by the CRS. In particular the latter were used, on Government orders, against the ORTF and two of the most obstinate automobile factories, Peugeot in Sochaux and Renault in Flins. In the last two cases the use of force resulted in the deaths already mentioned.[47]

In Sochaux an explosion was avoided only by the hasty calling-off of the CRS and the closing of the factory. The death of the schoolboy at Flins was followed by riots in Paris. As in the case of the banning of Cohn-Bendit there were spontaneous riots in the Latin Quarter as soon as the news arrived. The following day, Tuesday 11 June, demonstrations were called for by the student movements, the students proper at the Gare de l'Est, the schoolboys in the place Maubert. The police did all they could to prevent the demonstrations from forming up and, once they had begun, to prevent any concentration of forces. Nevertheless an orgy of destruction and violence covered a wider area of Paris than ever before, the students responding to the police tactics with effective guerrilla tactics of their own, using Molotov cocktails to devastating effect.[48] The Government retaliated by forbidding the holding of any demonstration anywhere in the country and by banning, under a law dating from 1936 and aimed at Fascist militias, a dozen left-wing unorthodox political parties and student movements.[49] However, the most striking result of the riots was their universal condemnation on the morrow; no commentator, not even those who had been most favourable to the students, thought fit to suggest how they should have reacted to what appeared to many of them as the murder of one of their number.

46. The management of many French firms are past masters in the art of organising elections so as to influence the result, either directly or by making the act of voting as difficult as possible for the worker (cf. Document 20C). Among such firms Citroën stands out. Some of the less objectionable methods employed by it on this occasion included barring journalists from attending, obliging those who wished to vote in favour of continuing the strike to ask for a special voting paper, and publishing the results in a misleading manner (cf. Le Monde, 9–10 June 1968).

47. Cf. Appendix 3.

48. Cf. Patrick Seale and Maureen McConville, op. cit., p. 220. There were also riots in Toulouse, a student demonstration in Lyon and a workers' one in Nantes.

49. Jeunesse Communiste Révolutionnaire, Voix Ouvrière, Groupe 'Révoltés', Fédération des Etudiants Révolutionnaires, Comité de Liaison des Etudiants Révolutionnaires, Union des Jeunesses Communistes Marxistes-Léninistes, Parti Communiste Internationaliste, Parti Communiste Marxiste-Léniniste de France,

For the wind had indeed changed. Many organisations, cadres, professors, even those whose original sympathy had taken the form of active support, were unsparing in their criticisms and in their advice to the students to settle down and pass their exams and to the workers to return to work and allow the economy to get going again. Every newspaper (not excepting *L'Humanité*, whose headlines on 6 June read *'Reprise victorieuse du travail dans l'unité'*) and every radio station emphasised the number who returned to work and scarcely mentioned those who were still on strike. Yet on 10 June, the day the election campaign officially opened, there were still well over a million strikers (the official estimate of the total number of strikers in 1936 is 1,500,000) including teachers, merchant seamen, aircraft and automobile workers, and shipyard and building workers. Renault did not go back to work until 18 June, and when Citroën, the last big firm to remain on strike, decided to go back to work on 24 June, the day after the first ballot, there were still 10,000 workers out.

The same thing was true as far as the students were concerned. Increasing emphasis was put on those faculties where agreements were being reached concerning exams, and less on those where the students were holding out for some form of student control. The Sorbonne was transformed from a symbol of righteous student indignation into one of unhygienic anarchy; when it was re-occupied by the police on 16 June enough had been said and written about the 'Katangais'[50] the rats and venereal disease(!) for hardly a non-student voice to be raised in protest. For the students themselves, one of the most disheartening and revealing results of this change in the climate of opinion was the ease with which a large number of their teachers and professors who had supported them in the beginning suddenly turned first into counsellors of moderation and then into active opponents. Yet the Government had not yet

Fédération de la Jeunesse Révolutionnaire, Organisation Communiste Internationaliste, mouvement du 22 Mars. Were it not for the error by which the CLER, which had dissolved itself in April 1968 to become the FER, was included the list could well have been drawn up by the Communist Party.

50. A small group of young unemployed workers (and their girl friends), one of whom claimed to have been a mercenary in Katanga. They had installed themselves in the Sorbonne where they formed the nucleus of an unofficial militia. Rumoured to have stockpiled arms, they had in fact only the crudest weapons and, when their presence was discovered by the press and they became a political liability, the students were able to expel them without too much difficulty. Afterwards most of them came to one sort of 'bad end' or another.

shown the slightest sign of even considering, let alone putting into practice, a single one of the reforms they themselves had advocated. The trouble was that many of them agreed with de Gaulle's '*La réforme, oui; la chienlit, non!*', an opinion repeated, in different but no less polemical language, by Raymond Aron in a series of articles in *Le Figaro* entitled 'On behalf of the silent ones'.[51]

Thus was order restored in the name of Liberty, and in the name of Order the flowerings of a different notion of liberty were crushed. Whether the victory will be permanent or not remains to be seen, but for the time being at least the perennial and unholy alliance of Order and Liberty triumphed, not so much with a bang as with a frightened whimper.

51. *Le Figaro*, 11–19 June. The articles are also reproduced as an Appendix in Raymond Aron, *La Révolution Introuvable*, Paris, Fayard, 1968. Raymond Aron is one of those whose enthusiasm for university reform, before the events of May, was in exact relation to the invulnerability of his own position (Maurice Duverger is another). One of the first to realise to what extent this position was menaced by the student revolt, he wrote the articles largely, if not entirely, as an act of revulsion against what he saw in the one general assembly, that of the *Ecole Pratique des Hautes Etudes*, at which he was present. He reveals in these articles the same genius for brilliant generalisation based on wide reading but little empirical evidence that is apparent in other of his works, but in descending to the same level of invective for which, rightly or wrongly, he castigates his opponents, he does less than justice to one of the most brilliant minds of modern France. It is probably fair to say that he did not relish becoming the rallying-point for all the outright reactionaries in the University, but his political intelligence is sufficiently acute for him to have foreseen that this would be the case.

DOCUMENT 25

How the strike began in Flins

A young worker (from the Renault plant):

There had already been a stoppage for two hours the previous day, when we heard that Cléon had gone on strike.

On the morning of 16 May the shop stewards came round the workshops to tell us we were downing tools at 10.15. We found ourselves outside, about two, three hundred of us; the shop stewards asked us to go back into the workshops to get the others to come out as well. We already knew that Cléon had stopped the previous day—they send us the engines, and we only have half a day's engines in advance to work with. We went back to the production lines until midday to explain things to the blokes; we went back again later in the afternoon, for the people on shift-work, and by the evening there were more than 8,000 of us outside, out of perhaps 10,500 in all. We started to get organised and to enrol blokes in the strike pickets and I spent the first night there; I spent at least seven other nights there afterwards, there must have been about eight strike pickets in the whole factory; there were rounds from one gate to another, guard duties etc. We could go into the yard, in the corridors, the changing rooms, but not in the workshops. At the beginning the watches were too long, but afterwards we soon got organised with turns on watch of four hours on, four hours off.

(Source: J.-Ph. Talbo, *La Grève à Flins*, Paris, Maspero, 1968, p. 13)

DOCUMENT 26

The turn of the tide: de Gaulle's radio broadcast to the nation at 16.30 on 30 May

Frenchwomen, Frenchmen, as the trustee of national and republican legitimacy, I have, for the past twenty-four hours, considered every possibility, without exception, which would enable me to preserve that legitimacy. I have made my resolutions. In the present circumstances I shall not resign. I have a mandate from the people. I shall fulfil it. I shall not dismiss the Prime Minister, whose value, solidity and ability deserve admiration from all. He will propose to me the changes which he thinks useful in the composition of the Government. I am dissolving the National Assembly today. I proposed to the country a referendum, which would give citizens a chance to prescribe a profound reform of our economy and our university, and at the same time to say whether or not they still had confidence in me by the only acceptable way, the way of democracy.

I find that the present situation materially prevents this referendum from taking place. That is why I am postponing it. As for the general election, it will be held within the time limit laid down by the constitution—unless it is intended to gag the entire French people, by preventing them from expressing themselves at the same time as they are prevented from living, and with the same methods which are used to prevent the students from studying, the teachers from teaching, and the workers from working. These methods are intimidation, intoxication and tyranny exercised by groups long organised for that purpose, and by a party which is a totalitarian enterprise even if it already has rivals in that respect.

If therefore this situation of force continues I shall have, in order to preserve the Republic, to adopt, in accordance with the constitution, other methods than an immediate vote of the country. In any case, civic action must be organised everywhere and at once. This must be done to help the Government in the first place, and then locally, to help the Prefects, who will assume or reassume the role of commissioners of the Republic, in their task which is to ensure as far as possible the livelihood of the population and to prevent subversion at every moment and in every place.

France is indeed threatened with dictatorship. People are trying to compel her to resign herself to a power which would impose itself in the midst of national despair. This power would then be essentially that of the conqueror, that is to say, the power of totalitarian communism.

Naturally, it would to start with be coloured with a deceptive appearance by using the ambition and hatred of discarded politicians. Later, these persons would carry no more than their own weight, which would not be much. I say no, the Republic will not abdicate, the people will come to their senses. Progress, independence and peace will win the day together with freedom. Long live the Republic! Long live France!

(Source: *The Times*, 31 May 1968 [amended].)

DOCUMENT 27
Some strike leaflets

French students are used to leaflets. Every time there is a student election, meeting or demonstration, hundreds of copies are distributed. However few had ever seen a strike leaflet. Here are two samples of some of the more orthodox ones. The total number produced and distributed by workers, politicians, and students during the two months is incalculable. Nearly everyone in France must have had at least one, and in some cases a great many more, thrust into his hands at one time or another.

C. G. T.   **F. S. M.**

Toutes et tous
à 15 heures
de la Bastille à la Gare St-Lazare

9 millions de grévistes ont contraint gouvernement et patronat à discuter.

Les travailleurs se sont prononcés sur le résultat des discussions, sur les concessions gouvernementales et patronales.

Dans l'immense majorité la réponse est nette :

C'EST INSUFFISANT !

Le mouvement de grève se poursuit et s'étend.

Pour exiger la satisfaction des revendications essentielles des salariés
Pour un changement politique ouvrant la voie du progrès social et de la démocratie

Tous en masse, à 15 heures
de la BASTILLE à la Gare St-LAZARE

L'Union Syndicale C.G.T. de la Région Parisienne appelle les travailleurs et la population de la région parisienne à exprimer, dans un puissant défilé,
— leur volonté d'obtenir la satisfaction de leurs revendications
— leur aspiration à des changements profonds assurant durablement le progrès social et la démocratie.

L'Union Syndicale C.G.T. de la Région Parisienne souhaite que se retrouvent solidaires et unies toutes les autres organisations syndicales, ainsi que l'U.N.E.F., pour les objectifs revendicatifs et démocratiques communs.

L'Union Syndicale C.G.T. de la Région Parisienne
Les Unions Départementales C.G.T.
de Paris, Hauts-de-Seine, Seine-Saint-Denis, Val-de-Marne, Essonne, Yvelines, Val-d'Oise.

I.G.P. - Paris

MAI-JUIN 1968

une lutte, un espoir

Après un mois d'une lutte intense et exceptionnelle, la plupart des travailleurs ont repris le travail. Parmi ceux-ci, deux secteurs principaux restent des points chauds :

— Les métallos face à un patronat qui refuse l'extension des droit syndicaux.

— Le personnel de l'O.R.T.F. à qui le pouvoir refuse l'honnêteté de l'information.

Si une avancée importante a été réalisée sur des revendications essentielles :

— Priorité aux bas salaires,

— Réduction progressive de la durée du travail,

— Extension des droits syndicaux,

de nombreuses revendications restent en suspens et n'ont reçu que des promesses comme réponse. Et ce ne sont pas les 0,27 F par jour aux personnes âgées qui lèveront notre septicisme quant aux promesses gouvernementales sur :

— les Allocations Familiales,

— l'emploi et la formation professionnelle,

— la Sécurité Sociale,

— le projet de loi sur les droits syndicaux,

— la réforme de l'enseignement.

Les 23 et 30 juin, les élections législatives marqueront une autre étape de la lutte engagée.

Tout au long de cette lutte, la CFDT a pris des positions originales qui ne se sont jamais démenties.

des revendications fondamentales

Devant l'ampleur de la lutte engagée par plus de 10 millions de travailleurs, la CFDT n'a mis en priorité l'augmentation des salaires que pour les plus défavorisés (salariés au SMIG, travailleurs immigrés, anciens travailleurs, handicapés, familles). Elle s'est refusée de mettre en priorité l'augmentation générale des salaires. En effet une hausse des prix risque très vite de rendre cet avantage illusoire.

Elle a exprimé sur ce point son originalité par rapport à la CGT.

CHAPTER SIX

THE OCCUPATION OF THE
FACTORIES

Question: Why have you occupied the factory instead of striking
in the normal way?

Answer: To show who is really master here.[1]

It is not easy to form an accurate and coherent idea of what the
motives and aspirations of the striking workers were. For one thing,
unlike the students, their output of words, both spoken and written,
was relatively limited. What there was, with very few exceptions,
emanated from the unions and, although some of the local CFDT
leaflets are not without interest, it should by now be clear that they
cannot be relied upon to give an unbiased picture of the workers'
mood. A further difficulty comes from the small quantity of evidence
collected by outside observers compared with what has been amassed
on the students, who were both more easily available and more
ready to talk. For example, nothing has been done on the workers
to match the excellent collections of student interviews, some of
which are quoted in Part 1. More material will certainly have
appeared by the time this book does, but by then the workers'
perceptions will have been distorted by their knowledge of the
outcome. The little that exists at the time of writing has been collected
by those who rightly believed that in the long run the workers'
revolt was much more important than the student one, but much of
it is coloured by antipathy towards the unions, and in particular
the CGT, and tends to reveal more of the ideology of the observer
than of the observed. For these reasons it seemed best to start by
taking a closer look at what actually happened in one or two cases.

One case that deserves mention, if only because it was passed over
in silence at the time, concerns not a single factory but the town of
Nantes which for one week, from 24 May to 31 May, was virtually
cut off from the rest of France and administered by the workers and

1. From the author's personal files. In French the answer reads 'Pour montrer
que les rapports de force ont changé.'

207

peasants themselves.[2] In the course of their demonstration on 31 May the peasants, as is their custom, set up road blocks round Nantes. These were taken over and reinforced by the lorry-drivers, dominated in Nantes by the local federation of FO whose positions are much more 'revolutionary' than those of the central Federation. Aided by students and schoolboys, their object was to reinforce the strike and ensure that only those engaged in transporting vital necessities could enter or leave the town. For this the co-operation of the agricultural unions was required, and when this was obtained a Central Strike Committee was set up, composed in the first instance of the CGT, the CFDT, the FO, the FNSEA and the CNJA; later the two student and teachers' unions, the UNEF and the FEN, were allowed to join. The Central Strike Committee further instituted petrol rationing, and so had control of the only sectors of the economy functioning in France at the time, food and road transport. The Prefect of the Loire Atlantique was isolated with one member of his staff, and the police were not strong enough to attack the road blocks which were manned, in some cases, by up to 500 workers and students.

At the same time, on 24 May, another movement was started independently of, and to some extent in opposition to, the Central Strike Committee (this may well have been due in part to ignorance, as it is by no means clear to what extent the inhabitants of Nantes were able to be informed of all these developments). A number of District Committees were organised, essentially by workers' wives in collaboration with local farming communities, with the object of ensuring a regular supply of food at reasonable prices by eliminating the middle-men. The Central Strike Committee had in fact had the same idea, and there was a certain amount of friction between the two organisations, but the system worked reasonably well; only those shops were allowed to open which agreed to sell at prices fixed by the Committees. However, it ended, as did the 'closed town' policy of the Central Strike Committee, on 31 May, the day following de Gaulle's broadcast. For with the coming of the Whitsun holiday, the freeing of petrol supplies and the risk of military intervention,

2. Although *Le Monde* had a special correspondent in Nantes, it is only with the benefit of hindsight and by reading between the lines that one can discern any reference to these events (see p. 96, n. 39). The only remotely comprehensive account is to be found in one of the journalistic products of the revolt, *Cahiers de mai*, 1, 15 June 1968, on which is based the vivid, but rather hasty, description in Patrick Seale and Maureen McConville, op. cit., pp. 163–8.

the only other possibility was to transform the situation into one of open insurrection. The road-blocks were therefore dismantled and the Committees' energies devoted to reinforcing strike pickets.

The question remains whether the situation in Nantes was, as some have claimed, a revolutionary one. The capital of one of the most depressed areas in France, it has a long tradition of militant, and sometimes violent, industrial and agricultural unrest. On this occasion Nantes was certainly the most extreme example of the breakdown of central government control over wide areas of the provinces, and there are some grounds for believing that the use of force against it was envisaged.[3] But even if there were some militants who believed that the revolution was just round the corner, the rapidity with which the precarious administrative structure was dismantled suggests that they were far from certain of carrying the population of the town with them. It is significant in this respect that no attempt was made in Nantes (although some were made elsewhere) to set up workers' management committees or some other form of alternative power structure in the factories themselves; it was as though it was generally accepted that once the strike was over and the claims granted things would go back to normal. For the steps taken arose directly out of the strike itself, and do not appear to have been motivated by the desire to introduce a permanent new administrative power structure.

This is not to say that what happened in Nantes is without interest. Just as the revolt in the *lycées* showed surprised parents and teachers that schoolboys are quite capable of organising themselves into discussion groups and putting forward highly intelligent and worthwhile proposals for their own better education, so the workers of Nantes revealed, what no-one should have doubted, that they are quite capable of running their own lives when the normal administrative machinery has seized up. Further, there were some who were well aware that mere wage-claims were not going to alter fundamentally the workers' condition, as the following slogan, put up on the walls by one of the District Committees, shows:

A huge wage increase with no change in the political and economic structures = an increase in the cost of living and a return to poverty in a few months' time.

3. According to unofficial reports, in at least one nearby garrison contingency plans were made and ammunition checked. Of course, if troops had been used they might well have provoked a genuine insurrection.

However, although time might have reduced the distance, there is still a long way to go before such political awareness can take the form of substituting new political and economic structures for old ones. If it can be said that Nantes was to the workers' revolt in France as Barcelona was to the Spanish civil war, saying it only points up the difference between Spain in 1936 and France in 1968.

If Nantes is in many ways an exceptional town, the following somewhat detailed account of the strike in one particular factory perhaps gives a better general idea of what the revolt meant to the majority of French workers.[4] Of course no evidence exists to show that the example is statistically typical, but the impression of quiet, disciplined determination (more menacing in the long run than a brief outburst of revolutionary fervour) is confirmed by other observers who have spoken to strike pickets,[5] even if, viewed as a whole, the revolt looked more like an explosion.

Técalémit, out by Orly (its clock tower can be seen from the airport motorway), manufactures accessories for aircraft and automobile engines. Founded in 1923, it now has branches in most European countries. The French one is relatively small, employing 970 men in all (the English branch, in Plymouth, employs 8,000), and, like so many French firms, has remained essentially a family affair. Management is practically an unknown quantity, so that technical know-how and ingenuity is found side by side with a 'take it or leave it' attitude to commercial, personnel, and organisational matters—delivery dates are not respected, workers sacked without notice, and finished products stored on the third floor before being taken down again to be sent off. Three years ago a Swiss technical manager was imported from the German branch. He did a time and motion study, reorganised the grouping of machines on the work-shop floor, and caused considerable surprise by greeting and shaking hands with the workers. Otherwise things went on much as before.

It is not easy to gain access to an occupied factory. Natural

4. The author spent the morning of 29 May inside the factory talking with the workers (an account of this first appeared in *New Society*, 6 June 1968). Any criticisms of the management are based on remarks made by the workers and do not necessarily correspond to the facts. It was however thought worth recording them since they not only represent the workers' perception of the running of the firm, but are also borne out by some of the younger generation of French managers—cf. Text no. 31.

5. Cf. the articles in *Le Monde* at the end of May and the beginning of June, as well as Appendix 1 (ii).

suspicion, fear of sabotage and wariness of agitators ensure that, even where there is an introduction to a member of the strike committee, the matter has to be put to the vote of the pickets. Once accepted, however, the stranger encounters no constraint, but only cheerful willing talkers. Inside all is calm and orderly; there are a few slogans on the walls around the courtyard, but none on the gate. The dominating impression is one of silence. There is no noise of machinery, cars, lorries or even typewriters. The only sounds are of groups of workers talking together or playing *pétanque*.

The headquarters of the strike committee have been set up in an office next to what has become the leisure hall. The office is shared by the delegates of the two unions represented in the factory, the CGT and the CFDT. Although their influence was negligible both with the workers and the management before the strike, they are now responsible for the organisation and running of it; and they have no difficulty in working harmoniously together as neither has enough members in the factory to justify rivalry. Only 10% of workers have union cards, and of these no more than eight turn up regularly for the union meetings, held during an hour's paid time once a month, an hour which has come to be known as the 'barber's hour'. Apart from that, authorised union activity within the factory is minimal. There are union notice-boards on each floor of the administrative block, but notices have to receive prior approval and it is not unknown for this to be withheld. No leaflets may be distributed inside the gates, no meetings held, and the unions have no offices to themselves. And of course the classic means are employed to discourage any union activist from going too far.

Técalémit, perhaps not surprisingly, had a reputation for good labour relations. When 24-hour strikes were called by one or other of the national unions from time to time, work would stop for an hour or two, but that was all. Such unrest as there was usually came from the toolshop, where the highest paid and most politically aware workers were to be found. On Monday 20 May, however, a different pattern occurred. Everyone came to work normally, but they all knew that over the week-end two million had already gone on strike. Some of the younger workers downed tools immediately, but the majority simply called for a meeting, and at their request this was organised by the union delegates. A series of claims were sent to the management who refused to consider them at once. As a result, at the end of a meeting that lasted two and a half hours, a secret ballot was held on whether there should be a 24–hour strike, or an unlimited one with occupation of the factory. Of the 500 present and voting, out of a labour force of 800, 422 voted for the second proposal. Despite propaganda efforts, the office-workers were not on the whole willing to give more than their moral support (remarks such as 'I'm all in favour, but I don't think the boss would like it' were heard among the typists). When the result was known, one group went to occupy the gate, while another went to tell the management.

The first day was spent in organising the 200 or so volunteers, among whom there were a large number of young workers, into three groups to relay one another at twelve hour intervals, and in taking the necessary security measures so that the factory remained insured. The factory fire service was taken in hand by striking firemen, and day and night security rounds organised. An inventory was made of the state of all machinery, and every precaution taken against possible sabotage.

If there was a certain amount of confusion and tension during the first two or three days, as the risk of an attack by the police diminished things became calmer and better organised. Each of the three groups formed a strike committee of about ten members, each with a particular responsibility, for the treasury, discipline, first aid, food, leisure, the switchboard, etc. Sleeping accommodation was organised in the conference room, and the canteen made available for those who could not bring their own food. By the end of the first week the strikers had settled into a regular routine, and their numbers increased. Some who had originally voted for the strike but remained sceptical, or perhaps even afraid of reprisals, came along to see how things were, and stayed as volunteers. More would probably have come had they lived nearer, but some lived as much as thirty miles away on the other side of Paris, and although the factory's petrol supply was commandeered transport difficulties were such that only the minority who lived close at hand could take an active part.

There was nothing to prevent the strike continuing, in the strikers' own words, 'as long as need be'. Money was no immediate problem as an advance on wages was paid and local shopkeepers were prepared to give credit (this did not always apply even in workers' residential areas, and the price of potatoes, for example, rocketed to over 2/6 a pound; a rather narrow conception of their own interests has always characterised shopkeepers, who were to be counted among those who had a 'good' war under the Occupation). Attempts to break the strike were on the whole limited to executives who tried to persuade the strikers to let them get at their files, and to threatening telephone calls. However, there was one more serious, and somewhat amusing incident.[6] When the strike had lasted sixteen days, an agreement was reached between the management, the strike committee and the unions according to which the results of the negotiations then going on between the Patronat and the metal-workers' unions would be applied at Técalémit. A secret ballot was held on the question of a return to work. The managing director, who is also on the board of nearly a dozen other firms, succeeded in persuading the rather naïve workers that he, as the first wage-earner of the firm, was entitled to vote; it naturally followed that all the executive staff were similarly entitled to vote. Nevertheless, a comfortable majority voted in favour of continuing the strike.

The result of this vote is significant in two respects. In the first place, it deals once and for all with the argument of the Patronat and the Government that the strike would have ended much sooner had all the votes been secret.[7] It may be true that in some cases (but, as Técalémit shows, by no means all) where the vote was taken by head counting, the pressure of the group to which the worker belonged may have had some effect; this is the obverse side of the principle of workers' solidarity. However, the strikers could use nothing like the pressure available to the Patronat, which (quite apart from the use of force) ranged from publishing the results of management-organised votes without giving the percentage of abstentions (and as the unions were invariably hostile to any vote not organised by themselves, this was high enough to invalidate the great majority of such votes) to outright blackmail, a form of argument frequently used against immigrant workers.

The result also raises the further and much more important question of why the workers of Técalémit, like so many others throughout the country, refused to go back to work even when some form of agreement had been successfully negotiated by their representatives. Their basic claims were much the same as those elsewhere: wage increases tied to the cost of living, a forty hour week without loss of pay, union rights, guaranteed employment, retirement at sixty, and an end to unemployment among the young.[8]

6. *Le Monde*, 6 June 1968.
7. Cf. M. Pompidou's appeal for secret ballots, *Le Monde*, 30 May 1968.
8. An additional reason for this, pointed out by the strikers, is that the law

And as elsewhere they saw that the Grenelle Agreements were not going to provide any long-term answers. But by the time they voted the political climate had changed and they were not to know that in fact the negotiations between the Patronat and the metal-workers' unions would not produce any results. Moreover they were comparatively isolated; there are no other factories of comparable size for several miles around, the nearest concentration of labour being at Orly Airport, where the Técalémit workers have always been considered as too docile for any interest to be taken in them.

Part of the reason probably lies in the working conditions and general atmosphere in this as in many other factories. Everyone has a grievance of one sort or another (the book set aside for noting them filled up very rapidly), and they have been simmering for some time. For example, although a certain amount of social work is organised by the worker-management committee, there are no sports facilities (although there is space for them), and promising young athletes have to find work elsewhere. There is a self-service canteen, but only 45 minutes are allowed for everyone to eat. No provision is made for those who prefer to bring their own meal, and there is nowhere to go to read or smoke during the lunch break. The shop floor is separate from the main administrative building, and looks like a slum in comparison with it. But even the former looks more like a barracks block than anything else, with stone stairways, dull paint, and no interior decoration to speak of. The manager's office was pointed out with something like admiration by the workers, as though they were surprised at their own audacity. Admittedly not plush by some standards, it is glass-walled and looks on to the draughtsmen's work-room; which means that not only are they under constant surveillance but they can see the manager as well (he may smoke, but not they, etc.).

However, such environmental considerations do not appear to be enough in themselves to account for the workers' obstinacy. At the beginning of the strike there were discussions about reforming the factory, and proposals for changing the whole organisational structure were debated. Problems that had never arisen before, such as those connected with automation, were now discussed openly.

forbids anyone under eighteen to be employed more than eight hours a day. As the apprenticeship system has fallen into disuse without being effectively replaced by anything else, employers often prefer simply not to employ anyone under eighteen.

Two or three automated machines had been installed alongside older traditional ones, but before the strike no-one thought that it concerned him directly; the same goes for the wider questions of trade unionism and industrial politics. But the impression was given that concepts like *co-gestion* (co-management by the workers) did not mean very much to them, and still less did terms such as capitalism, imperialism, the means of production, exploitation of the masses, etc. form part of their vocabulary. Recurrent themes were rather *la conscience professionnelle* and care for *les outils de travail* (work tools). This sense of responsibility was further shown by their knowledge of what the firm was doing, and of the markets that might be lost through the strike (exports account for 30% of production), with all the consequences which that could entail; knowledge that was acquired because the firm is small enough for those things to become known, and not as a result of any managerial policy of informing the workers.

It seems reasonable then to suppose that what motivated at least the workers of Técalémit was not simply a desire for a fatter wage-packet and better working conditions, although these were certainly important. It was much more a feeling of being isolated and cut off, of being mere puppets with no control over their destinies, in short, a feeling of alienation, at the very least in its crudest sense of estrangement from their work and their work-place. This is not the sort of thing that can be readily formulated in terms of easily understood bargaining points. In the France of 1968 they could only hope for one of two results: either there would be a revolution, with the expectation that in a different, more open, form of society the workers would have their rightful say; or the Government and the Patronat would be forced to capitulate, to listen seriously to what the strikers were saying, and to implement some of the devices which, in other industrial societies, have so far successfully served as safety-valves. In actual fact, neither of these results materialised. But the quiet, obstinate determination of the workers, more potent perhaps than any short-lived explosion of revolutionary fervour, should serve as a lesson which those in authority would do well to take to heart.

Técalémit may be considered typical of many, even most, French firms,[9] but the strike did not spare any sector of the economy.

9. This does not contradict what was said above, p. 194, since the workers' obstinacy was most usually expressed in terms of stiffer material demands.

There was even a move to organise a strike at Havas, one of the biggest advertising agencies in France, but the proposition was voted out. Another élite of a different sort are the workers of the *Imprimerie Nationale*: 2,400 strong, 80% are paid-up members of the CGT (out of 23 union delegates five are Party members). The workers there are relatively well off: wages are higher than in any other printing firm through a special combination of piece-work and hourly rates, good terms have been maintained with the management, and being among the most active and politically educated workers in France they had few real grievances. However, in 1967, the Government decided, as part of its decentralisation policy, to transfer the *Imprimerie Nationale* from Paris to Douai, near Lille. Since a job at the Imprimerie is a career position, many had bought flats or houses and had wives who worked in Paris (in some cases in offices that are threatened with transfers elsewhere). All are unanimous in not wanting to leave Paris. Despite innumerable protests, including a one-day strike and demonstration on 14 May, they did not obtain satisfaction and so, rather belatedly but unanimously, they joined the general strike and 500 workers occupied the buildings every day. Although they added claims for wage increases and a fifth week's paid holiday, their primary object was to protest against a typical example of the high-handed way in which the Government regularly implements what are doubtless very rational decisions over the heads of those most directly concerned.

Attempts were made by the strikers in some of the most technologically advanced firms to work out structures which would allow of a much more effective two-way information flow. Such was the case in the Brest branch of the CSF (Compagnie générale de Télégraphie Sans Fil). The plant was occupied on 20 May by the workers and 70% of the engineering, administrative and executive staff, and from the first day, after a strike committee had been elected, work started on a reform of the firm's hierarchy. Workers' committees would be set up at the level of each production unit (workshop, laboratory, office, etc.), and would have responsibility for everything which directly concerned the worker, from work conditions to salary and employment. Authority would be shared with the management, and in the case of disagreement the final decision would rest with a plant committee on which the workers would be represented.[10]

However, in general, and in the short run, the workers' revolt

10. For an account of reform proposals put forward by mixed commissions

216

was a failure. Few were the firms, such as Renault, where the workers obtained results that went substantially beyond the Grenelle Agreements. Here and there an extra 1% was accorded, here and there the existence of the unions in the plant was, in a limited but formal way, recognised. But this was not what the workers of that small electronics firm in Lyon (*la Compagnie Industrielle Française des Tubes Electroniques*) wanted when, some days after even Citroën had gone back to work, they took part in a secret ballot which the management had obtained by court order. Of a labour force of 629, 565 were present and voting; 224 voted for a return to work, but 338 to continue the strike. And so the strike went on for a few more days.

Yet every worker who was old enough to remember and compare said, when asked: 'No, this is quite different, it is more serious. In 1936 there were people who fought the pickets in order to go to work; today everyone accepts the strike.' Although when pressed to explain in what way 1968 was more serious, they were at something of a loss, it is hoped that the preceding chapters give some idea of why this impression was shared by at least one independent observer.

of striking workers, engineers and executives in three large, technologically up-to-date firms, see the economic supplement to *Le Monde*, 26 June 1968.

DOCUMENT 28

What some strikers wanted

A

A letter from strikers to the management.

C.G.T.—C.F.D.T.   FEYZIN, 25th MAY 1968
UNION BRANCHES
FEYZIN REFINERY
THE MANAGER

Dear Sir,

Following conversations with the staff during this week's strike, we have modified the demands we made on the 19th May last. You will find the altered list below:

1. Repeal of the regulations concerning social security.
2. Extension of union rights.
   (a) Freedom of action for union organisations within industry: collection of subscriptions, distribution of press and union literature, staff meetings and assemblies during working hours.
   (b) Application of article 2 of the law of 18 June 1966 concerning the social attributions of the worker-management committee, the text to be modified in the following way:
      the worker-management committee *participates* with the management, instead of cooperating.
      the committee *decides* what use to make of the 1% contribution out of salaries.
      the committee *decides on solutions* to general problems concerning professional training and finishing.
   (c) Application of article 3 of the law of 16 May 1946, which concerns the economic role of the worker-management committee, the phrase '*on a consultative basis*' being abolished.
3. Basic oil unit at 3·85 francs.
4. A 40 hour week with no reduction in salary.
5. Retirement at 60 years of age. For posted wage-earners or those working in particularly unpleasant or unhealthy conditions, retiring age should be put forward, with the same advantages

as for other workers, in terms of one year for every three years spent engaged in this work. This clause cannot make it possible for those concerned to be fully retired before the age of 55.

6. The 5th week of paid holidays.
7. Abolition of fines for delay in the performance of a contract.
8. Immediate engagement of staff on a contract basis.
9. Compensatory bonus (increased to 150 Fr.).
10. Indexing of the housing bonus.
11. Watch and seniority bonuses to be calculated in terms of real income.
12. Planning of relief timetables (teams to be made up in such a way that any unforeseen absences in the relief team should not lead to anyone having to stay at his post; guarantees of employment, classification and wages when a worker who is usually on shift or semi-shift work has to do a normal day because he is directed to, or for personal reasons).
13. Professional training.
14. Remuneration of days lost during the current strike.

B

The Renault (Cléon) action committee manifesto in draft form

Critical attitude in respect of legislative elections (and all forms of consultation of the electorate): the active force of the working classes is to be reckoned in terms of what they do in the street, and the occupation of factories, not the ballot box.

Unity of action of worker parties.

Basic indivisibility of unions (in the workshops and in the offices).

Obligation to belong to a union and to be a militant.

Fight for working class democracy (freedom of the press and freedom of expression).

United front: workers-students-teachers.

Solidarity between workers and students in the struggle (material and financial support).

Representatives to be controlled by those who elected them: they must report on their mandate.

CLAIMS

Wages (and working hours) to be on a sliding scale.
Guaranteed employment (abolition of temporary contracts).
Access to the books.
Short-term return to the 40 hour week.
Improvement of working conditions (under worker control).
Everybody to be paid on a monthly basis.
Wages to be equivalent to those at Billancourt.
Free health service.
An increase in low wages.
No overtime.
Uniform bonuses (away with the classification of bonuses).
One wage according to qualification.
Retirement at the age of 55 (as for civil servants).
Workers' supervision of implementation of Billancourt agreements.
The ending of age-differentials.
Public posting of work quotas.
Right to hold meetings during working hours.
Eligibility at the age of 18 or under.
Freedom of political expression in the factory.

(Source: *Notre arme, c'est la grève*, Paris, Maspero, 1968, pp. 89–90)

DOCUMENT 29

Statement by a delegate of Sud-Aviation (Nantes) to post-Grenelle Agreement negotiations in Paris

STATEMENT by comrade Yvon ROCTON, a member of the strike Committee at the Sud Aviation factory in Nantes, who was nominated as a member of the CGT, CGT-FO and CFDT delegation sent to negotiate with the management of Sud Aviation in Paris.

I came to the Paris negotiations with the firm intention of obtaining satisfaction as to the most important of the claims made by the Sud-Aviation workers, who were participating in the general strike by 10 million workers.

We Sud-Aviation workers in Nantes started the strike on 14 May by occupying the factory, in order to press home our demands, and this then became general:

—We reject dismissals, in particular those which are anticipated because of the closing of the Rochefort factory, decided upon by the de Gaulle–Pompidou Government.

—We want the 40 hour week immediately.

—No wages are to be inferior to 1,000 francs, as the Renault workers claim.

—Retirement at sixty.

—Complete payment for the hours spent on strike.

—The repeal of the (social security) decrees.

I consider that the evasiveness of M. PAPON, Chairman and General Manager of Sud-Aviation, who expressed a desire that the start of negotiations be put off until Tuesday, proves his determination to pressure Sud-Aviation workers into work again without their demands being satisfied.

When I came to Paris, I realised that although specific negotiations at professional and factory levels by federations and unions may result in some improvements, they in no way solve the problems which led the Sud-Aviation workers to join the general strike by 10 million workers.

I therefore consider it my duty not to take any further part in the negotiations, but to return to my factory in Nantes in order to explain to my comrades that they must continue the strike until the end, until they obtain complete satisfaction.

I have no doubt that my comrades from the CGT, CGT-FO and

CFDT, who are negotiating with M. PAPON, will do all in their power to extract concessions. But at present I do not think the solution to our problems can be found by negotiating.

SUD-AVIATION WORKERS!

WORKERS OF ALL PROFESSIONS TAKING PART IN THE GENERAL STRIKE!

We can gain complete victory. We can force the introduction of a sliding scale for wages; we can obtain worker control over prices and production. Our duty is clear if we are to obtain our ends:

LET US CONTINUE THE GENERAL STRIKE ON TUESDAY AND WE WILL WIN

3 June (4 o'clock in the morning).

DOCUMENT 30

How a housewife saw the strike

The point of view of the wife of a water board employee (Montsouris Reservoir) on strike in May

My husband is employed by the Water Board at the Montsouris reservoir. I have four children; the eldest daughter has just got married and, alas, the youngest is a mongol. For a month I had them all at home. The married daughter and her husband as well, because they couldn't go home. I am the wife and the mother-in-law of union representatives. The evenings were amazing; I had to revive my husband's spirits because he was afraid the fellows might give in, and calm down my young son-in-law who used to tell my husband that the union was too soft, that it had only accepted the strike because the majority of the fellows had forced its hand, or even that the 'big noises' in the union were in fact in agreement with the employers and Pompidou behind the workers' backs. . . . As for me, I prefer not to have any opinion about it, but sometimes my husband just didn't know what to reply.

Inconvenienced by the strike? I still am. Just think that my husband only got half his wage. Even when he gets all of it, it only comes to about 900 fr. per month, and that's after he's been working for them for twenty years. But what I liked about the strike was the unity between everybody: for the first time some members of the higher staff joined with the workers.

The students? It was not so clear. Of course one can think what one likes about Cohn-Bendit, but I say that without him nothing would have started.

My husband went on strike, and I agreed with him: I have confidence in him. If he did it again when the factory restarted, that's only justice: because in his factory there have been wage increases, but now they're in the process of reducing working hours, which cuts overtime by 25%. The bosses are busy getting back with their left hands what they gave with their right. And the rent is going up, so where do we go from here?

(Source: *L'Anti-Mythe*, 36, 2 August 1968, a leaflet produced by the Action Committee of the 14th *arrondissement* of Paris).

DOCUMENT 31

A Young Executive's View

Everything will be just as it was before!

[Many of us disagree with the CNPF] and nobody consults us before passing on to the government opinions which are often outdated, and above all hints about the threats of unemployment, financial difficulties and the same old stories!

Fortunately, there exist companies and heads of business who are not afraid of negotiating directly with top civil servants, their colleagues or their competitors, and with unions and their staff—whether one is referring to representatives, production committees or strike committees.

Physically and morally upright men, who, whatever their age, do not spend their time re-reading France's economic history, but are more interested in contemporary experiments in more advanced countries, who take the trouble to go and see what is happening in the East and in the West, who are able to talk to the great of the world in the field of industry or economics (most of whom are in the United States) in their own language, who are willing to see anyone who asks them and benevolently explain their successes or their failures with no regrets and in a free and easy way...

In France it is paternalistic to address someone in the familiar form, whereas in the United States people soon call each other by their first name, whatever their standing.

Men whose job it is to make industries produce and direct their staff, and who are physically capable of doing so, lost their illusions when, at the climax of the period of unrest, they were able to see on television such and such a defender of such and such a category, tired and confused because he had been negotiating all night at Grenelle, and such and such an industrial 'boss'—for that is the word—incapable of expressing himself unprepared in front of the camera, as Sauvageot, Geismar or Cohn-Bendit did without any difficulty.

That said, the remainder of us, we managers, were surprised to learn that the CNPF was saying that its members, though doubtless without knowing it, had always practised participation at all levels. Which means to say that they do not know much about companies, general assemblies, boards of directors, worker-management committees, strikes and the occupying of factories!

Having got that straight, it is only right that a believer in the capitalist system, a member of the ruling class, and a bourgeois into the bargain, should state that if France was not, the world of industry at least certainly was, astonished to learn that it had come to light during the occupations, strikes and barricades required to get the SMIG increased to 3 francs per hour, which is not very much, that a considerable number of people in our country were being paid 2.20 per hour.

Anybody who had the audacity to say that 'he' was satisfied, that 'he' was not asking for anything, that 'he' was happy to work fifty or fifty-four hours, ought to be banished for good from his position as an employer or head of a company, whichever you prefer.

All those who live too well out of capitalism, whose duty, right, good fortune or misfortune it is to be heads of companies and who make the most of their two houses, their domestic staff, their cars and their holidays, these people may be justified in doing so if they pay fit and correct wages, above the lower limit imposed by the law, to those who work for them; this is something which is open to discussion and is certainly discussed by all the theorists of equality and even decency. On the other hand it seems quite unacceptable that men and their families should live too well from the profit they come by not because of their own value, because they put all their capital into a project or because they have eminent people working with them, but because they suceed in paying wages which are below the legal limit and above all are not decent, and all this amply explains the unrest which can come to grief in a disastrous free-for-all.

Let there be no illusions; there are and there will continue to be people payed less than the SMIG.

A few days after the Grenelle agreements, employers used trickery or the threat of unemployment to persuade workers, who either lacked determination or had no resources to fall back on, to allow themselves to be employed for 2.20 francs or 2.30 francs. The employers listed their wages at 3.00 francs per hour for a reduced number of hours, and then made their employees work extra hours without pay. This sort of practice discredits the ruling classes. We are not certainly not very close to the CFDT's self-management or even the idea of election by plebiscite of the head of the company, which was put forward by M. Bloch-Lainé.

If anybody tells you that work inspection makes this impossible, allow me to inform you that this organisation does not have access to the most detailed company accounts, and while it may have the means to find out about the most important affairs, it is quite incapable of recognising the people who are really concerned amongst the small artisans, the little concerns which would, it is said, be in jeopardy if they were not able to use simplified accounting systems, undeclared labour, and, when the product can be easily handled, get part of the work done at home.

(extract from an independent column by Fred Lip in *Le Monde*, 15 August 1968).

PART THREE

THE POLITICAL AFTERMATH

Quis tulerat *Gaullists* de seditione querentis?

—with apologies to Juvenal, who wrote 'Gracchos'.

INTRODUCTION

IT is not intended in this Part to give a detailed account of the various French constitutions and parliaments, as excellent works on this subject already exist.[1] Yet one of the most striking aspects of the May uprising was the way in which it made all existing political institutions appear quite irrelevant. There was an enormous gap between what was going on in the country and what the party spokesmen were saying and the language they were saying it in. The June elections did little, if anything, to bridge this gap. But if the existing, traditional channels of dissent proved quite unable to cope with the great wave of revolt, they were not entirely swamped by it, and indeed their very existence did much towards restoring a certain calm. Before looking at French political parties from this angle, and analysing the election results, it is therefore worth venturing a few remarks on the way political institutions are traditionally regarded in France.

It is a commonplace to point out that since the Revolution France has known fifteen different constitutions, including three Empires and five Republics. Governments that have been too weak have alternated with ones that have been too strong. This is due not only to the fact that the French have never been able to agree on how or by whom they should be governed (although that is true as well) but also that since any government means Paris and Paris is not France they have never really agreed to be governed at all. If one may borrow the metaphor of the social contract, the situation in France is much closer to Hobbe's version than to Rousseau's. Government is accepted only as a necessary evil, and it should infringe as little as possible on the liberty of the individual; but partly because the latent hostility to it is so strong, government tends to be very powerful and authoritarian. It is thus always regarded with suspicion, and the concept of community does not enter into the question. Government is a problem that concerns only the central authority and the individual, who regard each other with mutual distrust.

1. The outstanding authority is Philip Williams. See in particular *Crisis and Compromise; politics in the Fourth Republic*, Longmans, 1964, which contains a very full bibliography: for the Fifth Republic see the same author's *The French Parliament (1958–1967)*, George Allen and Unwin, 1968.

It is clear that there is not much room for political parties in this scheme of things, and as recently as 1962 an opinion poll showed that 49% of Frenchmen considered that none of the main political parties represented their interests, and 29% did not mention any political party.[2] Roig and Billon-Grand, in their study of political socialisation, also confirm this tendency to ignore political parties,[3] and the difficulty the authors had in undertaking their research shows to what extent politics in France is considered as something essentially private, a matter of individual conscience. The historical origins of this attitude lie in the fact that deputies were elected to go to Paris, which in the nineteenth century was very often a long way away, to represent the interests of his electors, and even more to defend them against encroachments by the central government. The deputy himself was for the most part a local *notable*, a landowner, lawyer or schoolmaster, who, whatever his political affiliations, saw his role in the same light.

This did not of course prevent the formation of political parties under the Third Republic, nor did it prevent certain major issues of the nineteenth century, such as the conflict between Church and State and the closely connected choice between a democratic and an authoritarian form of government, being fought out and settled at the Parliamentary level. These issues deeply divided the country, but they were decided to a considerable extent by groups of deputies who formed first parties and then governmental coalitions. Yet divorced from their electors, except where local interests were concerned, deputies were free to formulate issues and wrangle over them in a way that accentuated rather than diminished the gulf between governing and governed. So long as France's economy remained static and protected, that is to say up to World War I, the system worked well enough. A conservative social and economic policy combined with a violently anti-clerical one enabled all the parties (the conservative right never formed itself into one or more coherent parties), and above all the one which was most typical of the Third Republic, the Radical party, to pose as inheritors of the French Revolution. This was important, as most people in France owed their position to the Revolution (or believed that they did); but

2. *Sondages*, 2, 1963, p. 69.
3. Op. cit., p. 90. 'Our study thus underlines the existence of a fundamental cultural characteristic of French political society, the absence of any political socialisation through political parties.' For the hostility which the authors encountered in the course of their research, see their introduction.

for these small independent farmers, small independent artisans, and small independent shopkeepers (France, far more than has ever been the case in Britain, was and is a nation of shopkeepers) progressive social and economic policies at home as well as an international free trade policy would have spelt disaster.

Between the wars the combined effects of international diplomacy and international economics, coupled with the emergence of a revolutionary Communist Party, made apparent the contradictions of a system which allowed for no compromise between the notion of a representative assembly and that of government. The electorate remained very stable (even the Popular Front only came to power as a result of a $1 \cdot 5\%$ swing) and with increasing regularity returned to power left of centre majorities which, by the time the elections came round four years later, had produced right of centre governments. All governments were coalitions, but as soon as one coalition looked like facing up to a series of more and more complex problems, it fell apart and was replaced by another coalition (or the same one with a different Prime Minister). Deputies, even when they were aware of the widening gulf between what went on inside Parliament and what went on outside, were prisoners of their mandate; elected not to govern but to prevent any government interfering with their constituents' lives, they would have lost their seats had they acted otherwise.[4] In an economically backward, atomised society like France, it is difficult for concepts like 'the greatest good of the greatest number' (whether interpreted by Bentham or by Marx) to take root.

In 1940, as in 1958, when the credibility gap became too great, the French accepted with relief the disappearance of the system and the emergence of a national figurehead. At the Liberation, however, there was a revival of revolutionary fervour which meant that the constitution of the Fourth Republic was not sufficiently different from that of the Third to prevent the same pattern recurring. The pressing need to decolonise and the second half of France's industrial revolution posed problems that were different from the pre-war ones, but Parliament was no better adapted to cope with them. Although the record of the Fourth Republic is by no means a meagre one, the persistence of social and political attitudes and

4. The title of one of the works of the great Radical philosopher, Alain, is very revealing; *Le Citoyen contre les Pouvoirs*. It is this sort of attitude which gave rise to the Poujadist protest movement in the 1950s, but it is also largely responsible for the fact that France has not yet succumbed to the temptations

traditions, despite great economic changes, rendered its demise inevitable.

Neither the electoral system nor the parties themselves were enough to change these habits and traditions. During most of the Third Republic a two-ballot single member constituency system was used, which favoured the Radicals who, being the least doctrinaire of all, could on the second ballot pose as anti-clerical or anti-socialist champions as the local situation demanded. The Fourth Republic instituted a system of proportional representation in the hope that it would be fairer and would encourage electors to vote for a party rather than for a man. Neither result was achieved. For instead of the country becoming one vast constituency, as in Germany, separate lists of candidates were presented and voted on in each department, and although some departments were broken up into two or more constituencies this tended to favour the rural vote and the survival of small regionally-based parties. The big parties did become bigger, but no one party ever obtained an overall majority of seats. Moreover, when the Cold War drove the Communists into Parliamentary isolation and the Gaullist RPF[5] became an electoral menace, the electoral law was amended in such a way as to penalise those parties who were too intransigent to enter into alliances with other parties. Thus both in 1951 and 1956 the elector had to vote in terms of local electoral alliances which did not necessarily correspond in any way to the coalitions which the parties would later form among themselves, and the gap between what happened at the polls and what happened in Parliament was as wide as ever. The only positive result of the new system was that the conservative right was forced for the first time to come together into a single party, the *Centre National des Indépendants et Paysans*, out of which came Giscard d'Estaing's *Républicains Indépendants*.

The parties themselves could do little to bridge the gap. Far from being a means of communication between the voter and the government, they have always been a cross between a club and a caucus: a caucus for electing deputies and a club for harbouring militants. Decisions were in general imposed from above whatever the organisational structure, although in the centre parties the deputies had more weight, and in the left-wing ones the militants. The militant is at once the life-blood and the bane of a French

of either Nazi Fascism or totalitarian Communism, and is unlikely to do so in the foreseeable future.
5. See below, ch. 7.

party. The party cannot exist without him,[6] and for the militant the party provides that sense of belonging to an intermediate community between the family cell and the state which is so lacking in the French social system; but at the same time it to a large extent replaces them both, so that the party becomes an end in itself. The militant's concern is less with recruitment, social change, or even with getting his party into power than with preserving his cocoon intact.[7] The most bitter enemies are those who threaten it from within or from next-door, and not those at the other end of the political spectrum. Thus parties tend to live by and for themselves; as a means of political socialisation and participation they are practically worthless.[8]

The Fifth Republic has not changed the situation in any fundamental way. Parties are relegated to the background, and the electorate has clearly approved, in successive referendums and the 1965 Presidential election, de Gaulle's policy of appealing to it over their heads.[9] In 1958, partly to prevent Jacques Soustelle's pro-'French Algeria' tendency from gaining too many votes and partly to appear as 'Republican' as possible, de Gaulle reverted to the traditionally republican two-ballot electoral system with single member constituencies.[10] However, since the parties divided essentially on the question of support or hostility towards the regime,

6. The case of the Christian Democrat MRP (founded at the Liberation,) in which there was continual conflict between the militants on the one hand and the majority of deputies and voters on the other, is very instructive—cf. Williams, *Crisis and Compromise*, ch. 8.

7. Williams, op. cit., p. 401, makes a similar point: '[The militants'] concerns were to press the party's demands even at inconvenient moments, prevent unceremonious treatment of its sacred cows, and so protect the enthusiasm and loyalty of the faithful which the compromises of the parliamentarians threatened to dissipate. Living in the closed world of the party and behaving as if it were in a political vacuum, they could play the sea-green incorruptible and win votes and applause at party conferences.'

8. See above, note 3.

9. Although the presidential election, when de Gaulle failed to obtain an absolute majority on the first ballot, was represented as a defeat for him, its popularity was in fact a victory for his constitution. In this sense it is clearly a democratic constitution, but equally clearly its plebiscitary tendencies contain dangers which the party system of representative democracy is designed to guard against.

10. Michel Debré has always advocated the adoption of the British electoral system, and it is interesting to note that if this had been used in the 1967 election the Gaullists, with over 300 deputies, would have been returned with an absolute majority.

this has if anything facilitated the formation of a coherent majority and a united opposition. Although the process is far from complete, the progress that has been accomplished has given Parliament more potential importance than it had in the early days of the Fifth Republic. Moreover, as de Gaulle's personal vote has declined, so the opposition has become more united, and the Gaullist party more confident. But habits die hard, and it is above all fear of the inevitable dissolution (and of how both the voters and de Gaulle would react) rather than political conviction that has prevented deputies from overthrowing the Gaullist majority between March 1967 and June 1968. The plebiscitary character of all elections and referendums does not encourage deputies to behave responsibly, and ensures that the political and sociological gap in France between government and governed is not appreciably narrowed.

CHAPTER SEVEN

THE CAMPAIGN: THE GAULLISTS

'Toute ma vie je me suis fait une certaine idée de la France.'

This is the first sentence from Charles de Gaulle, *Mémoires de guerre*, vol. 1, Paris, Plon, 1954.

THE extreme left in France, and particularly the Communists, define Gaullism in economic terms as *le pouvoir des monopoles*. Granted that the French economy, from before 1958, has been moving in this direction (and which industrial economy has not?), the most that can be said for this definition is that it provides a convenient slogan and battle-cry. Right-wing conservatives and economic efficiency experts[1] have rallied to the Gaullists, and rendered them to some extent their prisoner, but this is because Gaullism and the concentration of capital exist at the same time. This is not to say that there are no links of historical necessity between the economic system and the form of government in a given country, but the economic conditions in France do nothing to explain the rise of Gaullism (as opposed to any other form of conservative government) nor its popular success.

Gaullism is in fact one more attempt to impose on Frenchmen a sense of unity that mere geography and certain cultural characteristics have never been enough to provoke. It is idle to enquire whether the constitution of the Fifth Republic is more *Orléaniste* or *Bonapartiste* or anything else; it is in the tradition of all of these. The French Revolution having failed to solve the problem of the co-existence of a 'general will' and an all-powerful legislative assembly of representatives, it was open to all those (and not just the reactionaries who refused to accept the fact of the Revolution) who put more emphasis on the former than the latter to settle the problem once and for all by imposing a consensus by means of a strong, centralised

1. Commonly, but confusedly, described as technocrats. The trouble with this term is that it is used to refer both to those who work out policies in terms of economic efficiency and those who translate them into political decisions; the fact that in both cases the social consequences of the policies are often ignored does not make the two categories one.

235

executive authority which would not have to pay more than minimum attention to the particularist views of an elected assembly. Gaullism is but the latest, and by no means the most despotic in a long series of attempts to incarnate the 'general will', the State, the Nation, in the person of one man. The constitution of the Fifth Republic is itself an attempt to institutionalise this and, when amended in 1962 to allow for the election of the President of the Republic by direct suffrage, to render it permanent.

In what he considers as essential de Gaulle is nothing if not consistent; an outline sketch of the constitution of the Fifth Republic can be found in his Bayeux speech, delivered in 1946 after he had left for what he thought was to be a short stay in the political wilderness. But the basic problem, the attempt to create an artificial unity and impose it as a political programme by a series of personal and verbal symbols from the top, is to be found most clearly expressed in the writings and speeches of that most passionate, most doctrinaire (but not always most illiberal) of Gaullists, Michel Debré.[2] It explains de Gaulle's tight control over foreign policy, and indeed his inordinate emphasis on it (nationalism is very often the first resort of those who wish to create a factitious unity), as well as such chimera as an association of capital and labour. The idea, which was first formulated by de Gaulle at the Liberation, is that if capital and labour, which are naturally distinct entities, are not willing either to agree among themselves or to negotiate in good faith, some form of unifying association must be forced upon them.

A glance at the names that have been given to the various Gaullist movements is also instructive. The first was the short-lived *Union Gaulliste* of 1946.[3] Following de Gaulle's Strasbourg speech in the spring of 1947 the *Rassemblement du Peuple Français* (Gathering of the French People) was then formed; although never officially dissolved, it ceased to be active after just over five years.[4] After

2. Cf. for example, Michel Debré, *Au service de la nation. Essai d'un programme politique*, Paris, Stock, 1963. The title itself is revealing—it as though Edward Heath were to write a political 'credo' entitled 'For Queen and country'.

3. The *Mouvement Républicain Populaire*, composed mainly of leftish Catholic Resisters, declared itself to be the party of de Gaulle's followers, but it never received more than his tacit blessing: the parting of the ways came over the October 1946 constitutional referendum—cf. Williams, *Crisis and Compromise*, chs. 8 and 10.

4. Although its elected deputies continued to sit and hold office under different names—cf. Williams, op. cit., chs. 10 and 11.

de Gaulle's return to power in 1958, the *Union pour la Nouvelle République* was founded on 1 October of that year; at the Lille conference in November 1967 it changed its name to *Union des Démocrates pour la Cinquième République* and, having fought the 1968 election under the banner of the *Union pour la Défense de la République*, it has now become *Union des Démocrates pour la République*. Although each of these organisations has taken part in the normal electoral process, they have without exception sought to distinguish themselves from political parties in the ordinary sense of the term, in particular by studiously avoiding the word 'party' in their names.[5]

The reasons for this reveal a great deal about the nature of Gaullism. For Gaullists to describe themselves as a political party like any other would have meant accepting the traditional conception of representative democracy whereby each party represents a particular section (or interest group) of the population and all have equal right to exist. Now this is precisely what Gaullists do not accept; for them the only true Frenchmen are those who are prepared to be united (*Union*) or gathered together (*Rassemblement*) behind General de Gaulle.[6] This has the inevitable corollary that all those who are not Gaullists are not true Frenchmen and are to be cast into outer darkness. Whence the extraordinary animosity of Gaullists towards non-Gaullists; political adversaries are not considered simply as opponents, but as veritable enemies, not to say traitors, to be feared and hated.

This is understandable enough when it is realised that those who oppose the Gaullist undertaking are also opposing France. However, partly in order to unite a politically heterogeneous movement (Gaullists come from the right, the centre and the left), partly because of the logic of its own ideology, Gaullism cannot do without an enemy, and preferably a clearly identifiable one. At the Liberation it was all too easy, as the great purge showed, to distinguish between true and false Frenchmen. The unifying force of the RPF was an extremely virulent anti-communism. The UNR, as its name suggests, was opposed to all those who did not accept the 1958 Constitution and to all the existing political parties which had

5. Questions of vocabulary are very important for the Gaullists; for example, their party conferences are not called '*congrès*' but '*assises*' (sittings).

6. No mass movement was formed at the Liberation because de Gaulle thought that he could rally all Frenchmen to him over the heads of the political parties. It was when this proved not to be the case that the RPF was formed.

brought France and the Fourth Republic into such universal disrepute. As a result of the increasing acceptance of the constitution by the opposition parties, following the lead given by their electors, it became apparent that some new enemy was required. For the emergence of the Communist Party from its political ghetto into something like respectability, symbolised by its electoral unity with the non-Communist Left, produced a severe set-back for de Gaulle in the Presidential election of 1965, when he was forced to undergo the indignity of a second ballot, and disappointing results for the UNR in the 1967 general election. The answer was given at the Lille conference later the same year when, besides the usual scornful references to 'the parties of the old days', the Gaullists' anti-communism, never entirely absent even in the early days of the UNR, was given free rein. Nearly every important speech was full of it, and everyone present, militants and journalists alike, was given a fat brochure setting out all the reasons for hating the French Communist Party. The result was that when de Gaulle pointed out the enemy in his broadcast on 30 May 1968, the Gaullist militants, who had up to then been as perplexed as anyone else, knew exactly how to respond. But the depressing conclusion of this is that Gaullism, whose ideal is a united France, is bound inevitably to divide profoundly Frenchmen against themselves.

If this merely meant that the Gaullists are a governing party who are prepared to use every means in the book to remain so, it would not be so serious. But the violence which, in one form or another, has always been associated with Gaullism from the very beginning, means that the cleavages go very deep. For the two events in the twentieth century which split France radically in two were World War II and the Algerian War, and with both of these events de Gaulle was closely associated.

World War II saw the birth of Gaullism on 18 June 1940, and also the Resistance which left its mark of clandestine, but morally approved, violence on a whole generation. The Liberation as well was accompanied by a situation which in some places was not far short of civil war; de Gaulle established order, but the price paid was high. The RPF's anti-communism knew no bounds; among other acts of violence its *service d'ordre* shot dead a Communist at Grenoble in 1948. This, together with its cult of the leader and hostility to the constitution, lent some weight to the arguments of those who at the time were tempted to see in it a fascist threat. Even though it was virtually disbanded in 1953 such was the loyalty and mutual friendship of the key men that in May 1958 ten telephone calls were all that was necessary to put the network in place again.[7] Again, de Gaulle's return to power in 1958 took place in an atmosphere of suspicion, plotting and rebellion which, if it was not the work of Gaullists themselves, certainly made things easier for them.

The Algerian War was altogether an extremely nasty affair, and it would be unfair to blame the Gaullists for all of its atrocities (systematic torture was started under Guy Mollet's socialist government). But it was Roger Frey, the Gaullist Minister of the Interior, who 'covered' the Paris police when in October 1961 they threw over twenty Algerians into the Seine.[8] Similarly, the OAS and its sympathisers, some of whom like Jacques Soustelle were ex-Gaullists, used avowedly terrorist means to achieve their ends, but that is no reason why high-ranking Gaullist ministers and deputies should be implicated, directly or indirectly, in defeating them by the same terrorist methods. One such deputy, Lemarchand, was also implicated in the Ben Barka scandal in 1966; a practising barrister, he was struck off the rolls for unprofessional conduct but retained his seat in the National Assembly until the 1967 election. That such people can still be elected on a Gaullist ticket is shown by the conduct of Pierre Baudis, who in June 1968 became one of the deputies for Toulouse; on learning of his victory he joined a gang of supporters in wrecking the offices of the Radical newspaper, *La Dépêche de Midi*. The vast majority of Gaullists and their electors certainly disapprove of such methods, but it is clear none the less that on every occasion in the last thirty years when France has been deeply divided the Gaullists have not been found among those who seek a general reconciliation, but have actively, and sometimes violently, taken sides.

Insofar as the only valid 'conception of France' is the Gaullist one, and the only way to translate it into practical terms is the Gaullist way, there is something inherently totalitarian about Gaullism. De Gaulle himself is a typical example of the Weberian charismatic leader. His charisma may now be wearing a little thin,

7. According to one highly placed Gaullist, quoted in Jean Charlot, *L'Union pour la Nouvelle République; étude du pouvoir au sein d'un parti politique*, Paris, A. Colin, 1967, pp. 303–4.
8. Despite parliamentary pressure, Frey refused a committee of enquiry, but finally set up a judicial tribunal. As its findings have never been made public, it is reasonable to assume that the charges against the Paris police were justified.

but he has lost none of his Machiavellian intelligence which, combined with a very fine sense of what is possible, makes him one of the outstanding political leaders of the century. But he is no dictator. One of the accusations that future historians will level against him, the justice of which has now been confirmed by the May revolt, is that he did not use his popular mandate to force through some of the (compared with the Gaullist *weltanschauung*) minor reforms which are so badly needed in France. Moreover, he has succeeded time and again in getting his policies and actions, even the most unconstitutional ones, approved by a free popular vote, and he would have stepped down before the presidential election in 1965 if he had been convinced that the 1958 constitution was sufficiently firmly established for its institutions to function without him.

It is by no means evident, however, that his followers have such a self-effacing vision of their historical role as the leader. Jean Charlot[9] distinguishes three categories of Gaullists, the believers, the pragmatists and the doctrinarians. The first are those who have always followed de Gaulle blindly and will continue to do so as long as he is in the saddle; when he retires some will doubtless retire with him but others will continue as apostles of the faith. The most striking examples of the pragmatists are Georges Pompidou and Jacques Chaban-Delmas, speaker of the National Assembly and Mayor of Bordeaux; political realists of this ilk are quite content that Gaullism in 1968 should not necessarily be identical with what it was ten or twenty years earlier, and they have drawn into the Gaullist net traditional conservatives, such as Valéry Giscard d'Estaing's *Républicains Indépendants*, and strongly tempted some of Jacques Duhamel's right-centre *Progrès et Democratie Moderne* (the votes of some or all of these groups have been essential for maintaining a government majority in the National Assembly). On a different level this aspect of Gaullism, the possibility it offers of getting things done, has attracted to it a number of local personalities and militants who have helped to give the Gaullist party the beginnings of a solid foundation at constituency level. The third group, the doctrinarians, comprises people like Michel Debré on the one hand, and on the other left-wing and moderate Gaullists (or social and Christian democrats, in terms of their political origins) such as René Capitant and Louis Terrenoire. But none of them have been able to formulate a coherent body of doctrine;

9. Op. cit., ch. 11.

whether they talk in terms of the State, the interests of everybody or the common good, it is clear that Gaullism is for all of them essentially such as it has been described above, a permanent invitation, or even obligation, to all Frenchmen to transcend themselves and their everyday problems.

No less significant is the structure and organisation of the Gaullist party. French political parties are not in general addicted to renewing their leaders and national executives, but since the Liberation even less fresh blood has been injected into the higher echelons of Gaullism than of any other political movement. Gaullism was formed by and through the Resistance, and by 1945 the principal leaders of the Fifth Republic already formed a coherent group around de Gaulle;[10] and many of those who joined later were already known to the members of that group. And it is these men who have retained all the key posts in the Gaullist movement. Jean Charlot[11] has convincingly shown that the higher one goes in the hierarchy the more frequently party officials are coopted and the same men re-elected, and the smaller the percentage of newcomers. Gaullism is in fact very much an oligarchic movement. Whether or not it will remain so depends very much on when and how (and perhaps even more, if) the newcomers to Gaullism, who at the moment form the vast majority of militants in the local federations, accede to posts of greater responsibility. The events of 1968 and their consequences are not, from this point of view, very encouraging.

Both these aspects of Gaullism, its lack of any coherent doctrine and its oligarchic nature, go some way to explaining why the Gaullists have never fought an election on the basis of a political programme. It is true that this has never been a notable feature of election campaigns in France, but there have been times before the advent of the Fifth Republic (the latest was the 1956 general election) when the dominant issues of the day have formed the subject of open political debate. But despite its overall majority and stability the Gaullist party has not scorned to adopt at the local level the old Radical tactics of buying votes by promises of what the deputy could do for his constituents in Paris, and at the national level to take refuge behind de Gaulle and the institutions of the Fifth Republic. It is probably not too much to suggest that one, and

10. A list is given in Jean Charlot, op. cit., pp. 302–3.
11. Op. cit., ch. 9. The rank and file succeeded in obtaining a few relatively unimportant concessions at the Lille Conference in 1967—cf. *New Society*, 30 November 1967.

probably the main, reason for this is that to present a coherent electoral platform would be to invite voters to choose between that and other electoral platforms. Yet it cannot too often be stressed that Gaullism does not admit the possibility of such choice, and a tightly knit oligarchy does not encourage its members to face up to the possibility of losing power one day. So far a divided opposition has always helped the Gaullists to avoid the problem. In the meantime, the French voter remains as politically uneducated as ever.

The elections of January 1968 were not very different. Although the atmosphere was extremely tense, and sometimes violent, the campaign itself was relatively calm. In March 1967 the Gaullists had hired the services of a publicity firm to project their image. A year later this was not necessary. De Gaulle's speech on 30 May had set the tone. The Gaullists, who fought the election as the UDR, were identified with order, liberty, the Republic and indeed France as a whole. Opposed to them were the Communists who wished to establish a dictatorship, with or without the help of the various revolutionary movements that had sprung up during May. The choice, although it did not correspond in any way to the events that had shaken France to the core, was clear. Little or no attempt was made to preach the virtues of unity (there was one reference to it in a speech by Jacques Chaban-Delmas), and the wounds of May were if anything made worse by the atmosphere of fear, bordering on panic, which the Gaullist campaign tended to aggravate.

The sporadic violence which continued to break out in Paris and elsewhere served the UDR's purpose. As one opposition candidate put it, 'Every barricade loses me a hundred votes'.[12] There were also rumours that certain groups were planning to sabotage the elections. All this gave some slight semblance of justification to the Committees for the Defence of the Republic which went into action, quite literally, after de Gaulle's 30 May speech. They were responsible for many of the minor acts of violence which marked the campaign, the wrecking of local party offices and the beating-up of opposition bill-posters. There were, it is true, some attacks against Gaullist premises, but these were the work of one or two extremist movements and not of rival political parties. Yet it was a gang of thugs brought over from Corsica who shot dead a young Communist at Arras on the evening before the second ballot (the Communist, in accordance with the tactical alliance between the

12. Quoted in Le Monde, 18 June 1968.

242

Communists and the Federation, was loyally helping Socialist Party bill-posters). The Gaullists in fact conducted their campaign as though they were engaged in a cold civil war. Care was taken to avoid an open conflict, but coexistence, let alone national unity, was out of the question.

This was also apparent in the choice of candidates. The Gaullists, like the Communists, put up candidates in every constituency,[13] which meant opposing an ex-Gaullist minister like Edgar Pisani who had voted the censure motion, as well as those *Républicains Indépendants* who were not prepared to accept the investiture of the UDR. In a speech on 3 June, Georges Pompidou was very broad-minded in his approach; the investiture of the UDR would not be reserved exclusively for loyal Gaullists, but extended to all those who were willing to defend the Republic, and he let it be understood that once the election was over the doors of the majority (and therefore the possibility of ministerial office) would be open for the centre (Jaques Duhamel's PDM). However, as the campaign progressed, and it became clear that the great majority of electors were going to vote for 'order and freedom', attitudes hardened and no quarter was given. Some of the bitterest attacks were reserved for PDM candidates, many of whom adopted towards the events of May, and the young in particular, a much more liberal attitude than the Gaullists.

The campaign opened officially on Monday 10 June, but three days earlier de Gaulle was interviewed on television by Michel Droit, editor of *Le Figaro*. Although not supposed to be an election broadcast it contained a clear appeal to the voters. It also contained practically the only attempt at a serious analysis of what was happening in and to France. Profound changes in the University were called for, as well as in the working conditions and dignity of the workers, but the account of the events of May left much to be desired.[14] The final sentence summed up, in some ways, the essence of Gaullism: 'I call on French men and women by their vote to come together in the Republic around its President'. Thus as usual there were a few magic words, such as 'participation', and a call to unity, but a unity that by definition excluded a large section of the population. The same theme was repeated in a short broadcast delivered on 29 June, the day before the second ballot (quite illegally, as of course the President is not allowed to intervene in election campaigns).

13. Except in those of the four PDM deputies who had not voted the censure motion.
14. Cf. *Le Monde*, 9–10 June 1968.

In these circumstances the Gaullist candidates had a relatively easy time. Few campaigned actively, and many contented themselves with distributing photographs of themselves framed in the red, white and blue of the French flag. The identification of Gaullism with France and violent attacks on the Communists and their allies were in most cases enough. Even in those cases where there was a vigorous campaign the emphasis was on the past, on General de Gaulle as the saviour of the nation, and on the importance of maintaining order and preserving the basic freedoms. Hardly a word was said about the future. And this was as true of local campaigns as it was of party political broadcasts. It was as though the Gaullists had not only failed to understand the significance of what had happened, but had not even thought it necessary to ask themselves whether there was anything to understand.

CHAPTER EIGHT

THE CAMPAIGN: THE OPPOSITION

'. . . old hat and phrases which have been debased and worked
to the bone . . . .'

Letter to *Le Monde*, 21 June 1968.

T HE *Le Monde* reader had begun by examining the electoral platforms of all the political parties, and he found each one wanting;
his conclusion was that he scarcely felt any stronger urge to vote
than to hurl a cobble-stone. While his strictures are doubtless somewhat exaggerated, they are typical of many—apart from the students
—who felt that no political party was equal to the situation. Apart
from the Gaullists, the choice lay essentially between the *Centre
Démocrate*, with its parliamentary off-shoot *Progrès et Démocratie
Moderne*, the *Fédération de la Gauche Démocrate et Socialiste*,
and the Communist Party. Separately none of these stood for the
kind of profound renovation which the May uprising seemed to call
for, and together, in whatever combination, they did not look like
being able to form an alternative government. This is a sad comment
on parties that had spent ten years in opposition. If some of the
responsibility lies with the French political system itself, the fact
remains that the parties did not take the opportunity to transform
and adapt themselves to mid-twentieth century conditions.

The attempt to unite the centre and the non-Gaullist right in an
organised movement dates from Jean Lecanuet's comparative success
in the presidential election of 1965 when he took a sufficient number
of votes away from de Gaulle to force a second ballot. The first
French politician to make use of an advertising agency, he projected
a 'new frontier' type of image, modelled on that of John Kennedy,
which attracted to him a number of young people besides the
traditional Catholic vote. But the *Centre Démocrate*, which was
born in February 1966, could not make up its mind whether it was
going to be a completely new party or simply an inter-party committee
comprising everything from right-wing Radicals to non-Gaullist
conservatives. The difficulties were aggravated by the fact that
Jean Lecanuet was a senator and so could not control his centre

deputies in the National Assembly. When as a result of the March 1967 general election the centre found itself with forty deputies, it formed a parliamentary group, *Progrès et Démocratie Moderne,* under the leadership of Jacques Duhamel, which kept itself distinct from Lecanuet's *Centre Démocrate.*[1] For all practical purposes, the latter ceased to exist.

The majority of PDM deputies come from the MRP, the others from the Radical Party or right-wing groups; some of them were Gaullists in the early days, others have always been hostile. But despite the diversity of their political origins, most of them have in common the fact they they are relatively young (very few were deputies under the Fourth Republic), and also that they were elected in a manner much more reminiscent of the Third Republic than of the Fourth or Fifth. That is to say that they had no need of a party organisation; their local prestige and influence were enough to ensure that they were sent to Parliament not to take part in a government but to represent local interests.[2] Insofar as they have a common programme it can be summed up in the words: order, liberty, progress.[3] The first two are the traditional slogans of the centre and right-wing Catholic vote, on which they all depend, the third is an appeal to a more dynamic younger generation some of whom were attracted to Lecanuet. The centre, which is aware that the next election will see the youngest electorate that France has ever known, is gambling on attracting the young voter who is as tired of Gaullism as he is of the traditional Left; but the young are in general more ready to vote for one or other extreme than for the sort of uneasy compromise represented by the PDM. The deputies are also divided on parliamentary tactics in a way that is typical of the whole situation of the centre; some will join with the FGDS and the Communists in censuring the government, others will abstain and thus save it.

Although Jacques Duhamel himself often speaks well and to the point (his speeches during May and June 1968 were those of an enlightened conservative), the real influence of the PDM is negli-

1. Under the present constitution only parties with at least 30 deputies can form parliamentary groups and enjoy the privilege of official recognition, proportional representation on committees, etc.
2. The analysis on which this conclusion is based is given in an article by Roland Cayrol and Jean-Luc Parodi in *Revue Française de Science Politique,* 18 (1), February 1968, p. 102 and note 16.
3. Ibid., p. 103.

gible. In spite of a vigorous campaign based on the theme of avoiding the division of France into two irreconcilably hostile blocks they lost fifteen seats in the 1968 elections. They have never been strong enough to make an alliance with the FGDS plausible in terms of a possible majority, and whatever the more liberal views of some of them their electors will eventually compel them to align themselves with the conservatives. But as many of their leaders are opposed to Gaullism, this will not happen until Gaullism has either disappeared or been radically transformed. And, as the 1968 results show, it may by then be too late.

The birth of the FGDS is also directly due to the presidential election of 1965, and to the need to find a rival candidate to de Gaulle. The first suggestion was Gaston Defferre, mayor of Marseilles and leader of the liberal wing of the Socialist Party (more ready to decolonise than Guy Mollet, he has nevertheless been consistently opposed to any suggestion of joint action with the Communists). His candidature was approved by the Socialist Party but was torpedoed mainly by Guy Mollet at a meeting of leaders of the non-Communist Left in June 1965. The reasons were partly connected with rivalry inside the Socialist Party, but also with the fact that Defferre would never have obtained a single Communist vote, so that his candidature would have been little more than a gesture. Until the last minute the Communists threatened to put up their own candidate, but agreement was finally reached on François Mitterand, who had the double advantage of not belonging to any of the main political parties and of being one of the very few members of the non-Communist Left (another is Pierre Mendès-France) not to have approved of de Gaulle's come-back in May 1958. Having obtained the great majority of left-wing votes (Communist and non-Communist alike) on the first ballot, Mitterand established himself as a national figure. He determined to use his prestige to forge the unity of the French Left, and as a first step bullied some of the political clubs (see below) and the Radical and Socialist Parties into forming a loose federation, the FGDS. Ideally the federation should have superseded its constituent parts, but the main ones, the Radicals and the Socialists, refused to lose their own structure and identity. In the 1967 election it was the FGDS and not its members which nominated candidates, and in the following Parliament it functioned as a single group under the tactful leadership of Gaston Defferre; but lacking a unified structure, doctrine, and even programme, it

247

remained very much an alliance of political leaders and deputies at the national level.

That even this much was achieved is largely due to the untiring efforts of François Mitterand himself. His surest ally was the *Convention des Institutions Républicaines*, whose president is Charles Hernu. In the last years of the Fourth Republic and at the beginning of the Fifth some twenty political clubs were founded as part of a revolt against the traditional parties and against the threat of fascism. To begin with they did not seek to have any parliamentary influence, but simply to be a means of promoting political education and discussion. Some, such as the Club Jean Moulin, have a nation-wide audience, while others are more regionally based, like the Club Tocqueville in Lyon. For the most part they are simply elitist discussion groups whose members profess a strong attachment to the values represented by the French Revolution[4] and the Liberation, but some of them played an active role in the campaign to get Gaston Defferre accepted as the Left's candidate in the 1965 presidential election. Others joined together to form the CIR whose main object was to support François Mitterand. Thus, although it was contrary to the spirit in which the majority of them were founded, many came to have a more politically active role, and several of them have disappeared altogether as a result. The CIR itself has survived, reinforced by a number of left-wing Radicals, and has in fact transformed itself into a political party not unlike the Radical Party, insofar as it is becoming an elitist group of parliamentarians of different origins and allegiances but with certain basic ideas in common, ideas which are considerably to the left of the present Radical Party. In the 1967 Parliament the FGDS's deputies were composed of fourteen CIR, sixteen Radicals, and seventy Socialists. Perhaps because it is the weakest member of the trio the CIR was always the driving force behind the creation of the FGDS and the attempts to transform a loose electoral and parliamentary federation into a completely unified party. That by June 1968 it had not succeeded is due to the resistance of the Radicals and the Socialists.

The Radical Party is not only the oldest party of the French Republic,[5] it is also its most typical and representative. For if the

4. Cf. names such as Club des Jacobins (to which belonged Mitterand and Hernu), Cercle Sain Just, Club Robespierre, Atelier Lafayette, etc.
5. The *Parti républicain radical et radical-socialiste*, to give it its full title, was formed in 1901.

Socialist and Communist Parties between them have a virtual monopoly of what is the normal left-wing vote in an industrialised society, the Radicals represent that large middle and lower-middle section of the population which gained most from the French Revolution and stands to lose most from any further change in the *status quo*. Until the advent of the Fifth Republic it played the role accorded to the conservative right in other countries, but with a conscience eased by the knowledge that its electorate believed it was voting 'Left', that is to say against the Church, against militarism and against a strong central government. As apart from these very general themes all that Radical electors demand from their deputies is a certain amount of local financial and personal favouritism, the deputies are left with all the room for manoeuvre that they need in order to be part of the governing majority and, if possible, leader of it. Under the Third Republic no government, whether of the right or the left, and under the Fourth Republic very few, could hope to survive without the active support of the Radicals, and the Radical Party, even when weakened and divided as under the Fourth Republic, produced nearly as many Prime Ministers as every other party put together. Such flexibility of principles demanded a very flexible organisation, and although the party's formal structure is classically democratic, its functioning is not. Local committees may have considerable influence at election time, but all important policy decisions are taken in Paris by a committee dominated by the deputies.

The real nature of the Radical Party, as the representative of the dominant class in a comparatively backward and stagnant economy, is shown by what happened to it when France achieved her economic 'take-off' under the Fourth Republic. Held to be responsible for the political failure of the Third, and contaminated by 'Pétainism' during the war, it lost a lot of votes and seats at the Liberation when the Communists, the Socialists and the new MRP carried all before them. However, with the exclusion of the Communists from the government and in effect from any future coalition by the Socialist Prime Minister, Paul Ramadier, in 1947, the Radicals again became an indispensable part of any governing coalition. The curious electoral system of 1951 ensured that the Radicals nearly doubled the number of their seats in Parliament with fewer votes; in 1956, after five years when every other Prime Minister was a Radical, they lost one seat, but their votes went up by over 50%. Their collapse in 1958, which in terms of votes if not of seats was greater than that of 1945, showed how precarious this popularity was. Moreover, it was foreshadowed on another level by an attempt, which was bound to come sooner or later, to adapt the party to economic and international conditions which were totally different from those which it had been founded to cope with. In the mid-1950s Pierre Mendès-France[6] made a gallant effort to transform the party from a defensive coalition of local interests into a modern, properly organised party with a coherent governing programme.

His failure irrevocably divided, and probably destroyed, the Radical Party. The 1958 elections showed that its electoral basis had diminished but not changed; its most impregnable bastion was still the south-west of France, an area which has considered itself as being on the left ever since the Revolution and indeed has the record for the number of *lycées* built this century, but in every other respect presents all the conservative characteristics of a rural, at best semi-industrialised, community, including that of a static or decreasing population. Those Radical leaders who realised what was happening turned either to Gaullism, as did Edgar Faure, or to the CIR. Those who remained in the Radical Party did so either because they could not make up their minds or because they considered that they still had a duty to represent their electorate (which, so long as the economic transformation of France remains incomplete, is a fair point). But in either case they are extremely suspicious of the FGDS and have no intention of losing their identity in a movement which calls itself socialist and which they agreed to join only in order to survive.[7] In view of their electorate this may turn out to be a blessing in disguise for the Left as a whole.

6. For a full account of the conflict see Williams, op. cit., ch. 9. Pierre Mendès-France is a man devoid of public charm, but of great intelligence and integrity. It is these latter qualities which brought him considerable popularity, particularly among young intellectuals, and this, combined with a reputation for efficient and ruthless government, has made him appear as a viable alternative to de Gaulle on several occasions, the last of course being May 1968. His political position has always been that of a radical in the English sense of the term (the French Radical Party, which was founded by such men, has always managed to attract a few of them into its ranks): someone who would have joined Harold Wilson's cabinet in 1964, but would have resigned within two years.

7. This is not to say that they have not co-operated loyally as far as electoral and parliamentary strategy is concerned, but from the point of view of their general attitude to the FGDS it is significant that when their President, René Billères, came to the closing session of the Socialist party conference in January 1968 he did not, unlike François Mitterand, even go through the motions of singing the Internationale.

The *Parti Socialiste Français, Section Française de l'Internationale Ouvrière*, is the largest and most intractable of the members of the FGDS. Founded in 1905 it has been continually subject to internal conflict, but it has been dominated and held together by three men, Jean Jaurès until his assassination in 1914, Léon Blum between the wars, and Guy Mollet since 1946. A Marxist party, the SFIO did not participate in any government until the *Union Sacrée* of World War I. At the *Congrès de Tours* in 1920 the great majority of federations broke away to form the French Communist Party; under the leadership of Léon Blum a few stalwarts rebuilt '*la vieille maison*' and from 1924 onwards the SFIO regularly formed part of governing coalitions with the Radicals, although only once, in 1936, did a Socialist become Prime Minister. But the party remained a Marxist one, terribly suspicious of the Communists on its left and of all bourgeois parties on its right. The position was, and still is, an untenable one, and the fragile unity of the party was constantly threatened by those who considered it was losing its revolutionary purity and by those, such as the 'Neo-Socialists' of the 1930s, who sought to give the party a real reforming potential. The 'purists' were most often to be found among the militants, and on more than one occasion they forced the deputies to abandon a governing coalition with the Radicals. In 1946, having purged from its ranks all those who had voted for Pétain in 1940, the SFIO emerged as the third strongest party in the National Assembly with more deputies than it had ever had before. Instead of taking advantage of the opportunity to complete the transformation into a left-wing governing party, as Léon Blum hoped, the 'purists', led by Guy Mollet, an ex-English teacher and Mayor of Arras, reasserted their authority, reaffirmed the party's Marxist vocation, and so condemned it to sterile inefficacy. The party's structure and organisation is probably the most democratic of any French party's, but since Guy Mollet has been secretary-general, a post which he has kept since 1946 and which he did not relinquish even when he became Prime Minister in 1956, the authentic voice of the traditional militants has been less and less often heard. A tight disciplinary control has been kept by Guy Mollet and his henchmen on the executive, and all attempts to change either men or ideas or both have failed. In the ten years or so that followed World War II nearly every socialist party in Europe went through a period of agonising reappraisal in the course of which they tried to adapt their doctrine to the exigencies of the post-war world. For the SFIO this occurred in 1951 and 1952, and the leader of the reformist movement was Jules Moch.[8] The movement failed, and since then the gap between doctrine and practice has been so great that socialist deputies began to behave to an increasing extent like Radical ones. Principles went by the board, and the party gained a reputation for corruption, patronage and abuse of power.[9]

The Algerian War and the return of de Gaulle in 1958 left the SFIO badly shaken. But the long period of opposition has enabled it to survive, and indeed to regain strength, by reinforcing its unshakable sense of mission. For the SFIO is not, and has never been, a class party, however much it may protest to the contrary. The working-class vote counts for less than half of its electorate, and even that tends to be concentrated in areas where light industry is predominant (the south-west and the south-east and the textile industries of the extreme north) and not in the heavily industrialised east and north-east regions. The rest of its vote comes from white collar workers of one sort or another, state and municipal employees, and of course teachers. It is this which makes the SFIO a party of local administration. From the time when the socialist primary school teacher was secretary to the local mayor to the time when the party was dominated by the Mayor of Arras and the wealthy Mayor of wealthy and efficiently run Marseilles, Gaston Defferre, the party has tended to do better in local than in national elections.

The SFIO then has never been a Marxist party in anything but name. It has always been what it was in the beginning, the party of Jean Jaurès,[10] the party with a mission to educate Frenchmen into making the Republic not simply secular but also socialist. As is the case in the field of general education, the tradition inherited from the French Revolution meant that what the French socialists had to teach, like the culture the schoolmasters teach, was at once unique and universal. Indeed, a recent study of primary school-teachers in the early days of the Third Republic[11] has shown that many of them, ardent socialists, believed wholeheartedly in the

8. Who wrote the introduction to the French edition of John Strachey's *Contemporary Capitalism*.
9. None of this of course was new to French politics, but it is a striking fact that most of the malpractices commonly associated with Gaullism, from the muzzling of radio and television to the condoning of torture, have direct precedents in Guy Mollet's 1956–1957 government.
10. It was also of course to a large extent the party of Jules Guesde, but the anarcho-syndicalist tradition, with the exception of a small but vocal bastion in the *fédération du Nord*, had practically disappeared after 1920.
11. Jacques Ozouf (ed.), *Nous les maîtres d'école*, Paris, Julliard, 1967.

French colonial mission: to educate the colonial peoples to be good Republican Frenchmen. The same faith in the same mission has always animated the Socialist militant with regard to France. It is this faith which has enabled Guy Mollet to represent the SFIO as being the sole repository of all the values which Gaullism by definition denies. It has thus enabled him to prevent the SFIO being entirely absorbed by the FGDS, and so, incidentally, to preserve his own power and position in the face of François Mitterand's growing prestige. His task has not always been an easy one, as the party is not only old in years but also in the age of its leaders and militants, and many of the latter particularly are tired and discouraged, and would be happy to accept some sort of merger immediately.[12] But on the other hand Guy Mollet has been forced to go some way with the FGDS, and probably further than many other militants approve, simply because unification is the only viable parliamentary strategy in the Fifth Republic.

However the real problem, which divides both the Socialist and the Radical Parties, concerns the attitude to be taken towards the Communist Party. Electoral statistics show that the Left cannot hope to come to power without the Communists, but many on the left, including most Radicals and a good many Socialists led by Gaston Defferre, would prefer an alliance with the centre and moderate right, as in the days of the Third and Fourth Republics. Anti-Communist attitudes are deeply rooted in the French political culture,[13] and it is possible to hear the Communist Party attacked just as bitterly at a Socialist party conference as a Gaullist one. If there are still Socialist militants who hark back to the days of the Popular Front, most of them realise that it is not a paying proposition from the point of view of votes. It is one thing to form and respect an electoral pact with the Communists in order to reduce, and if possible overthrow, the Gaullist majority, as happened in 1967; it is quite another for the voter to commit himself in advance to being governed by a coalition of which the numerically strongest[14] member would inevitably be the Communist Party. In February 1968 the Communist Party and the FGDS published a document which, although full of ambiguities and mutual reservations, con-

12. Such as that proposed by Gaston Defferre at the January 1968 party conference, which involved an immediate merger with the CIR but left the Radicals, at least for the time being, out in the cold.
13. Cf. Roig and Billon-Grand, op. cit., p. 136.
14. At least in terms of votes cast if not of seats won—see below, ch. 9.

stituted a first statement of principles or outline on which a more detailed programme could later be hung. In March the FGDS announced the setting up of a new executive committee in which the Socialists would no longer have an overall majority. But before either of these hesitant but positive steps towards unity could be put to the test, the events of May and June swept away the whole edifice which François Mitterand had so bravely constructed. The contradictions of the Federation, multiplied by the contradictions of each member of it, contradictions which are best summed up by the fact that in March 1967 it was the Gaullists and not the Federation (or even the Communists) who obtained between 30 and 55% of possible votes from the oldest electorate since the war in the dynamic half of France; these contradictions meant that the success of his enterprise was always in doubt, and they were shown up with pitiless clarity by the May uprising and general strike. For the FGDS, unlike the Gaullists and Communists, was scarcely even directly concerned by these happenings; François Mitterand's bid for power in the final days of May failed partly because his electorate was not among those who were in the vanguard of the movement. On the contrary, it contained many of those who had no understanding of, and little sympathy for, what was happening. In short, the FGDS can be said to represent left-wing opinion in France only if 'left' is still defined in the same way as it was up to and during the Third Republic, even if some of its ideas may be appropriate to a moderate left-wing party in the Fifth.

The French Communist Party is no less full of contradictions than its rivals. To begin with, it has never been an exclusively working-class party, but has always had a strong rural vote. Indeed, it was created in 1920 by a majority vote made up for the most part of the small country federations of the SFIO; it lost many of these soon afterwards when its membership fell drastically (although it retained Jean Jaurès' newspaper, *L'Humanité*), but it did not begin to make serious inroads on the urban working-class vote until the 1930s. Even now, if 70% or so of its votes come from workers, less than 40% of the workers vote Communist, and at no time have more than 50% voted Communist (comparable figures for the SFIO would be 40–45% and 15–20%).[15] A large proportion of the rest of the Party's votes come from farm labourers, who can be thought

15. Cf. Mattei Dogan in Léo Hamon, ed. *Les nouveaux comportements politiques de la classe ouvrière*, Paris, A. Colin, 1962.

of as the proletarians of the land, but also from small independent land-owners. One of the most solid bastions of Communism has always been the *Massif central*, one of the poorest and most backward regions of France in which peasant families, each with its individual plot of land, eke out a precarious living. The Communist vote is certainly more homogeneous than that of most other parties, but not enough to qualify as a class vote. Neither is it simply a 'protest' vote by those for whom society as it is offers no hope. A large proportion of its working-class vote comes not from the poorest but from better-off workers. In 1951, only a few years after the revolutionary fervour of the Liberation, less than half of its electors thought that the party should take power by force or favoured progress by revolution, and the percentage is certainly even smaller now.[16]

The party solves this problem by denying its existence. It claims to be the party of the working class, and its doctrine and policy, acts and statements are in general based on this assumption. But the assumption is in contradiction not only with the voting statistics of the party, but also with its leadership and membership. Although more of its deputies are workers than those of any other party, more than half are from white collar or 'intellectual' professions,[17] and the same is true of delegates to party conferences. Theoretically, the key element in the party's organisation and structure is the work cell, based on the shop-floor of the factory. Yet barely a fifth of all cells are work cells, the rest being rural and local ones, based on residence. This is partly due to sociological factors (the Frenchman's horror of forming face-to-face discussion groups), but it also reflects the difficulty the party has in maintaining its working-class membership. Since the only figures available are the official party ones or those given by ex-party members, and both are somewhat suspect, it is difficult to give an accurate idea of membership. At the Liberation it was probably over half a million, but it has certainly dropped to a fraction of that figure now; even so the Communists can reasonably claim more members than all the other parties put together. Moreover membership has declined in quality as well as in quantity. In 1946 the Communist Party was by far the youngest party, both in its deputies and its conference delegates. But the leadership remained unchanged from before the war (Maurice Thorez was

16. Williams, op. cit., Appendix VII.
17. However since they only keep for themselves a proportion of their salary equivalent to the wages of a skilled worker and give the rest to party funds, they are assimilated to workers by their standard of living.

secretary-general from 1930 until his death in 1964; he was replaced by Waldeck Rochet, who was born in 1905), and the party is now as old as any of the others. Further, since the virtual dissolution of the student movement, the UEC, in 1965, it can no longer count on a regular supply of young intellectuals as in the past.

The decline in numbers is still compensated for by the loyalty and efficacy of those who remain. For much more is demanded of the Communist member and militant, and much more is given him than by any other party. The Communist Party has institutions which cover every sphere of working and private life, from newspapers, women's and children's magazines and sporting clubs to organisations for the defence of the small family farm, trade unions, youth movements, women's associations, writers' and artists' associations, etc. The party has an answer for every militant's problem, whether it be theoretical or practical. Far from being an intermediate socialising institution, the Party is an organisation within which and for which the militant can live his whole life; it becomes, in a sense, his country. This explains both the passionate, if not always public, debates within the party as well as the bitterness that accompanies expulsions and resignations.[18] It also explains the attraction of Communism for large numbers of French intellectuals of all kinds; rather as large numbers of German philosophers and intellectuals accepted Fascism because an excessive pluralism of values rendered all doctrines equally unjustifiable (and hence equally justifiable), so the absence of any institutionalised political socialisation in France makes Communism particularly attractive to those who are aware of the need for both a means and an end to political action. The result is that despite the great wedge which Communism drives between those who regularly vote for the Communist Party and those, including many workers, who would never vote for it under any circumstances, Marxism in general and membership of the Communist Party in particular are quite respectable in intellectual circles.

The one occasion when this intellectual respectability was combined with popular and political respectability was not so much the Popular Front in 1936, when the Communist Party supported

18. No one is harder on the blindness of those who remain in the Party than the ex-Communist—cf. David Caute, *Communism and the French Intellectuals (1914–1960)*, London, 1964. At the other extreme the author knows of a Communist schoolteacher who burst into tears on announcing her resignation from the Party.

256

Léon Blum's government without accepting a post in it, but the Liberation. At that time, flushed with a reputation for patriotism earned in the Resistance and having accepted to work with de Gaulle rather than against him, it was the biggest single party in Parliament with between 160 and 180 seats (there were three elections within two years), and Communists were members of every cabinet, including de Gaulle's, until they were expelled from the government by Paul Ramadier when the cold war hit France in 1947. They then found themselves almost as ostracised as they had been after the Nazi-Soviet pact, and the brief period when they were considered as Frenchmen first and Communists second was over. After five years of concentrating on extra-Parliamentary action such as strikes, they began a long struggle back to political respectability, which began when they voted in favour of Pierre Mendès-France's government in 1954.[19] The Party was handicapped in this task by its refusal to follow Khruschev all the way in condemning Stalin, by its support of the Soviet invasion of Budapest, and by its ambivalence towards the Algerian War. Although the second decision in particular gave weight to the widespread view that the Party was but the tool of Moscow, it is probable that they were all taken with a view to the need to preserve internal unity; the rank and file militant has always been used to looking up to the Soviet Union as the one example of 'socialism in our time'.[20] And the protest against the Algerian War started among students and intellectuals, and not among the workers. Moreover, it was a period when membership and votes were declining. The Communists could claim $21 \cdot 9\%$ of the electorate in 1946, $20 \cdot 5\%$ in 1956, and only $14 \cdot 3\%$ in 1958 and 1962, when many workers preferred to vote Gaullist, partly because the Communist Party had achieved so little for them.

Forced to choose between returning to being a solitary but pure revolutionary party and trying to create an image of itself as a democratic parliamentary party like any other, the Communist Party chose the latter course. The former would have enabled them to preserve intact their revolutionary ideals at the cost of losing most of their votes and many of their members; the second, however much

19. Although Mendès-France refused to accept their votes as part of his majority—which is an example of how complicated was Parliamentary arithmetic under the Fourth Republic.
20. This is borne out by the crisis that was provoked in 1968 when the opposite reasoning prevailed over the Soviet invasion of Prague—i.e. the image of the Party was put above internal unity.

it tried to disguise the fact that it had become a reforming and not a revolutionary party, entailed the risk of sooner or later being overtaken on the left. In electoral terms the Communists' choice was justified by the results of the 1967 general election, but their image among students had already been tarnished by their conduct during the Algerian War and by the relatively conservative attitude of their student movement, the UEC. May and June 1968 showed that there was no going back. Faced with a movement which, whatever the final judgement on it may be, appeared to be a revolutionary one to those who took part in it, the Communists were unable to divert it into even their own pseudo-revolutionary channels. Once they had accepted to play the electoral game on the Gaullists' own terms (and the Communist Party made this clear the day after de Gaulle's speech on 30 May) it was obvious to everyone that the Communists no longer represented the most left-wing movement in France, and that they did not even stand for the sort of radical change the need for which had been so clearly expressed by students and workers alike.

The only party that made any attempt to make political capital out of the uprising was the *Partie Socialiste Unifié*, a tiny splinter group composed of dissident Socialists who broke away from Guy Mollet's reactionary SFIO in 1958, a small Catholic group called the *Union des Gauches Socialistes*, a few dissident Communists, and Pierre Mendès-France and some of his leading Radical followers.[21] After much hesitation and internal dissension the PSU finally decided not to join the FGDS, but to continue to preach a pure left-wing doctrine from outside. As it makes a point of emphasising the importance of practising what is preached it appears to be far to the left of both the FGDS and the Communist Party, but although it managed to win three seats in the 1967 general election, its public is almost exclusively limited to left-wing intellectuals of the sort who read *Le Nouvel Observateur*. Among them, however, its influence is considerable, and it has a large following in the UNEF, the SNESup., and similar intellectual institutions (both Alain Geismar and Jacques Sauvageot were members of the PSU). In May it came out more openly than any other party in favour of the students, encouraged every move, such as the Charlety meeting on 27 May,

21. Mendès-France himself did not become a member, preferring to remain *apparenté*, that is to say an independent ally of the PSU. To all intents and purposes, however, he was identified with the PSU in the popular image.

designed to promote student-worker unity, joyfully welcomed into its ranks deserters from other parties, particularly the Communist Party (such as Andrè Barjonet), and consolidated its contacts with the CFDT. In June, after having denouced the holding of elections as a diversionary tactic, it presented over three hundred candidates, including one in every Paris constituency, organised meetings at which people like Alain Krivine of the JCR spoke (on 19 June), based its campaign on the slogan 'power to the people', and warned that the danger of a betrayal by the traditional Left was as great as the Gaullist menace.

As in the 1967 campaign when the Gaullists, and especially Georges Pompidou, succeeded in luring their opponents away from policy debates to sterile arguments about the constitution and institutions of the Fifth Republic, so in 1968 the campaign was fought along the lines proposed by the Gaullists. France was menaced by disorder, subversion, and Communist dictatorship? From their very first election meeting on 11 June the Communists replied by blaming the government for the uprising, underlining the role of the Communists in saving France from anarchy, and declaring that the Communist Party did not seek power for itself alone. The help that the Communists had given the workers during the strike and their part in the success of the wage claims were of course mentioned, but the dominant theme was that the Communist Party was as much a French party as the Gaullist party, and had as much right to represent the free choice of French voters. At all election meetings the red, white and blue flag of France was to be seen alongside the Communist red flag, and the *Marseillaise*[22] was sung more often than the Internationale. The real revolutionaries were not the Communists, but the various anarchist and ultra-left-wing grouplets, supported by the PSU, who relied on hysteria and violence to achieve their ends, and indeed Communist speakers often reserved their bitterest attacks for these pseudo-revolutionaries. Forced on to the defensive by the Gaullist attacks, the Communists contented themselves with denying the charges and attacking in their turn those who were further to the left than themselves. The tone was set by Waldeck Rochet's opening electoral speech:

22. *Les Deux Marseillaises*, referring to the Gaullists and the Communists, is the title of a film about the election campaign in the Paris suburb of Asnière. It is also worth noting to what lengths René Andrieu, the editor of *L' Humanité*, is prepared to go in his book, *Les Communistes et la Révolution*, to prove the patriotism of French Communists during the Occupation.

259

'The choice is not between the continuation of Gaullism and the setting up of Communism. . . . Unlike the Gaullist party, which claims the right to govern alone, we Communists do not claim power for our party alone, we say that the building of a truly democratic society in France is not the task of a single man nor of a single party, even our own, but the task of the people as a whole. . . .'

The French Communist Party had given up even pretending to be a revolutionary party, and this timidity, combined with the role it and the CGT had played during May, was to cost it many votes.

The Gaullists tarred all the Left with the same brush, and the position of the FGDS was an exceedingly uncomfortable one. Their hopes of returning to power were linked to an alliance with the Communists, but it was clear very quickly that Gaullist propaganda was successful, and that its links with the Communist Party could only be a disadvantage to the Federation. Some of the more right-wing Radicals, such as Félix Gaillard, seized the opportunity to speak out openly in favour of an alliance with the Centre, and Gaston Defferre managed the extraordinary feat of conducting his whole campaign in Marseilles with scarcely a mention of the Federation. Moreover, François Mitterand, and with him Pierre Mendès-France, were compromised by their statements made in the last days of May, when they publicly considered the possibility of the government's collapse and the necessity of installing a provisional government headed by themselves; their bid for power, having failed, left them weaker than ever. Although between the first and second ballots the FGDS urged its voters to respect the electoral agreements with the Communists, little mention was made during their campaign of what form the government would take should the Left defeat the Gaullists at the polls. Instead, most of the FGDS candidates followed the example of François Mitterand in his telecast of 13 June, of which the theme was that 'the whole of the France of tomorrow rejects the official France of today'. But since the France of tomorrow was not yet of an age to vote, they could do little but point out some of the obvious responsibilities, and suggest some of the most urgent remedies, without much hope of being able to do anything about it themselves.

Those in the centre, the PDM, were not in a very happy position either. Some of them had voted the censure motion on 22 May, but others had abstained, thus in fact supporting the Government.

The same dilemma was evident in their campaign. The fact that they were officially part neither of the majority nor of the left-wing opposition enabled them to make great play in their posters of the danger of dividing France into two irreconcilable blocks; the idea was that the more votes there were for the centre, the less France would be divided. But this theme was much less evident in their campaign speeches, which in many ways were difficult to distinguish from those of the Independent Republicans. The Gaullists represented the best Government available, but it could be made even better if its priorities were changed and its methods made more democratic. In a situation in which extremist passions had been aroused, such moderate proposals found little echo, and the PDM whose only hope was to be accepted as the liberal wing of a right-wing majority was bound to lose.

In fact, as will be seen in the next chapter, all the traditional parties lost, and lost heavily. But what was remarkable was less the fact that the 'party of fear' won, but that the Gaullists were able to capitalise on the fear of disorder and anarchy that seized many Frenchmen in the final stages of the uprising while not a single one of the opposition parties was able to capitalise on the immense hope to which the uprising had also given birth. Sad though it is, this is an accurate enough reflection of the state of politics in France.

CHAPTER NINE

THE GENERAL ELECTION, JUNE 1968

'If hopes were dupes, fears may be liars'

Clough

THE elections were held, as they have been ever since the beginning of the Fifth Republic, according to the single-member constituency system, but with two ballots. Thus if any candidate obtains an absolute majority of votes on the first ballot, he is declared elected and no second ballot is required. Unlike the presidential election[1] in which only two candidates can contest the second ballot, any number can do so in a general election, and the winning candidate is the one with the greatest number of votes, irrespective of whether his total represents a relative or an absolute majority. Under this system any party that does not have an absolute majority in the country is at a disadvantage on the second ballot, provided its opponents can unite. This came out very clearly in the 1967 general election, when the electoral alliance between the Communists and the FGDS was respected by both partners. Under the terms of the alliance the Communist and Federation candidates were to stand down on the second ballot in favour of whichever of the two had obtained the most votes on the first ballot; this agreement was loyally respected by the candidates, with one or two rare exceptions who were promptly expelled from their respective parties, and, what was even more surprising, by the voters. For if Communist voters can usually be relied on to respect their party's orders, it was estimated that as many as 40% of the Federation's electors would never vote under any circumstances for a Communist candidate; in actual fact this figure dropped to 20–30%, which in itself goes a long way towards accounting for the success of the Left, since the percentage of votes obtained on the first ballot by the Left as a whole was only fractionally superior to that which it had obtained in 1962.[2] But that was in 1967.

1. Provided that the candidate obtains 10% of possible votes on the first ballot; until 1967 only 5% was necessary.
2. Cf. François Goguel, 'Les élections législatives de mars, 1967', in *Revue Française de Science Politique*, 17 (3), June 1967.

Another characteristic of the electoral system is that it depends for its fairness, to a large extent on how the constituency boundaries are drawn. Electoral laws are not determined, as in Britain, by common agreement between the different parties, but in such a way as to suit the majority at the time, and the same goes for the drawing of constituency boundaries. The problem is further complicated by the fact that in France the great majority of the 487 constituencies are rural, which makes it particularly difficult to balance the number of electors in each constituency. However, the result is that, as might be expected, the centre and the right have a much easier time than the left. It can, and often does, happen that it takes three times as many votes to elect a Communist candidate as it does to elect a Gaullist one.

The deposit demanded of every candidate, and which becomes forfeit if he does not obtain at least 5% of possible votes, is only 1,000 francs (just over £80), but television time is allotted only to parties putting up at least 75 candidates. These rules enable minor parties and even individuals to pose their candidatures, but makes it difficult for them to have access to a wider audience. Thus Edgar Pisani, the ex-Gaullist minister who voted the censure motion, founded a party called *Le Mouvement pour la Réforme*, but was not able to find 75 candidates willing to risk their political careers for him. One of the clubs, however, *Technique et Démocratie*, put up nearly eighty candidates, of whom thirty were in the Paris region alone, thus obtaining the right to seven minutes television time. But all their candidates as well as most of Edgar Pisani's lost their deposits.[3] The all-important television time is divided equally between the majority and the opposition; within each camp it is divided up in proportion to the size of the party.

The first ballot was held on Sunday 23 June, but before turning to the results it is worth briefly recalling the atmosphere in which the campaign was fought. Officially it only lasted for a fortnight, but as has already been said, when it opened there were still more workers on strike than in 1936. In the first few days there were renewed

3. Yet such was the uncertainty of the outcome at the beginning of the campaign that, according to one *Technique et Démocratie* candidate, they were all offered considerable sums of money by the UDR to stand down. The system obviously encourages this sort of back-stage bargaining, which was widely employed, particularly between the two ballots, in the Third Republic. For another example of such bargaining between the ballots in 1968, cf. Georges Chaffard, *Les Orages de Mai: histoire exemplaire d'une élection*, Paris, Calmann-Lévy, 1968, p. 175.

263

outbursts of violence, by the workers at Sochaux, and by the students in Paris after the death of a schoolboy. Many wondered where the escalation of repression, violence and repression would lead, and the atmosphere was not calmed by the return to France of OAS exiles like Georges Bidault and the release from prison of General Salan. The strike continued at the ORTF and the refusal of the Government to negotiate made many doubt its intentions. Rumours of a military or fascist government coup were countered by rumours that the extremist grouplets were planning to sabotage the elections by blowing up the voting booths, etc. In actual fact the elections took place calmly enough, but the atmosphere was far from calm. Even in those many rural constituencies which had been completely untouched by the events of May, there was some doubt whether the elections would really provide the answer.

Under these circumstances the very high turn-out (80·01% as against 80·93% in 1967) on 23 June was a remarkable achievement, and is a tribute to the habit-forming effects of democratic institutions, even when, as was the case, the very notion of democracy appeared to many to be in danger from one or other of the two principal adversaries. The result was an undoubted success for the Gaullists. Of the 154 candidates elected on the first ballot, 142 were UDR (of these 28 were Independent Republicans), and the Gaullists increased their percentage of all votes cast from 37·73% in 1967 to 43·65%, an increase of just under 6%. The Communists, the FGDS and the PDM all lost between 2 and 2½% of their votes compared with 1967 (for exact figures see end of chapter). The only opposition party to gain votes was the PSU, but except in isolated cases this was due to an increase in the number of constituencies in which it presented candidates; as the second ballot was to show, far from winning any seats, it lost the three which it had already.

The results of the first ballot thus clearly presaged the final results a week later. A total swing of some 3% produced results out of all proportion, but it should not be forgotten that in 1967 twenty-five seats were won with a margin of 500 votes or less, and more than double that number by less than 1,000. Moreover, the swing was not directly from left to right, as closer analysis will show. The following results are taken from the constituency of Aubervilliers, La Courneuve and Stains in the department of Seine-Saint-Denis. The successful Communist candidate was Waldeck-Rochet, secretary-general of the Party and one of the six Communists to be re-elected on the first ballot.

	1967	1968	Difference
Electorate.	66,976	65,265	−1,711
Turn-out:	55,009	52,163	−2,846
Communists	31,106	27,036	−4,070
FDGS	4,389	2,289	−2,100
Other left	1,239	2,274 (PSU)	+1,015
UDR	15,226	16,264	+1,038
PDM	2,554	4,300	+1,746

The Communist and FGDS combined vote dropped by some
6,000, whereas the UDR and PDM combined vote only increased
by some 3,000. It is possible that some who had voted Communist
in 1967 voted PSU in 1968, and that some who had voted FGDS in
1967 voted PDM or UDR in 1968, but that still leaves 2,000 of the
1967 Communist or FGDS votes unaccounted for. They must
therefore have abstained, and in fact there were roughly 1000 more
abstentions in 1968 than the previous year, if the difference in the
electoral roll is taken into account. But the number of former
left-wing voters who abstained is probably considerably greater
than these figures suggest. For many of those who abstained in 1967
were partisans of the extreme right who could not bring themselves
to vote Gaullist because of de Gaulle's abandonment of 'French
Algeria'. The total amnesty granted to all those who had fought for
'French Algeria' enabled many to follow the lead given by Tixier-
Vignancourt, whose hatred of Communism now outweighed his hatred
of Gaullism, and vote UDR. Studies have already been made which
suggest that this was a fairly widespread phenomenon, and in any
case it has been shown that a great deal of voting change takes place
by the intermedium of abstentions.[4] If this also occurred in Waldeck-
Rochet's constituency, and the additional UDR and PDM votes were
to be largely explained by the votes of those who had abstained the
year before, this would mean that the 4,000 Communist defectors
in 1968 did not vote for another party, but abstained. And this is
certainly the most plausible hypothesis. For although there certainly
are marginal Communist voters who may vote differently from one
election to the next, this is not likely to be the case in a constituency
such as this one, situated right in the heart of traditional Communist
territory, the 'red belt' that surrounds Paris. In such an area a

4. Cf. Alain Lancelot, *L'abstentionnisme électoral en France*, Paris, A. Colin,
1968; and 'Les élections des 23 et 30 juin 1968' in *Projet* 28, Sept.-Oct. 1968.

Communist voter is likely to be someone who has voted Communist all his life, and whose mates have done the same; however much he may have disapproved of Communist policy during the strike, he is much more likely to abstain than to 'betray' the Party at the first opportunity.

Moreover, the drop in the Communist vote was uniform throughout the whole Paris region. In the department of Seine-Saint-Denis alone it was of the order of 5%, over twice the national average, and the Communists did not increase their vote in a single constituency. They have lost votes before, but that they should lose them from among their most reliable electors after a general strike which they claimed to be an unmitigated success shows just how far they had misjudged the temper of at least some of their troops. Although, as will be seen later, it is possible that many of their defectors were women, the fact that in the fourteenth *arrondissement* of Paris seven Communist cells went over lock, stock and barrel to the Maoist faction suggests that in Paris at least it was the workers themselves who were disgruntled.

In 1967 it was the Gaullists who, between the two ballots, were over-confident and failed to predict the way that the electorate would act when it came to their second vote. In 1968, however, the opposite happened, and what appeared after the first ballot as a serious setback for the Left became a rout on the second ballot. It is possible that de Gaulle's unconstitutional speech on 29 June had something to do with it, but it is much more likely that the Left, disheartened, lost faith. The result in any case was an overwhelming victory for the UDR who, with a total of 294 seats, gained 97 and an absolute majority; the Independent Republicans gained 21 seats, bringing their total up to 64. All the other parties lost heavily; the PDM ended up with 22, having lost 15, the Communists with 34, having lost 39, the PSU lost all three seats, and won none, but the heaviest losses were incurred by the FGDS which was reduced from 118 to 57, having lost 61 seats.

The most spectacular defeat was that of Pierre Mendès-France who was beaten by Jean-Marcel Jeanneney, ex-Minister of Social Affairs and responsible for the hated social security decrees,[5] by a mere 132 votes at Grenoble. But there were plenty of others just as startling, although not involving such well-known national figures.

5. See above, p. 167, n.14.

A candidate who is also mayor of the local town is usually assured of victory in France, but on this occasion there were a good many mayors, Communist, Socialist and Radical, among the victims. Many traditional bastions of the Left, whether in the mining districts in the north of France, or in the independent farming communities in the Dordogne and the Languedoc, fell before the Gaullist onslaught.

In the remoter country districts there is no doubt that the generally accepted explanation of 'fear' is the correct one. Although some parts of the French countryside were affected, sometimes in quite remarkable ways, the May uprising was essentially an urban, industrial phenomenon, and many farming communities felt themselves directly menaced by it. Traditionally they had voted Radical, Socialist, or even Communist, to protect their own interests and to defend themselves from the results of increasing urbanisation. Yet these parties were all to some extent directly implicated in the May uprising, and their consequent fear and suspicion were increased by Gaullist propaganda. So many of them preferred to vote for the 'party of order', as the UDR styled itself.

This became very clear at the second ballot, when voters had to choose between parties that were not their own first preference. The electoral agreements between the Communist Party and FGDS were respected by the candidates, but the FGDS in particular failed to rally its voters to vote for a Communist candidate in order to defeat the UDR one. This was not because the voters abstained; the turn-out, 77·83% of those concerned, was good for a second ballot. An IFOP poll[6] indicates that whereas 82% of Communist voters, both in 1967 and 1968, followed their party's instructions and voted for an FGDS candidate on the second ballot when their own candidate stood down, only 63% of FGDS voters returned the compliment as opposed to 70% in 1967. The difference, as might be expected, is even more striking in the case of PDM voters; only 23% were willing to vote for an FGDS candidate against a UDR one in 1968 against 37% in 1967, and the figures are 10% and 25% in the case of a Communist candidate. Moreover, there was a striking difference between behaviour in the provinces and in Paris. In the capital city 80% of FGDS voters were willing to vote for a Communist candidate in both 1967 and 1968, but in 1968 this figure dropped to 55% in the provinces. The remainder either voted

6. Cf. *Sondages*, 30 (2), 1968.

UDR or abstained. This in itself is enough to explain why, for example, fourteen Communist candidates were defeated in constituencies in which the Left as a whole had obtained an absolute majority on the first ballot, a majority which in one case (Le Cateau) was of the order of 57·57% of votes cast.

In 1967 a combination of enthusiasm inspired by the spectacle of a united Left and a dislike of Gaullist government had resulted in a large number of floating voters supporting Communist or FGDS candidates on the second ballot even though they had not voted for either on the first. Thus in several cases the single candidate of the Left had obtained more votes than all the Left's candidates put together on the first ballot. In 1968 the reverse was the case. Not only were the combined votes on the first ballot fewer than in 1967, but more often than not the single candidate at the second ballot obtained still fewer. Fear, and the Gaullists' anti-Communist propaganda, did their work very well, and the drive for unity on the left has suffered a setback from which it may take a very long time to recover.

However, although much can be explained by a switch to the centre or to Gaullism in traditionally left-wing country areas, or by abstentions or anti-Communism in many other places, a certain number of awkward questions remain, particularly concerning the behaviour of Communist voters in traditionally left-wing industrial regions. In the *Nord* department, for example, where the Communists and Socialists have always been strong, the UDR obtained on the first ballot 77,522 more votes than in 1967, making a total of 488,605. As the centre vote remained fairly stable, this difference is too great to be explained by Communist or FGDS abstentions, and one of the successful Gaullist candidates, Maurice Schumann, Minister of State for Social Affairs, was probably right in declaring that a large number of the 22,658 Communist and 18,103 FGDS defectors must have voted Gaullist. Yet the vast majority of workers, including, it is reasonable to suppose, all those who normally vote left-wing, were on strike during May and part of June. The same thing happened at Sochaux, where there was fighting between Peugeot workers and the CRS a bare ten days before the first ballot; Sochaux is part of the constituency of Montbéliard, and although the FGDS candidate was eventually elected, the UDR one was top of the list on the first ballot, and more than that, he was ahead of the Communist candidate[7]

7. Whose vote dropped from 17,739 in 1967 to 12,706 in 1968.

in Sochaux. At first sight it seems incredible that workers who had been in a state of open insurrection a few days earlier should vote nevertheless for the government in power.

The detailed studies needed to answer these questions have not been made, and possibly never will be. But, in the absence of any other reasonable explanation, it is perhaps worth putting forward the hypothesis that it was the women's vote which was responsible. Women always tend to vote more conservatively than men (which is one reason, if not the only one, why de Gaulle gave them the vote in 1946), and this tendency increases in times of stress. A strike always bears hardest upon the housewife, and little imagination is required to see that the exceptional circumstances of May made this truer than ever. The whole movement was a movement of general protest, against the existing structure of society, against all forms of authority, and for a different way of life. Not only was the housewife, who had to stay at home and feed the family under increasingly difficult financial conditions, excluded from all this, she also had to listen to the older children abusing their elders in general and their parents in particular, as well as to the husband coming home and explaining how the boss had been kicked out of his own factory and how they were going to organise things differently in the future. The May revolt was essentially a masculine affair. Only intellectuals and girl students were able to join in, or even to go out and see for themselves what was happening. In the faculties day and night nurseries were organised, but except in a few towns with left-wing councils nothing similar was organised for workers' families. The only people who could have done anything about this were the primary school teachers, by keeping the schools open. But their union, the *Syndicat National des Instituteurs*, is dominated by Communists, and when it reluctantly called a strike it called for a classic one with the closing down of the schools. It is possible that if they had decided to make it an 'active' strike, and to continue to look after the children without teaching them, a great many women would have been able to take a more active part in the movement. As it was, tied to their homes and responsible for the whole family, they doubtless came to the conclusion sooner than their husbands that enough was enough, and that the only answer to renewed outbreaks of violence, such as that at Sochaux, was to vote for the party which promised to bring things back to normal as quickly as possible.

There is of course no way of verifying this hypothesis, but discussions that the author has had with those, particularly women, most actively engaged in the movement tend to confirm it. Moreover it does explain a certain amount of otherwise inexplicable voting behaviour. The only conclusion to be drawn from it is one that this whole analysis tends to support, namely that when the chips are down the French parliamentary Left does not inspire confidence either in its traditional conservative-minded electorate or in those who fought and went on strike in May in order that radical solutions might at last be applied to really pressing problems.

DOCUMENT 32
Some campaign leaflets

ELECTIONS LEGISLATIVES DE JUIN 1968.   17ᵉ circonscription de Paris

Pourquoi un candidat P.S.U.?

Le P.S.U., à Paris comme dans toute la France, a décidé de présenter un candidat par circonscription aux élections législatives. Ces élections vont se dérouler sans réouverture des listes électorales, sans abaissement de l'âge du vote, et avec un mode de scrutin qui privilégie les notables : elles ne peuvent en aucun cas régler les problèmes que l'action populaire vient de poser. Le mouvement parti du Quartier Latin ayant abouti à la mise en cause du pouvoir dans la société actuelle doit être renforcé. Le P.S.U. pense que les élections sont l'occasion d'expliquer les objectifs de ce mouvement à l'ensemble de la population. Chacun pourra par son vote exprimer son adhésion.

CANDIDAT :

Pierre NAVILLE

est directeur de recherches au Centre National de la Recherche Scientifique où il dirige le Centre d'Etudes Sociologiques. Militant du Syndicat National des Chercheurs Scientifiques et membre du Comité Politique National du P.S.U., il est rédacteur à Tribune Socialiste.

Ancien militant socialiste de gauche et de la Résistance, il est l'un des fondateurs du P.S.U. et militant actif de l'actuel mouvement universitaire.

Pierre NAVILLE a déjà représenté le P.S.U. lors des élections législatives de 1967 dans le quartier Saint-Lambert.

SUPPLÉANTE :

Francine SMOLIANOFF

Née en 1932 à Paris. Contrôleur aux Chèques Postaux de Paris et militante syndicaliste C.F.D.T. Membre du Comité de liaison de la Sécurité Sociale. Sympathisante du P.S.U., Francine SMOLIANOFF, qui milita activement au sein du Comité central de grève des Chèques Postaux, lors des derniers événements, a accepté d'être suppléante afin d'exprimer son adhésion au mouvement populaire du mois de mai.

UNION POUR LA DEFENSE DE LA REPUBLIQUE

avec
DE GAULLE

contre le drapeau noir de l'anarchie
contre le drapeau rouge du communisme stalinien
pour les couleurs de la liberté et de la paix

Roger Barberot

Union de la Gauche 5e République
Compagnon de la Libération
Grand officier de la Légion d'Honneur
Rosette de la Résistance
Croix de Guerre (11 citations, 11 palmes)
Ambassadeur - 52 ans - marié - 2 enfants

Suppléant
Paul Pin

Union des Démocrates pour la 5e République
Professeur de l'Enseignement Supérieur
Docteur en médecine, Docteur ès Sciences
Pupille de la Nation - Officier de la Légion d'Honneur
Rosette de la Résistance. Croix de Guerre
Conseiller général d'Issy-les-Moulineaux - marié - 4 enfants

Votez en masse : Union pour la Défense de la République

pour barrer la route à l'anarchie et à la dictature
pour maintenir la paix, l'indépendance et la liberté,
pour un nouveau bond en avant et pour renouveler les structures de la France
sur la base de la participation de tous les citoyens à toutes les responsabilités
dans le respect de la République   vu : le candidat

DOCUMENT 33

General election results

1968

		%
Registered electors	28,171,635	100
Abstentions	5,631,892	19·99
Votes cast	22,539,743	80
Spoilt papers	401,086	1·42
Net number of votes	22,138,657	100
Communists	4,435,357	20·03
PSU	874,212	3·94
FGDS	3,654,003	16·50
Other left-wing parties	133,100	0·60
PDM	2,290,165	10·34
Other moderates	410,699	1·85
UDR, Independent Republicans and other Gaullists	10,201,024	46·05
Others, including extreme right	140,097	0·63

1967

		%
Registered electors	28,291,838	100
Abstentions	5,404,687	19·10
Votes cast	22,887,151	80·89
Spoilt papers	494,834	1·74
Net number of votes	22,392,317	100
Communists	5,029,808	22·46
PSU	506,592	2·26
FGDS	4,207,166	18·79
Centre parties	3,017,447	13·47
Other moderates	878,472	3·92
Gaullists	8,558,056	38·22
Others, including extreme right	194,776	0·87

COMPARISON

		%
Difference in votes cast	−253,317	
Communists	−594,451	−2·43
PSU	+367,620	+1·68
FGDS, etc.	−420,063	−1·69
PDM, etc.	−1,195,055	−5·20
UDR, Independent Republicans and other Gaullists	+1,642,968	+7·83
Others, including extreme right	− 54,679	−0·24

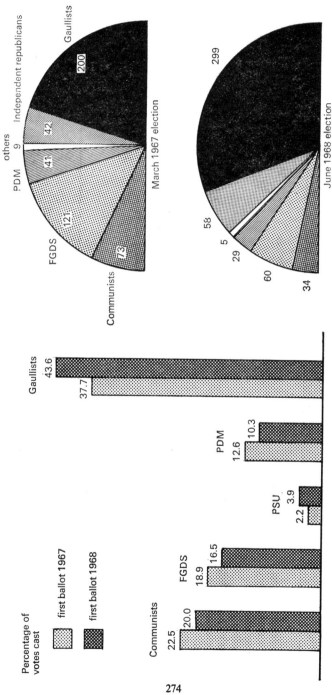

Percentage of votes cast

first ballot 1967

first ballot 1968

Gaullists
43.6
37.7

PDM
10.3
12.6

PSU
3.9
2.2

FGDS
16.5
18.9

Communists
20.0
22.5

Gaullists

Independent republicans

200

others 9

PDM 42

41

FGDS 121

73

Communists

March 1967 election

299

58

5

29

60

34

June 1968 election

Seats in the national assembly

274

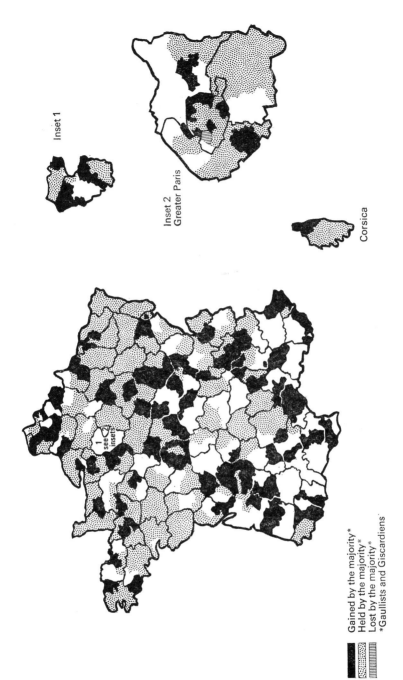

Inset 1

Inset 2
Greater Paris

Corsica

1
see
inset

Gained by the majority*
Held by the majority*
Lost by the majority*
*Gaullists and Giscardiens

275

CONCLUSION

Nobody has gained very much from the student revolt and general strike. Inflation and an economic crisis have eaten up most of the wage increases the workers obtained, and the spate of firings of union militants in firms like Citroën and Renault during August and September suggests that the law on union rights in the factory is not necessarily going to be very effective. The students were thrown an Act of Parliament which, if it were loyally put into practice, would go a long way towards meeting their demands, but at the time of writing the combination of conservative interests in the Government and the teaching profession and among parents of schoolchildren has had the effect of rendering it virtually null and void. Old habits, old methods look like creeping back under new names. For there are few fears as powerful, at least in France, as the fear of losing one's status and authority. The continuing agitation, which is to a large extent the result of this bad faith, means that in most universities and Paris *lycées* very little work is being done.

Conservatives always have an easy time of it when they say that the young, the workers, are not ready for responsibility. This is to some extent true, but those who use this argument forget that one learns responsibility only be exercising it, and responsibility is rarely if ever delegated in France. Long established traditions die hard, and it takes more than one summer's crisis to change them. Institutions may be altered, and these may in time affect attitudes of mind, but it is a slow process and time is short. French commentators frequently use the term 'cultural revolution' (first coined to describe the upheavals in China) to refer to the student revolt, and there is some truth in this. For May and June 1968 saw a large number of young Frenchmen protesting against existing cultural institutions and, in some small way, trying to change them. But a cultural revolution, like any other revolution, must succeed since otherwise it is only a revolt and the reaction is likely to make things worse than before. There are some men in France, even among the Gaullists, who are to some extent aware of the significance of what happened. The problem is whether there are enough of them with enough influence to carry on where the students and workers left off, and so prevent France's cultural revolt from being written off as a total failure.

For if the revolt took the violent form it did, it is because changes are not only necessary, they are long overdue. Some commentators, looking at France's history, tend to see her periodic revolts as an institution in themselves, as though Frenchmen cannot survive without occasionally throwing off every social shackle (only, in most cases, to forge themselves new ones). It would be more accurate to describe France as a society without adequate safety-valves. Not only is there no efficient warning system, no links between primary groups and the nation, but even the 'opium' of life in an advanced industrial society is less attractive in France than it is elsewhere. A comparison of advertising in France and Britain would probably show that what is within the reach of most Frenchmen is at once more standardised, more uniform, and less colourful, while what is out of his reach appears all the more glamorous for being further away; the consumer in France is in fact more blatantly manipulated than elsewhere (and there is of course no *Which?* to help).

But to say this is not to explain what happened or to give final answers concerning why it happened or whether it will happen in other countries. For there are no final answers. All that can be said is that the rate of change in advanced industrial societies continues to increase, and that there are signs that France is not the only country which in one sphere or another has got out of step. Everybody will look at what happened, and interpret it, according to his own lights. But those who are tempted to look at 1968 as Burke looked at 1789 would do well to ponder deeply before damning it in the same way.

APPENDICES

THREE CASE STUDIES

(i) The Student Revolt in Dijon[1]

DIJON is a town of some 184,000 inhabitants, an important railway junction and the capital of the Burgundy wine-growing district. As in many French provincial towns, a rather uniform and unimpressive façade often hides courtyards and buildings of great historical and architectural interest; also as in many French provincial towns its politics are those of the dominant nineteenth century-type bourgeoisie. In Dijon's case, however, these were rendered more colourful by the eccentric personality of Canon Kir, a right-wing liberal of independent mind and forthright speech, who was Mayor of the town for many years until his death early in 1968 and its deputy until 1967 when the seat was won by Robert Poujade, now the secretary general of the Gaullist party. The generally conservative, Catholic and paternalist nature of Dijon politics can be judged from the title of its leading local paper, *Le Bien Public*, which systematically minimised all except right-wing counter-demonstrations during the month of May.

Dijon university is, with that of Besançon, one of the smallest in France, although it now has some 10,000 students, mostly divided between the faculties of arts, law and science. As everywhere the numbers have doubled in the last five years, and the beginnings of a campus with new buildings and hostels have been built on the north-eastern outskirts of the town. But the university is far from being a homogeneous unit. As communications with Paris are easy, both by road and rail, a considerable number of even the younger lecturers prefer to live in Paris and go to Dijon for only two or three days a week. Nor are the students drawn uniquely from Dijon; some come from as far away as Bordeaux, and in normal times the university is practically deserted over the week-end. However, mainly because examinations were not far away, the majority of both students and staff remained in Dijon at least during the first half of May.

1. Much of what follows is based on conversations with Jacques Roubaud, *maître de conférence* at the Dijon science faculty.

On Saturday 4 May the SNESup. and UNEF called a strike which was effective principally in the arts and science faculties; as everywhere else the SNESup. was particularly strong in the science faculty, but at no time during the following week did the staff have the impression that they would be on strike for any length of time, so that strikes were decided on for one or two days at the most and renewed accordingly when necessary. The following Monday there was a small demonstration of some five to six hundred students organised by the UNEF, in which a few of the junior staff took part. At the same time there was a counter-demonstration by some thirty members of *Occident* carrying banners which read '*Les enragés* to the lunatic asylum'.[2] It is worth noting that many of those who both then and later took part in counter-demonstrations were not university students, but were from the commercial and technical colleges. Whether or not this is a general characteristic of *Occident* is difficult to say, but it was certainly the case in Dijon where, as in all provincial universities, anyone who demonstrates is likely to be recognised and identified sooner or later.

On Tuesday 7 May the strike became general in the arts faculty as well as in the science one, but the law faculty continued to function more or less normally. As the arts and law faculties are next door to one another, strike pickets were in place in front of them both, which caused a certain amount of scuffles between striking and non-striking students. The following day the picket in front of the law faculty was reinforced to about thirty students, but found itself faced with a demonstration of 600 to 700 law students and members of *Occident* who were determined to force an entry. The situation would probably have degenerated into a bloody battle if about thirty members of the staff, including the Doyen of the law faculty, had not positioned themselves between the opposing forces. After long hours of discussions and negotiations a compromise was reached and in particular the president of the law AGE, who had a very difficult task to control the more extremist elements of his group, announced that he would take part in the demonstration march organised for the next day by the UNEF and the SNESup.

This demonstration march, on Thursday 9 May, was unique in that four days before the token general strike on 13 May workers marched side by side with students. This was due above all to the fact

2. Cf. *Le Monde*, 8 May, which did not report the UNEF demonstration and estimated the *Occident* one at 100 students.

that one of the lecturers was also the local representative of the Communist Party, which meant not only that the relationship between the UNEF and the CGT was a much smoother one than it was elsewhere, but also that someone whom the workers' delegates naturally respected was able to put across the students' point of view. Every day that week there were meetings of between twenty-five and thirty representatives of the principal student and professors' unions, the workers' unions and the Communist Party, the FGDS and the PSU at the *Bourse du Travail*. Finally the CGT, the CFDT and the FO agreed to a joint demonstration with the UNEF and the SNESup. on the Thursday afternoon. A discreet route was decided on, but the grouplet FER held out for a much more provocative one which would take the demonstrators in front of the prefecture. By midday agreement had still not been reached, but such was the degree of cooperation between the students' and workers' unions that some of the departmental representatives of the three workers' unions accompanied a few lecturers to the student restaurant to continue the discussion with the FER and to dissuade them from taking any unilateral action. The FER finally agreed and the demonstration march of 5,000 workers and students went off without incident, despite the existence of a small counter-demonstration.

All the organisers, and particularly the workers' unions, were concerned to avoid any unnecessary provocation, and this was particularly evident on Saturday 11 May, the day following the Gay-Lussac battle in Paris. Telephone calls from Paris at 05.00 alerted the union representatives and it was decided at a meeting at the *Bourse du Travail* at 08.00 to hold a similar demonstration march to that which had taken place two days earlier, although the route chosen this time went right through the centre of the town. However, partly because of the rain and partly because word had already come through of the general strike call for Monday 13 May, there were fewer workers than on the previous occasion, and in all there were only some 3,000 marchers. The following Monday 8,000 to 10,000 students and workers demonstrated. There were no incidents with the police, who kept well in the background, but although it had been decided that there would be no red flags the FER insisted on carrying them, and at one stage onlookers were able to witness the curious spectacle of the CGT *service d'ordre* wresting red flags from the FER and throwing them into the basement areas of respectable Dijon houses.

Dijon is indeed a very respectable town and the sight of students and workers demonstrating together must have deeply impressed the population; this may possibly be one of the reasons why the Gaullist, Robert Poujade, was re-elected with an absolute majority hearts singing the Internationale since, thanks to their solidarity and on the first ballot. Moreover, although that first week of the student revolt in Dijon was in some ways exceptional, it does show to what extent, at any rate at the local level, individual personalities counted. The fact that one man had a foot in both camps meant that students and workers were able to come to an understanding which was not repeated on the national level and only rarely elsewhere.

(ii) Strikes and Politics in Grenoble[1]

The population of Grenoble and its suburbs has risen by over 400% since World War II. 80,000 in 1945, it rose to 261,000 in 1962, and is now 332,000. To some extent this figure is artificially swollen by vast numbers of rootless immigrant workers, Italians, Algerians, Portuguese, who come not to settle but simply for a particular construction job with no security. This in itself is a sign of the great economic boom which has in twenty years transformed Grenoble out of all recognition so that it is now in many respects one of the most modern-looking towns in France. Much of this has occurred in the last five years, since it was largely in order to provoke the investment necessary to bring the urban infrastructure up to the level required by its economic expansion that Grenoble was chosen as the site for the Olympic winter sports in 1968. This inevitably meant that considerations of prestige interfered with long-term planning, so that the results are very uneven. The urban motorways and arteries are impressive by any standards, and alongside a magnificent new railway station is a new, but miniature, coach station. Yet Grenoble is virtually a dead end as far as rail traffic is concerned and essential communications depend on the road network. Again, the new university campus gives the impression of having been designed by someone in an office in Paris; aesthetically, the site is a very beautiful one, and some of the buildings are fine, but they appear to be unconnected with one another, and the green spaces between have an unfinished look about them. One of the buildings on the campus is *La Maison de la Promotion Sociale*, one of four such in the whole of France designed for the further education

1. Some of what follows has already been published in article form in *New Society*, 4 July 1968.

of workers but, apart from the fact that it can only house sixty at a time, it has not been related either to the other institutions already existing with more or less the same object, or to the concrete problem of further educating the workers. The one undoubted success is the miniature new town built on the outskirts of Grenoble and called the Olympic Village. Architecturally it is very good, and the whole is coherent, so that it would be a pleasure to live there; but it is a drop in the ocean. With the Olympics over it is unlikely that any-thing else will be done for a long time. As with everything else, planning was done in at best a five-year perspective, and little account was taken of the needs of ten or twenty years hence. Added to all this was the bitter disappointment felt by the population of Grenoble in the results of the Olympics. For contrary to what had been prom-ised, a few people made a great deal of money before the games started (from building, from the organisers, from American TV), while the majority made practically nothing from the tourists during the course of the games.

Grenoble, besides being in the forefront of industrial development, has also been a centre of political activity. The area is predominantly a Catholic one, and this tendency has been reinforced by earlier generations of Spanish and Italian immigrants who have settled and taken French nationality. But the Catholicism is by no means an exclusively right-wing conservative brand. Grenoble was a very active centre of Resistance during the Occupation, and it was mainly for that reason that the reformed UNEF held its 1946 conference there and so produced the Grenoble Charter. The town thus began to acquire a reputation for being 'left' that was not entirely justified. For besides the modern dynamic elements that make it an exception among French provincial towns, there remain many much more traditional elements. For example, Grenoble, as the gateway to the Alps and surrounded on all sides by mountains, is the meeting-point of a series of radiating valleys, such as the Grésivaudan and the Drac. These valleys are semi-industrialised, often on one bank only, and the population is still essentially rural. Perhaps as many as 50% of the workers come from families whose basic income is still derived from the land. They are of course Catholics and the great majority vote 'right'; they are not highly unionised.

The reputation however was given a fresh boost in 1964 when a certain Hubert Dubedout of the Nuclear Centre formed a pressure group to get the town's water supply improved. Encouraged by the success of his campaign he formed the *Groupe d'Action Municipale* to contest the municipal elections in 1965. With the aid of the CFDT, and at the head of a list including the SFIO and the PSU (the GAM candidates represented a quarter of the list), he succeeded in wresting the mayoralty from his Gaullist rival. His success was heralded as representing the entry into the political arena, on the side of the Left, of a new class of salaried technicians, junior managers and intellectuals with a social conscience—the products, in fact, of a modern industrial boom. Although these people were certainly well represented on Dubedout's list, a closer analysis of the election results shows that it is not obvious that this class as a whole did not vote Gaullist.[2] However that may be, the myth stuck, and Grenoble became a rallying-point for the Left in France. In 1966 a national conference was held there with the object of preparing a programme of action for a future Popular Front government—and *le colloque de Grenoble* became part of the left's mythology. In March 1967 Pierre Mendès-France, who had retired into the wilderness after he lost his seat at Louviers in 1958, staged a political comeback at Grenoble; after a hard-fought campaign in which volunteers from all over France participated he was elected on the second ballot by a majority of 5,500 out of an electorate of 84,000. The Left seemed assured of Grenoble and of the dynamic image that went with it.

The ex-Prime Minister's defeat in 1968 by less than 150 votes was due to a combination of personal factors (he was rarely seen in his constituency and was directly associated with the Left's bid for power in May), local factors (deception with the results of the Olympic Games), and of course the general backlash common to all France. The fact that this backlash affected Grenoble no less than everywhere else shows that what had been taken for a definite swing to the left was at best no more than the sign of a growing awareness of the complexity of contemporary society and a need for more efficient management of it; but when the chips are down, as they were in May and June 1968, the need for social order, even if it means the old order, comes before the desire for social progress.

In the field of industrial relations also Grenoble has pioneered in a leftward sense, and the results may prove in the long run more lasting than the political myth. The university has always closely co-operated with local industry,[3] but in 1963 this took on a new

2. Cf. the articles by Christiane Marie and Georges Lavau in *Revue Française de Science Politique*, 15 (5), October 1965.
3. Such co-operation, although common in the United States and Britain, is virtually unknown in France.

significance when some members of the law faculty played an active part on the side of the workers in the Neyrpic strike. Neyrpic (turbines and hydraulic research) and another large firm, Bouchayer, were taken over by outside firms; this resulted in a refusal to increase any wages and the laying-off of a number of workers, which in the case of Neyrpic involved breaking negotiated agreements, the *convention collective*. Moreover, besides the university, a large number of engineers and managerial staff took part in the strike on the grounds that all the employees were suffering the consequences of bad financial and commercial policies in which they had no say; their specific demands were for full union rights within the factory. The strike was a long and bitter one, with the Patronat doing everything in its power to break it, and to some extent succeeding.

Although the situation remained fairly calm after the Neyrpic strike (apart from some trouble on the railways over the Olympic Games), there was as elsewhere a restiveness among the rank and file which the unions either did not know of or chose to ignore. For the Neyrpic strike marked the highest point of left-wing Catholic militantism in Grenoble; the CFDT, which had considerable influence even among the engineers and junior management, had always been very active, and indeed many CGT militants have either started life in the CFTC or in one of the various Catholic youth organisations. But in May 1968 it was, as elsewhere, the rank and file who started the movement, led in some cases by ex-Catholic militants. One such man was the local CGT representative in the Coquillard factory at Froge in the Grésivaudan valley. A charming, cultivated and very intelligent man he was by no means an 'orthodox' member of the CGT, but he was tolerated and even respected in the local union hierarchy since his was the only factory in the area to have nearly 100% union membership. This was almost entirely due to his own personality and the fact that he was willing to devote practically all his spare time to talking and discussing problems with his fellow-workers. The factory was one of the first in the area to go on strike and the last to return to work. It was on strike for five weeks in all and work did not resume until 27 June. But when the workers at Coquillard went back, they did so with joy in their hearts singing the Internationale since, thanks to their solidarity and the negotiating genius of their representative, they had succeeded in bringing the management to its knees. It was not so much what they obtained (which in some respects was less than some other factories such as the Renault ones), but that the management had fought every inch of the way and had finally been forced to concede everything they asked for, including the recognition of the union on the factory premises. The workers had the impression that the balance of power within the factory had decisively altered in their favour.

The workers in the other factories, like the great majority throughout France, had gone back to work with the feeling that if much had been obtained, there was much more that could have been; once again, they felt, they had been duped. The unions, including the CGT, began a period of heart-searching and self-criticism based on the recognition that they had become too concerned with the organisation of the union and too little with maintaining contact with the rank and file; and in some cases the over-riding authority of Paris headquarters was disputed.[4] But whatever the final outcome, the recent history of Grenoble has shown the unions and everyone else that in existing conditions strikes are a more effective means of making grievances known than traditional politics, even when these are conducted by such exceptional people as Dubedout and Mendès-France.

(iii) Avranches: a Normandy market town

Avranches is a combination of a Normandy market town and a centre for middle-class retirement. Perched on a hill ten miles from the sea it is not particularly attractive, but it has certain claims to historical interest: Henry II came there to make amends for the murder of Thomas à Becket, and it is there that in 1944 General Patton broke through the German lines. Conservative, Catholic and commercial (out of a population of over 10,000 there are only 600 or 700 industrial workers divided among half a dozen small firms), Avranches has always voted to the right and has, like many such places, become a Gaullist stronghold. In the 1967 election two ballots were necessary to see whether the population preferred a *Centre Démocrate* candidate who proclaimed his support for the Gaullists or an Independent Republican. By June 1968 the elected *Centre Démocrate* had become a fully-fledged Gaullist and there was no Independent Republican candidate; the Gaullist was re-elected on the first ballot with 85% of the vote, the rest being divided be-

4. An authority which is symbolised by the fact that at one point nobody could telephone from the departmental headquarters as the lines had to be kept permanently clear for calls from Paris.

tween the FGDS and the Communist Party. Nearly 190 miles from Paris, and with the nearest University centre some 50 miles away in Caen, there was no reason why it should have been in the least bit affected by the May uprising. Yet on Saturday 25 May, 1,500 people marched through the centre of the town; there were few 'revolutionary' banners and little or no singing of the Internationale. Shopkeepers had been asked to put up their shutters for the day; some did so out of solidarity, but many waited till the procession had gone past to open up again only to find that, contrary to the programme, the procession came back down the high street as well. It all went off very peacefully, but if anyone had any doubt what the majority of the population thought of it, the election results were there to dispel it. Indeed, it must have taken considerable courage to demonstrate at all in Avranches.

The marchers, some of whom came from neighbouring towns, were composed for the most part of the municipal employees and civil servants (who were members of unions and on strike), schoolteachers from both the State and the Catholic schools, and agricultural workers. There were no students of course and no schoolchildren (firmly kept at home by the parents), nor were there any industrial workers. For in only one of the few family firms were there any union members (and that one was a branch of a Rennes firm) and none of the workers were on strike. Wages in the area are appallingly low—it is not unknown for a factory owner to run two houses and two cars while paying his workers less than the legal minimum wage—but to strike would have been to be fired, as there is no lack of available labour in this as in many other rural parts of France. The protest at Avranches was principally due to the action of young Catholic agricultural workers and teachers.

In the Manche department 49·5% of the working population is engaged in agriculture; of these only 40% own the land they work on, the rest rent it. The average size of a farm is 30 acres, which means that some have as little as ten. Moreover, the Napoleonic laws of inheritance have meant that the land is fragmented into dozens of little plots which may be no larger than 1½ acres each. Attempts have been made to encourage, and sometimes to compel people to constitute coherent farming units, but the legal difficulties, quite apart from the natural resistance of the farmers, are immense, and lawyers and landowners do not hesitate to take advantage of them. Moreover, the rural population is gradually getting older and older as fewer young people stay to earn what is at best a precarious living, and those that do stay have to buy out their brothers' shares exactly as though the land belonged to a stranger; and so the process of fragmentation goes on. Farming techniques have improved enormously since 1945, but investment is prohibitively expensive. Whereas in 1945 it was enough to sell two horses to buy a tractor, it is now necessary to sell ten. Needless to say, this puts it out of the reach of most farmers, but they still buy tractors by going heavily into debt to Government-sponsored lending societies. Since they refuse to work together as a co-operative team, there are now far too many tractors which do not in fact repay their cost.[1]

Agricultural workers have by now a long tradition of sometimes violent protest behind them, but most of it has been of a reactionary nature, designed to protect a vested interest that was without any future. However, a certain number of younger members of the CNJA have come to realise that the only hope is to abandon the increasing isolation of the farming community and to integrate it into society as a whole. Aided by increasing unemployment, some of them are now persuaded of the fact that the long-term interests of farmers and workers coincide. Very few farmers accept this as yet, but where there is a dynamic and forceful representative of the CNJA some of them are coming to do so. Such was the case at Avranches, a few miles from which is the farm of the CNJA representative for the Manche department. Like many other militants of the CNJA he gravitated there from the Catholic young farmers' association, the JAC, and if he is far from being a revolutionary, he is very much aware that agriculture is part of a much wider social problem. Invited to speak at the meeting which preceded the protest march in Avranches, he ended his speech with an open reference to the common interests of industrial and agricultural workers. As a result of this there was a suggestion that the FGDS, PSU and Communist candidates should stand down at the election in favour of him as the single candidate of the Left; if this suggestion had materialised, it would have created an important political precedent.

The other main force behind the Avranches demonstration was the schoolteachers. Most of the organisation of the protest meetings and commissions was undertaken by the inter-union committee, on which the State primary and secondary school teachers were

1. Most of this appendix is based on interviews in Avranches: for a fuller and more general discussion of French agriculture cf. John Ardagh, op. cit., ch. 4, and his bibliography.

most prominently represented. But what most shocked respectable Avranches society was the action of some of the teaching priests at the Catholic secondary school, who went on strike before (although it was only a matter of hours) their State school colleagues. Moreover, five of them took part in the protest march and such was the scandal caused by this that local parish priests would not speak to them. However, far from recanting they published a statement in *Ouest France* of 31 May, in which they set out the reasons for their action (see Document 34). If these men are typical of the younger generation of Catholic priests, then the Church in France is going to be forced to change quite a number of its received ideas. One of those who signed the statement, the Abbé Manneheut, only finished his studies in October 1967, and joined the CFDT three days before the strike. His brother farms 50 acres in a nearby village (he is one of three farmers out of a hundred to have as much or more land), and the Abbé can talk as knowledgeably and as passionately of the problems of the agricultural community as he can of those of the educational system; and he took his holidays in Czechoslovakia.

The student revolt and general strike did not produce many positive results in Avranches, but they left their mark there as they did in hundreds of other small towns throughout the country. One day this will have to be taken into account.

DOCUMENT 34

Statement by six priests of Avranches

The following statement appeared in *Ouest France* (on the Avranches page) on 31 May 1968. It was signed by six teaching priests of the Catholic secondary school, the *Institut Notre Dame*.

It is impossible to ignore the fact that young people are demonstrating in the events taking place at present and that they want to take over responsibility for a future which is a source of worry to them. Teachers are questioning the validity of unsuitable methods and programmes. Workers are reacting against conditions which deprive them of their liberty and make their lives insecure.

It is the gravity of present events which decided us to take part in a public demonstration. Our sole aim was to show that we share the desire for justice, liberty and freedom as expressed by a people to whom we belong. Thanks to our meetings with different people involved in the present movement, we have seen voiced by human lips a hope which is more in conformity with the message of the Gospels. In the course of reforming the schools, the young and their teachers are trying out a new sort of relationship. The workers are discovering that they have a common lot for which they want to be responsible. Everyone wants to contribute to the emergence of a new society in which the dignity of every human being would be recognised.

While we reject the concept of the priest as a man who is in favour of conciliation at any price, we do not approve of violence, but at the same time we are just as much opposed to a state of affairs in which acts of violence are committed every day against people who are unable to express themselves freely because they are paralysed by fear and insecurity. Our attitude may have surprised some, but we are of the opinion that the grave problems raised by present events can be overcome not by fear, but by seeking intelligently to set up a more equitable system of justice between men.

COMMUNICATIONS

LONG after the stocks of bicycles in the shops had been exhausted the boom in the sale of transistor radios persisted. Daily papers continued to appear locally, but they were obviously unable to keep their readers informed of what was happening while it was happening. This service was performed by the two commercial radio stations, Radio Télé-Luxembourg and Europe Number One. Although, as will be seen, their independence is considerably less than total, as long as there were only students involved they successfully resisted all Government pressure (mostly in the form of threatening telephone calls from either the Ministry of the Interior or the Postmaster-General's Office); their impartiality was such that on 24 May they were forbidden to use their radio-telephones (although they were again able to use them for the Gaullist demonstration on 30 May), and reporters from both stations were at different times beaten up by the police. On the other hand everything to do with the workers' strikes was dealt with much more discreetly, and after 1 June everything was played down and certain news suppressed, as was the case with the newspapers, in a way that can perhaps be justified, but not by the criteria of objective news coverage.

However, the most remarkable thing was that this service was performed by the peripheral stations and not by the official *Office de Radiodiffusion et Télévision Française*,[1] which was paralysed by a strike from the middle of May until, in some cases, well into July. Governmental control of radio and television was not invented by the Fifth Republic; to take just one example from the Fourth, Guy Mollet's government interfered regularly. But the Gaullists have institutionalised control to such an extent that it has become a habit, and although there have been flagrant examples of sanctions being taken against individual producers or journalists, the knowledge that the Government had the final say in all news programmes was enough to induce many journalists to censor themselves. This form of self-censorship was of course aided by a judicious

1. For a fuller account of the organisation and history of the ORTF see John Ardagh, op. cit., pp 420-430

recruiting policy, but its existence explains to a large extent the Government's surprise, which later turned to vicious anger, when 90% of all the 12,000 employees of the ORTF, journalists, technicians and administrators, finally decided to rebel. The trouble started at the end of the first week of student riots when a television news programme featuring student leaders was taken off; as a result of the protests of the team responsible it was shown a few days later, but on 15 May a *comité pour le respect de l'objectivité* was set up, and two days later journalists announced that they would no longer pay any attention to Government directives. However, interference did not cease, and on 20 May the radio technicians and journalists went on strike, although 'objective' news bulletins were assured. The 'objectivity' did not survive the taking-over of the ORTF by the police on 4 June, but the strike continued until 27 June. The television staff went on strike on 25 May after the Director of the ORTF had refused to pass a programme containing opposition criticisms of de Gaulle's broadcast on 24 May. The strike had the support of informed public opinion (it had relatively little support in the provinces, where the absence of anything on the screen—except for an evening news bulletin read, after a brief period, only by non-strikers—was greatly resented), and the last journalists on strike did not report back for work until 12 July.

The main purpose of the strike, apart from wage-increases for the very badly paid technicians and junior staff, was to ensure that the ORTF be freed once and for all from all governmental interference and be controlled by a truly independent council; new statutes were drawn up and submitted to every parliamentary deputy. To begin with the Government was conciliatory, but it soon became obvious that its only object in negotiating was to gain time. Once the election was over its attitude hardened to the point of becoming vindictive. Not only were no important concessions made, but despite repeated promises to the contrary roughly a hundred journalists, among whom were some of the best known and most popular with the public, were either told that their services were no longer required or transferred to less important positions, often in the provinces. Moreover the victimisation did not, any more than Government censorship as a whole, provoke the kind of public outcry which in some other countries would have put a stop to it. For as in nearly every sphere of life there is little contact between the top and the bottom; no daily or weekly paper carries a regular correspondence column, and although the press is reasonably free, it is much more fragmented and much less powerful than is the case elsewhere. This may have certain advantages, but in a country where communication tends to be a one-way affair, its inability to mobilise public opinion is perhaps a greater disadvantage. It is at any rate one reason why the May revolt saw such a proliferation of students' and workers' tracts, posters and newspapers. A brief survey of the press and mass media in general will show just how anarchic the situation is.[2]

In normal times relatively few Frenchmen read a daily paper. In 1965 there were 26 copies of daily papers sold for every 100 inhabitants; the figures for Britain, the United States and Western Germany were, respectively, 49, 32·1 and 30·6. Moreover the 26 dailies are for the most part made up of provincial papers as there are no 'national' newspapers in France. Apart from *Ouest-France*, which varies its middle pages from one region to another, only *France-Soir* sells more than a million copies a day, and only *Le Figaro* and *Le Progrès de Lyon* more than 400,000 (and possibly now *Le Monde* which was printing—ruinously—over 650,000 copies during May). Otherwise there are just Paris papers and provincial ones, and there are fewer and fewer of each.

At the Liberation many pre-war newspapers disappeared in the purge; some reappeared under new names; others, like *Le Figaro*, escaped by the skin of their teeth. But there was a great surge of new papers inspired by the Resistance, of which the best known is Albert Camus' *Combat*. In 1946 Paris had 28 dailies, the provinces 175. Eight years later, with still only 125,000 television sets in France, there were 12 dailies in Paris and 116 in the provinces. Now, with close on nine million television sets, Paris has ten distinct titles, and the provinces 75 (not counting regional editions of the same paper). The greatest part of this decline took place before television had made its full impact. As everywhere, rising costs, powerful printers' unions and inefficient management have taken, and continue to take, their toll. The process has been checked in a few cases by take-over bids, but the trend now is towards cartel agreements, like the one concluded in 1967 between Lyon's *Progrès* and Grenoble's *Le Dauphiné Libéré*. Lyon, followed by Toulouse and others, has also been experimenting with weekly free supplements to attract more advertising.

2. Much of what follows is based on an article which appeared in *New Society*, 20 June 1968.

At the moment the French press gets 40% of all money spent on advertising (before the introduction of advertising on television), but this does not mean a great deal in view of the fact that France comes twenty-sixth in the world, after countries like Colombia and Jamaica, in terms of the percentage of the gross national product devoted to advertising. Most French newspapers derive about half of their income from advertising, although this can go up to 80% in the case of *Le Figaro* or down to 20% in the case of *La Croix*, which is subsidised by the Church. Many newspapers have sought to protect themselves against undue outside influence (there are no press barons, but Hachette, for example, has a vested interest in a vast number of publications and publishing houses besides a virtual monopoly of distribution) by turning themselves into limited companies and forming editorial associations with a financial interest in the non-public company. *Le Monde*, which led the way in 1951, went further than any of the others at the end of 1967 by splitting a controlling interest among all its staff.

Another reason for the lack of a French newspaper empire is the republican tradition which militates against any too powerful concentration, at least as far as the daily press is concerned. From 1880 to 1914 newspapers (often read aloud in the local *Café du Commerce*) shared with primary school teachers the task of 'republicanising' the countryside. Thus the largest and most influential part of the provincial press has remained the mouthpiece of the Radicals and Socialists—such as *Le Provençal* (Marseilles, socialist), *La Dépêche du Midi* (Toulouse, radical), and *La Voix du Nord* (Lille, socialist). This is one reason why it took so long for a new political movement such as Gaullism to become firmly implanted in the provinces. It also explains the Government aid to the press which, in paper, postal and transport subsidies is considerable.

The republican tradition, founded in a missionary protest movement against the established order, has as its corollary the idea that the role of the press is not to aim at an illusory objectivity of news presentation, but to provide a means for every shade of opinion to express itself freely. The trouble is that although some newspapers may take what they consider to be their readers' views into account, the Frenchman does not consider that his views, even if he could express them, would have much influence.[3] The result is that dailies

3. Even where he can express them, in opinion polls, the results are treated with profound mistrust by politicians and journalists alike; pre-election ones in particular are considered as tampering with the workings of the normal

are not often read for the opinions they express. It is true that *Le Figaro* is read essentially by the middle-class and *Le Monde* by deputies, civil servants, economists and intellectuals, but the Parisian worker in the metro reads not *L'Humanité*, which is more often bought as a second paper by both intellectuals and workers, but *Le Parisien Libéré*, whose politics (when they exist) are well to the right of centre. It is partly for this reason that it is now virtually impossible for any new daily to establish itself, even in Paris. When Marcel Dassault, the manufacturer of Mirage jets, one of the earliest and most powerful financiers of Gaullism and himself a Gaullist deputy, tried to launch a new tabloid, *Vingt-Quatre Heures*, it did not last much longer than its title (the new revolutionary paper, *Action*, which began as a daily but later became a weekly, has so far done much better).

The daily press has in general done very little to modernise itself, so that it perhaps had good reason to raise such an outcry early in 1968 against the advent of advertising on television. Some of the weeklies, however, have and in particular both *L'Express* and *Le Nouvel Observateur* underwent a radical transformation in 1964 which have left them, if somewhat less 'pure' politically, much more financially secure. During the strike, which did not affect the dailies, both of them were sufficiently prosperous to be able to get special editions printed abroad. But the biggest profits of course come from the illustrated weeklies and the commercial radio stations. If women's children's and youth magazines are included, there are over 600 titles, with a total circulation of over 50 million. The biggest of them tend to be concentrated in a few hands, and the two with the largest circulation, *Télé-7 Jours* amd *Paris-Match* (the latter prints 1½ million and is read by nearly 6 million) are controlled by Jean Prouvost, a textile magnate, who besides owning *Le Figaro* has acquired a 13% interest in Radio Luxembourg. This has enabled him to gain control of the news service, and to bring with him many journalists from *Paris-Match*.

The other main interest in Radio Luxembourg, apart from the Luxembourg State, is a Government-controlled company known as SOFIRAD (Société Financière de Radiodiffusion), which owns 30% of it. Formed precisely for this purpose it also has a 50% interest in *Image et Son*, the parent company of Europe Number One. Further, 47% of the latter also belongs to its director, Sylvain

political 'game'. Insofar as there appear to be some grounds for thinking that some surveys are subject to political influence, this mistrust may be justified.

Floirat, who also controls Radio Monte-Carlo, Matra motors and cars, the Bréguet factories (until they were recently sold to the Government), and has also become director with a 30% interest in the *Compagnie Française de Télévision*, formed to promote French colour television and techniques.

If the State subsidy to the press is taken into account (it represents some £25 million a year) it is clear that a very large and influential portion of French mass media are directly or indirectly open to Government pressure. The result is a certain timidity, from which not even *Le Monde* is exempt; it is only in moments of grave national crisis (or after one of de Gaulle's press conferences or broadcasts) that one of the leading newspapers of the world will venture a clear and unequivocal editorial opinion. Moreover, whether or not direct Government pressure was involved, *Le Monde*, like every other newspaper and radio station, radically changed its attitude to the strikers, not to mention the students, after 1 June. In short, if the newspapers and radio stations were able to talk so much during May and June of *la prise de la parole* (lit. the taking of one's turn to speak) it is partly because they had not been doing, or had not been allowed to do, their job. Communication, after all, is a two-way process.

VIOLENCE AND THE POLICE

FRENCH as well as foreign observers were shocked both by the savagery of the street fighting during May and June and by the conduct of the police. The latter did not have an easy time; cobble-stones, bolts, sparking-plugs and, in the later stages, Molotov cocktails were among the weapons used against them—quite apart from the grenades which were sometimes rashly hurled back in their faces. Among the municipal police alone 480 were wounded seriously enough to require hospital treatment, and the total number on both sides must have been well over 2,000. Exact figures are impossible to come by as most of the students refused, unless they were very seriously wounded, to go into hospital (where they could have been identified and later arrested). But among those who did there were many with permanently impaired eyesight, fractured skulls and mutilated hands and feet; and one student known personally to the author spent five weeks in hospital and underwent three operations to have grenade splinters removed from his leg after the night of 10 May. At least two policemen died, one in Lyon and one in Sochaux on 11 June, when a member of the CRS, cornered by a body of demonstrating workers, panicked, fired and killed a worker, and was in his turn stoned and drowned in a butt of oil. Two workers died that day, although only one was shot (the other fell while climbing a wall to escape a police charge); one student was killed on 24 May by a grenade splinter, and a schoolboy was drowned at Flins on 10 June. According to some witnesses he was pushed off a bridge into the Seine, but even if he preferred to jump into the river rather than fall into the hands of the police, he was a direct victim of police action.

Were there any more unacknowledged deaths? In France it is impossible to be certain that the truth will out, so that the answer will probably never be known for sure. However, quite early on there were police who believed that some of their number had died (prisoners at the Beaujon depot heard them talking about it). This may have been deliberately put about to keep up the fighting spirit of the police, like the student tract announcing three deaths after the fighting on 3 and 6 May. But it may also have been true. Similarly, there may have been some truth in what a large number of students believed. After the first week the figure of six dead was heard on all sides, and when the unofficial commission of enquiry published a list of missing people it added that there were six others whose parents did not want the names revealed (*Le Monde*, 6 June). There is also some apparently reliable evidence which suggests that a few of those brought into hospital were already dead. None of this can be considered in any way conclusive, as it is very difficult to imagine how the parents of students, even supposing that the deaths could be disguised as car-accidents, could be persuaded to keep quiet. But if this appears improbable, it is equally difficult for those who saw and heard what went on in the fighting not to believe that some deaths were inevitable.[1]

For the fighting was of a deadly bitterness that resembled nothing which had occurred in France since 1948; Algiers in 1960–2 is the nearest parallel. The violence of the students took everyone by surprise, including the police, but it should perhaps be remembered that few, if any, saw half a dozen students attacking a fallen police-man, whereas the opposite was a common occurrence. However, if all this can be considered (as it tends to be in France) part of the rules of the particularly nasty game that was played, the police 'cheated' in a manner that was inexcusable on any grounds. CN and CS gas and offensive grenades were used in confined spaces (cafes and police cars full of prisoners); people obviously unconnected with any demonstration (passers-by, journalists, etc.) were beaten up and arrested; those already on the ground, the wounded on stretchers, and even Red Cross helpers were beaten up (a police officer was on one occasion seen using his truncheon on another policeman to stop him beating a stretcher-case); and finally there was the cold-blooded beating-up, humiliation and sometimes torture of arrested students. Forced to run the gauntlet between rows of policemen who beat them with fists or truncheons, both in local police stations and in the Beaujon depot, they were crowded 75 at a time into cages

1. Since writing the above, the author has heard of the death of one student as early as 6 May. The story as told by an older person who knew relations of the student, and who were in no way involved in either the riots or the movement, has the ring of truth about it. A student, who was not demonstrating, had his skull cracked open in the course of the heavy fighting round Saint-Germain-des-Près during the evening; the nature of his wound was not noticed when he was taken off by other students to the Sorbonne, and he died soon after. The parents refused to take any action on the understandable grounds that any publicity at that stage could only have made matters infinitely worse.

12 ft by 18 ft and kept there for anything up to twenty-four hours. The worst treatment was reserved for the girls, who were dragged by the hair, beaten up, stripped (one girl was driven naked into the street from her flat), tortured and, probably on at least one occasion, raped. Apart from the brutality, the memory which most of those who found themselves at Beaujon will carry with them for a long time is the horrid, hysterical laughter of men turned beasts.[2]

A few disciplinary measures were taken as a result of these atrocities, but there was no public enquiry and therefore no public trial of those responsible. For the amnesty which was voted for the students by Act of Parliament also applied to the police. Apart from the fact that the police wear no numbers and so cannot be identified, the notion of a purely formal and arbitrary reciprocal equality before the law is so firmly implanted in French tradition (and has so often served to cover police abuses in the past) that no one protested at the amnesty, or pointed out that the police have an infinitely greater responsibility than those whose disorderliness they exist to quell.[3] The French are far too used to the idea that the police are at the service of the Government and not of the people, and many of those on the Opposition benches who protested most violently against police atrocities had 'covered' similar acts in the past and doubtless would do so again.

The ordinary police force dates from the nineteenth century, but in France there are also special para-military forces created largely because the loyalty of the Army cannot always be counted upon. The first of these was the mobile gendarmerie created by Clemenceau in 1907; it is in fact part of the Army, comes under the Ministry of Defence, and is used for internal security. The CRS (*Compagnie Républicaine de Sécurité*) was created in 1945 by a Socialist Minister of the Interior, Adrien Tixier, who in fact did little but change the name of the *Garde Mobile de Réserve*, which was an invention of the Vichy government.[4] It was another Socialist Minister of the Interior, Jules Moch (he held that post under

2. Plenty of irrefutable evidence exists for all this; cf. the letters published in *Le Monde, Combat,* and *Le Nouvel Observateur,* as well as UNEF and SNESup. (ed.) *Le Livre Noir des Journées de Mai,* Paris, Seuil, 1968.
3. Except Casamayor, the pseudonym of an eminent appeal court judge, in *Esprit,* June–July 1968. Casamayor's integrity and courage is all the more admirable because he had already been severely and officially rebuked for writing in *Le Monde* what everybody thought about the Ben Barka case in 1966.
4. This is the germ of truth (although few, if any, were aware of it) in the students' taunting slogan 'CRS: SS.'

successive governments throughout a large part of the Fourth Republic) who welded the various forces into an effective order-keeping instrument. This first proved its mettle in October 1948 when a pitched battle, which resulted in considerable loss of life, was fought with striking miners.

The police as a whole have always been regarded as a race apart, whom no Frenchman loves. This was accentuated by the Algerian War when they found themselves being used first against Algerians and then against OAS Frenchmen. Several policemen lost their lives, which explains, if it does not excuse, the fact that although France has always tolerated an astonishing degree of brutality on the part of its police, it was then that real atrocities (the torture and murder of suspects) began to be committed and tolerated by the authorities; the seeds of a vicious racialism, which was evident in the 1968 riots, were also sown then. In May the police were again faced with a situation they did not understand and given orders that were quite inadequate; for they are trained to deal with insurrections and not with demonstrations. Furthermore, George Pompidou's *volte-face* on 11 May seemed to many like a disavowal of their action during the previous week, and there was a great deal of unrest in the lower ranks. The municipal police force, after the first few days, refused to take part in any further order-keeping operations—but they took their revenge on prisoners brought into the police stations. At one point there was even a serious possibility of a strike (since 1948 it is illegal for the police to go on strike, but that did not prevent them doing so in the early part of 1958).

At present there are 68,700 uniformed police, of whom 13,500 are in the CRS and 22,000 in the Paris police force alone. In addition there are 16,000 members of the mobile gendarmerie. Impressive though this total is, it was barely enough during the summer of 1968; at one point the corps of physical training and unarmed combat instructors were called in to help. Moreover, their quality is not high. A police commissioner must have a law degree, but the ordinary CRS, often recruited in the poorest parts of the countryside, is sometimes barely literate; the double ration of wine he is given before going into 'battle' does not say much for the esteem in which he is held by his superiors.[5]

5. For a fuller account of the history and organisation of the French police see Marcel Le Clère, *Histoire de la police*, Paris, Presses Universitaires de France, 1964 (2nd edition), and Claude Angeli and Paul Gillet, *La police dans la politique, 1944–54*, Paris, Grasset, 1967.

Maurice Grimaud, the Paris Prefect of Police, condemned the atrocities both publicly and in a letter sent to each policeman under his command. But given the traditions and quality of the French police force it is difficult to see how any important changes for the better can be made. Meanwhile their massive use remains the surest means of uniting any extra-Parliamentary opposition movement.

TABLE OF DATES

OCTOBER 1967–APRIL 1968

October

2   Violent demonstrations of agricultural workers, particularly in west.

12   Further demonstrations, including industrial workers.

17   Demonstration of students and dons at the Paris science faculty.

19   Demonstration of parents and teachers at the Porte de Clignancourt (a new *lycée* had been repeatedly promised but never built).

26   Violent fighting between police and demonstrators in Le Mans.

27–28   Workers and students demonstrate in Madrid and Barcelona.

November

9   5,000 students demonstrate in Paris.

17–27   Teach-in strike in the sociology department at Nanterre; creation of a departmental assembly.

24–26   At its Lille conference the UNR becomes UDVème.

December

2   Creation of mixed student-teacher commissions at Nanterre.

7   *Bureau d'aide psychologique universitaire* at Nantes forced to close down.

13   Joint action day by the CGT and the CFDT.

17–18   Wildcat strikes and lock-out at the Rhodiacéta factory in Besançon.

January, 1968

6   Scuffles between strikers and police in Caen.

8   Cohn-Bendit insults the Minister for Youth and Sport at Nanterre.

18   5,000 students on new campus at Bordeaux boycott student canteen.

23   Expulsion of a boy from the *lyceé* Condorcet for 'activism'.

23–24   c. 100 girl students occupy the boys hostel at Nantes.
26   The police called in to Nanterre—and repulsed; fighting in Caen between police and demonstrating students and strikers (from the Saviem factory).

February

2   Nanterre sociology dons (including Touraine and Crozier) condemn measures envisaged against Cohn-Bendit.
6   de Gaulle opens Olympic Games in Grenoble.
7   Clash in Paris between police and 2,500 pro-Vietnam student demonstrators.
11   Students in revolt in Italy.
12–13   Demonstrations, hunger strike and occupation of student canteen in Nice.
14   Action day by UNEF and occupation of girls hostels on nearly every campus in France; incidents at Nanterre, Lille, Strasbourg and Nantes.
19–20   Student riots in Rome; further incidents in Nice.
20–21   48 hour strike by members of the *Centre national de recherche scientifique*.
24   Joint declaration by the CP and the FGDS.
26   Secondary school teachers strike in the northern zone.
29   Students demonstrate in Rennes against the Government's feeble proposals for reforming the hostel system.

March

4   Secondary school teachers strike in the southern zone.
14   3,000 students demonstrate in Paris against university reform and hostel rules; similar protests in Saint-Etienne, Clermont-Ferrand, Nantes, and Dijon.
17   UNEF general assembly disrupted by Trotskyite students.
17–18   Explosion in the Paris branch of the Chase Manhattan Bank.
20   6 people, including a student from Nanterre, arrested after an attack on the American Express in Paris.
21   Student protests in Dijon.
22   As a result of arrests 2 days earlier, 142 students occupy the administrative block at Nanterre, and the *mouvement du 22 mars* is born.
28   Lectures suspended at Nanterre; UNEF and SNESup. demonstrate in Paris against overcrowding; demonstration in Besançon against hostel rules.

29   Students occupy a lecture-hall at the Sorbonne; disciplined protest against hostel rules at Rouen.

29–30   Nanterre faculty closed.

30   The Nanterre faculty board recognises the students' right to hold political meetings on the campus.

31   Meeting at the Sorbonne and birth of the MAU (police massed outside).

April

11   Rudi Dutschke victim of an attack in Berlin.

20   2000 students demonstrate in Paris in sympathy with Dutschke.

21   Tumultuous conference of UNEF: the president forced to resign by left-wing extremists, and not replaced: fighting between left and right-wing elements.

23   Beginning of student agitation at Columbia University.

25   Birth of the *mouvement du 25 avril* at Toulouse, where fighting breaks out between left and right-wing students.

26   The communist deputy Juquin prevented from speaking at Nanterre by extreme left-wing students.

27   Another student having lodged a complaint for assault, Cohn-Bendit is questioned for 12 hours by the police; the departmental council of the Loire-Atlantique decides to suspend its subsidy to the AGE of Nantes.

27–28   Birth of the FER.

30   Cohn-Bendit, officially the object of a judicial enquiry, organises a meeting at Nanterre to demand 'an explanation of the repression'.

MAY–JUNE 1968

(All figures, with minor exceptions, are taken from *Le Monde*)

May

1   First traditional May Day march for 14 years; some students succeed in joining CGT procession.

2   Faculty of Nanterre closed; Pompidou leaves for Afghanistan.

3   Police arrest students inside the Sorbonne; riots in the Latin Quarter (over 100 wounded); the Sorbonne closed; UNEF calls a strike.

5   13 summary convictions of rioters, including 4 prison sentences.

6   Protest marches and riots in Latin Quarter all day: 345 police wounded, nearly 600 students; SNESup. calls a strike.

7	30–40,000 students in long protest march across Paris; the Internationale is sung at the Arc de Triomphe; some fighting late at night.
8	Calm demonstration of students and teachers.
9	An increasing number of student strikes and demonstrations in the provinces; open meeting of the JCR in Paris.
10	Faculty of Nanterre reopened and occupied by students; in the evening a demonstration of students, schoolboys and teachers in the Latin Quarter; barricades are built.
11	During the night, the battle of Gay-Lussac: 367 (including 251 police) seriously wounded, 720 slightly wounded, 468 arrests, 188 cars damaged (including 60 burnt out); workers' unions call for a strike and demonstrations on Monday 13; student occupation of various faculties at Nanterre, Strasbourg, Bordeaux, Rennes and the Sorbonne annexe at Censier; Pompidou returns and gives in to student demands.
13	General strike throughout France, and protest marches in many big towns; over 700,000 in Paris; the Sorbonne evacuated by police and occupied by students.
14	De Gaulle leaves for Roumania and announces a broadcast for 24 May; National Assembly debates student riots and university reform; workers occupy Sud-Aviation factory near Nantes.
15	Occupation of Odéon Theatre in Paris and of Renault factory at Cléon.
16	Short and firm telecast by Pompidou; spread of strikes and occupation of work-places.
18	De Gaulle returns from Roumania.
19	De Gaulle, 'La réforme, oui! la chienlit, non!'; declaration by Mendès-France.
20	The strike, with occupation of work-places, becomes general throughout the country, and by mid-week France is paralysed; primary and secondary school teachers go on strike.
22	Failure of opposition censure motion in National Assembly; Cohn-Bendit forbidden to return to France; demonstrations in the Latin Quarter.
23	Disorganised riots in Latin Quarter.
24	Agricultural workers demonstrate in the provinces, particularly in the west; strikers in Nantes move towards a 'closed town' policy; CGT organises 2 marches in Paris; students demonstrate Gare de Lyon; de Gaulle broadcasts and announces a referendum on social and university reform; violent riots during the evening in Paris (one student killed) and in the provinces (police commissioner killed in Lyon).
25	André Barjonet announces resignation from CGT and CP;

beginning of Grenelle discussions between the government, the Patronat, and the unions; the strike at ORTF becomes general.

27 Signature of Grenelle Agreements and their rejection by Renault and other workers; UNEF, FEN and PSU organise mass meeting (over 30,000) at Charlety stadium; no incidents.

28 Minister of Education resigns; Mitterand holds press conference, announces candidature for the presidency of the Republic, and appeals to Mendès-France; Cohn-Bendit smuggled back to Paris.

29 De Gaulle leaves Paris; 500,000 take part in peaceful CGT march; Mendès-France declares himself willing to head an interim government.

30 De Gaulle returns, broadcasts and announces dissolution of National Assembly and general election; most political and union leaders accept election; massive Gaullist demonstration (over 500,000) on Champs-Elysées.

31 Cabinet reshuffle; CRS take over some postal centres and petrol supplies; Gaullist demonstrations in the provinces.

June

1 30,000 in UNEF Paris march; Parisians flee the capital for Whitsun week-end (68 road deaths); riots in Strasbourg.

2 Some agreements reached in nationalised industries.

3 Government ultimatum to ORTF journalists.

4–6 Workers of essential services (power, transport and communications) return to work.

5 ORTF occupied by the police.

7 Fighting between police and strikers at Flins; de Gaulle interviewed on television by Michel Droit of *Le Figaro*.

7–11 Teachers gradually go back to work.

10 Election campaign officially starts; more trouble at Flins, and a schoolboy is drowned during police operations; minor riots in Latin Quarter.

11 Fighting between police and strikers at Sochaux, resulting in the deaths of two workers and one policeman; desperate and very violent riots all over Paris.

12 Government bans all demonstrations throughout the country and outlaws extreme-left movements.

15 General Salan and ten other political prisoners or exiles amnestied.

16 Reoccupation of the Sorbonne by the police.

18 Renault strikers go back to work.

20 Peugeot and Berliet strikers go back to work.

23 General election: first ballot.

ABBREVIATIONS

AGE	Assemblée générale des étudiants.
CJP	Centre des jeunes patrons.
CNIP	Centre national des indépendants et paysans.
CNJA	Centre national des jeunes agriculteurs.
CNPF	Centre national du patronat français.
CEG	Collège d'enseignement général.
CES	Collège d'enseignement secondaire.
CAL	Comité d'action lycéen.
CDR	Comité de défense de la République.
CODER	Commission du développement économique régional.
CP	Communist Party.
CRS	Compagnie républicaine de sécurité.
CFDT	Confédération française démocratique du travail.
CFTC	Confédération française des travailleurs chrétiens.
CGC	Confédération générale des cadres.
CGT	Confédération générale du travail.
CIR	Convention des institutions républicaines.
FEN	Fédération de l'enseignement national.
FER	Fédération des étudiants révolutionnaires.
FGDS	Fédération de la gauche démocrate et socialiste.
FNEF	Fédération nationale des étudiants de France.
FNSEA	Fédération nationale des syndicats des exploitants agricoles.
FO	Force ouvrière.
IFOP	Institut français d'opinion publique.
INSEE	Institut national de la statistique et des études économiques.
JAC	Jeunesse agricole chrétienne.
JCR	Jeunesse communiste révolutionnaire.
JEC	Jeunesse étudiante chrétienne.
JOC	Jeunesse ouvrière chrétienne.
MAU	Mouvement d'action universitaire.
MJR	Mouvement de la jeunesse révolutionnaire.
MRP	Mouvement républicain populaire.
ORTF	Office de radiodiffusion et télévision française.
OAS	Organisation de l'armée secrète.
PSU	Parti socialiste unifié.
PDM	(Centre de) progrès et démocratie moderne.
RPF	Rassemblement du peuple français.
SMIG	Salaire minimum interprofessionel garanti.
SFIO	Section française de l'internationale ouvrière.

SGEN	Syndicat général de l'enseignement national.
SNES	Syndicat national de l'enseignement secondaire.
SNESup	Syndicate national de l'enseignement supérieur.
SNI	Syndicat national des instituteurs.
UDR	Union pour la défense de la République; later Union des démocrates pour la République.
UDVème	Union des démocrates pour la cinquième république.
UEC	Union des étudiants communistes.
UJCM-L	Union de la jeunesse communiste marxiste-léniniste.
UNEF	Union nationale des étudiants de France.
UNR	Union pour la nouvelle république.

BIBLIOGRAPHY

GENERAL

IT is not intended to provide a comprehensive bibliography on modern France nor even on student movements in general. The following is a list of those works which have been found useful in the course of this study. It contains a certain number of standard works in which further bibliographical material can be found.

Books

Angeli, Claude; Gillet, Paul, *La police dans la politique (1944–1954)*, Paris, Grasset, 1967.

Ardagh, John, *The New French Revolution; a social and economic survey of France, 1945–1967*, London, Secker and Warburg, 1968.

Bernot, Lucien; Blancard, René, *Nouville, un village français*, Paris, Institut d'Ethnologie, 1953.

Bon, Frédéric; Burnier, Michel-Antoine, *Les nouveaux intellectuels*, Paris, Cujas, 1966.

Bourdieu, P.; Passeron, J. C., *Les Héritiers; les étudiants et la culture*, Paris, Minuit, 1964.

Caute, David, *Communism and the French Intellectuals (1914–1960)*, London, Deutsch, 1964.

Charlot, Jean, *L'Union pour la Nouvelle République; étude du pouvoir au sein d'un parti politique*, Paris, A. Colin, 1967.

Debord, Guy, *La société du spectacle*, Paris, Buchet/Castel, 1967.

Ehrmann, Henry, W., *Organised Business in France*, Princeton University Press, 1957.

Fauvet, Jacques, *Histoire du parti communiste français, 1917–1965*, (2 vols.) Paris, Fayard, 1964–1965.

de la Fournière, Michel; Borella, François, *Le syndicalisme étudiant*, Paris, Seuil, 1957.

Hamon, Léo, (ed.), *Les novueaux comportements politiques de la classe ouvrière*, Paris, A. Colin, 1962.

Hoffmann, Stanly, et al., *France: Change and Tradition*, London, Gollancz, 1963.

Lafont, Robert, *Sur la France*, Paris, Gallimard, 1968.

Lancelot, Alain, *L'abstentionnisme électoral en France*, Paris, A. Colin, 1968.

Lesire Ogrel, Hubert, *Le syndicat dans l'entreprise*, Paris, Seuil, 1967.
Lipset, S. M. (ed.), *Student Politics*, New York, Basic Books Inc., 1967.
Mallet, Serge, *La nouvelle classe ouvrière*, Paris, Seuil, 1963.
Marcuse, Herbert, *One-Dimensional Man; studies in the ideology of advanced industrial society*, London, Routledge and Kegan Paul, 1964.
Marcuse, Herbert, *Negations; essays in critical theory* (with translations from the German by Jeremy J. Shapiro), London, Penguin Press, 1968.
Monod, Jean, *Les Barjots; essai d'ethnologie des bandes de jeunes*, Paris, Julliard, 1968.
Morin, Edgar, *Commune en France; la métamorphose de Plodemet*, Paris, Fayard, 1967.
Ozouf, Jacques (ed.), *Nous les maîtres d'école*, Paris, Julliard, 1967.
Prost, Antoine, *Histoire de l'enseignement en France: 1800–1967*, Paris, A. Colin, 1968.
Reynaud, Jean-Daniel, *Les syndicats en France*, Paris, A. Colin, 1967 (2nd edition).
Roig, Charles; Billon-Grand, F., *La socialisation politique des enfants; contribution à l'étude de la formation des attitudes politiques en France*, Paris, A. Colin, 1968.
Vaneigen, Raoul, *Traité de savoir-vivre à l'usage des jeunes générations*, Paris, Gallimard, 1967.
Vincent, Gérard, *Les professeurs de second degré; contribution à l'étude du corps enseignant*, Paris, A. Colin, 1967.
Williams, Philip, *Crisis and Compromise; politics in the Fourth Republic*, London, Longmans, 1964.
Williams, Philip, *The French Parliament (1958–1967)*, London, Allen and Unwin, 1968.
Wylie, Laurence, *Village in the Vaucluse*, Harvard University Press, 1957.

Reviews and Articles

Bosc, Serge; Bouguereau, Jean-Marcel, 'Le mouvement des étudiants berlinois', *Les Temps Modernes*, 265, July, 1968.
Bourdieu, Pierre, 'L'école conservatrice; les inégalités devant l'école et devant la culture', *Revue Française de Sociologie*, 7 (3), September, 1966.
Bourdieu, Pierre; Isambert-Jamati, V., (eds.), *Sociologie de l'éducation*, special issue of the *Revue Française de Sociologie*, 1967–1968.
Burnier, Michel-Antoine, 'L'enseignement inadapté', *L'Evénement*, 25 February 1968.
Cayrol, Roland; Parodi, Jean-Luc, 'Le centrisme, deux ans après', *Revue Française de Science Politique*, 18 (1), February 1968.
Goguel, François, 'Les élections de mars 1967', *RFSP* 17 (3), June 1967.

Goguel, François, 'Les élections législatives des 23 et 30 juin 1968', *RFSP* 18 (5), October 1968.

Kravetz, Marc, 'Naissance d'un syndicalisme eludiant', *Les Temps Moderness*, 213, February 1964.

Lancelot, Alain, 'Les élections des 23 et 30 juin, 1968', *Project* 28, September–October 1968.

Legoux, Y., 'Disparité de la formation des adolescents: l'exemple des petites villes', *Etudes et Documents*, 21, 1968.

Lerner, Daniel, 'The Hard-headed Frenchman,' *Encounter*, 8 (3), March 1957.

Lipset, S. M., (ed.), special issue of *Daedalus*, 97 (1), winter 1968, devoted to student activism.

Ridley, F., 'The French Educational System; policy and administrative aspects', *Political Studies*, 11 (2), June 1963.

Usami, Shō, 'Zengakuren', Japan Quarterly, 15 (2), April–June 1968.

The review *Sondages* regularly publishes the results of polls carried out by IFOP; see in particular 30(2), 1968.

MAY–JUNE 1968

In English

Bourges, Hervé (ed.). *The Student Revolt: the activists speak*, London Cape, 1968, (translated from the French by B. R. Brewster).

Cohn-Bendit, Daniel and Gabriel, *Obsolete Communism; the left-wing alternative*, London, Deutsch, 1968.

Glucksmann, André, *Strategy and Revolution in France, 1968*, translated from the French in the special issue of New Left Review, 52, November–December 1968.

Quattrochi, Angelo; Nairn, Tom, *The Beginning of the End; France, May 1968*, London, Panther, 1968.

Seale, Patrick; McConville. Maureen, *French Revolution 1968*, London, Penguin, 1968.

In French

A hundred or so titles have already appeared in France. The following is intended as a guide to some of the more interesting ones.

The most general account, and the only one to attach as much importance to the workers' as to the students' movement, is by two reporters of *Le Nouvel Observateur*: Lucien Rioux and René Backmann, *L'explosion de mai*, Paris, Laffont, 1968. The best day-by-day account is P. Andro, A. Dauvergne, L-M Lagoutte, *Le mai de la révolution*, Paris, Julliard, 1968; Philippe Labro, *Les barricades de mai*, Paris, Solar, 1968, is less good but contains a collection of photographs from the Agence Gamma. Marc Kravetz, Raymond Bellour, Annette Karsentz, *L'insurrection étudiante 2–13 mai 1968; ensemble critique et documentaire*, Paris, Union générale des éditeurs, 1968, and Jean Bertolino, *Les trublions*, Paris, Stock, 1968, give good accounts of the student movement during the first part of May, while Georges Chaffard, *Les orages de mai; histoire exemplaire d'une élection*, Paris, Calmann-Lévy, 1968, gives an excellent account of local politics in Vendôme (Loir-et-Cher) during those two months.

The few collections of primary material (interviews, documents, leaflets, etc.,) are uneven both in the ground they cover and their presentation. The best general collection is Philippe Labro et al., *'Ce n'est qu'un début . . .'*, Paris, Denoël, 1968. A. Deledicq, *Un mois de mai orageux; 113 étudiants parisiens expliquent les raisons du soulèvement universitaire*, Paris, Privat, 1968, presents what some science faculty students wrote instead of an examination paper during the second week of May. Michelle Perrot, Madeleine Rebérioux, Jean Maitron, *La Sorbonne par elle-même: mai-juin 1968*, in a special issue of *Mouvement Social*, 64, July–September, 1968, assembles and comments on a mass of documents produced during the student occupation of the Sorbonne; less good is *Centre de regroupement des informations universitaires, Quelle université? quelle société? (textes réunis)*, Paris, Seuil, 1968. For the *lycéens* there is only *Comités d'Action Lycéens, Les lycéens gardent la parole*, Paris, Seuil, 1968. Jacques Duran-deaux, *Les journées de mai; rencontres et dialogues*, Paris, Derclée de Brouwer, 1968, has some unstructured interviews with students. The Fine Arts students have produced their own collection of posters, *Atelier Populaire, présenté par lui-même: 87 affiches de mai-juin 1968*, Paris, Usines Universités Union, 1968. For the ORTF there is Claude Frédéric *Libérer l'ORTF; documents et témoignages*, Paris, Seuil, 1968, and on police atro-cities, UNEF/SNESup., *Le livre noir des journées de mai*, Paris, Seuil, 1968. Finally, very little exists on the workers, which makes invaluable the two books that have so far been published, J-Ph. Talbo, *La grève à Flins*, Paris, Maspero, 1968, and *Notre arme, c'est la grève*, Paris, Maspero, 1968, by a group of members of the action committee of the Renault factory at Cléon.

A lot of people felt the need to justify their actions and positions. *Le mouvement du 22 mars* gives its own analysis of events in Emile Copfer-mann, (ed.) *'Ce n'est qu'un début, continuons le combat'*, Paris, Maspero, 1968, and the Situationists do the same in Eliane Brau, *Le situationnisme ou la nouvelle internationale*, Paris, Debresse, 1968, and René Vienet, *Enragés et situationnistes dans le mouvement des occupations*, Paris, Gallimard, 1968. More interesting are the four dons (three sociologists and one social psychologist) from Nanterre who have published their apologias and comments: Henri Lefebvre, *L'irruption de Nanterre au sommet*, Paris, Anthropos, 1968; Alain Touraine, *Le mouvement de mai ou le communisme utopique*, Paris, Seuil, 1968; Michel Crozier, 'French Students: a letter from Nanterre-la Folie' in *The Public Interest*, 13, Fall 1968 (the whole of the review is devoted to student protest, and contains articles by eminent American sociologists such as S. M. Lipset, Daniel Bell and Talcott Parsons); and Epistémon, *Les idées qui ont ébranlé la France (Nanterre novembre 1967—juin 1968)*, Paris, Fayard, 1968. All these should be read less perhaps for the analyses they contain, interesting though they often are, than as ducuments expressing attitudes which should themselves be analysed. Edgar Morin, Claude Lefort, Jean-Marie Coudray, *Mai 1968: la brèche; premières reflexions sur les événements*, Paris, Fayard, 1968, is what it says it is. Raymond Aron's hostile, *La révolution introuvable; réflexions sur la révolution de mai*, Paris, Fayard, 1968, contains, besides his articles in *Le Figaro* during June, the transcript of an interview conducted by Alain Duhamel of *Le Monde*.

On the political level one of the most interesting apologias is that of André Barjonet, *La révolution trahie de 1968*, Paris, John Didier, 1968. Several leading Communists have published justifications of the party line; among them Waldeck Rochet, *Les enseignements de mai-juin*, Paris, Editions Sociales, 1968; Jacques Duclos, *Anarchistes d'hier et d'aujour-d'hui; comment le gauchisme fait le jeu de la réaction*, Paris, Editions Sociales, 1968; René Andrieu (editor of *L'Humanité*), *Les Communistes et la révolution*, Paris, Julliard, 1968; and Laurent Salini (correspondent of *L'Humanité*), *Mai des prolétaires*, Paris, Editions Sociales, 1968. The PSU is represented by Gilles Martinet, *La conquête des pouvoirs*, Paris, Seuil, 1968, the Independent Republicans by Alain Griotteray, *Des barricades ou des réformes*, Paris, Fayard, 1968, and the Socialists by André Philip, *Mai 1968 et la foi démocratique*, Paris, Aubier-Montaigne, 1968. Ministère de l'Intérieur, *Objectifs et méthodes des mouvements révolutionnaires d'après leurs tracts et journaux*, Paris, Ministère de l'Intérieur, 1968, gives the point of view of the Gaullist Government.

Other books include: Julien Besançon, *Les murs ont la parole*, Paris, Tchou, 1968 (a collection of literary graffiti); Jean Cassou, *Affiches mai 1968*, Paris, Tchou, 1968 (a small and expensively produced collection of posters); J. Joussellin, *Les révoltes des jeunes*, Paris, Editions Ouvrières, 1968 (a Catholic's view of the conflict of generations); Maurice Clavel, *Combat de Franc-Tireur pour une Libération*, Paris, Pauvert, 1968 (an ex-Gaullist columnist's passionately committed view of everything); Jean Bloch-Michel, *Une révolution du XXe siècle; des journées de mai, 1968 Paris*, Laffont, 1968; Club Jean Moulin, *Que faire de la révolution de mai*, Paris, Seuil, 1968; François Fonville-Alquier, *Les illusionnaires*, Paris, Laffont, 1968; Jean-Claude Kerbouc'h, *Le piéton de mai*, Paris, Julliard, 1968; Guy Michaud, *Revolution dans l'université*, Paris, Hachette,

1968; Max Paillet, *Table rase 3 mai-30 juin 1968*, Paris, Laffont, 1968; Jacques-Arnaud Penent, *Un printemps rouge et noir*, Paris, Laffont, 1968; and Jacques Perret, *Inquiète Sorbonne*, Paris, Hachette, 1968. Frédéric Bon and Michel-Antoine Burnier, *Si mai avait gagné*, Paris, Pauvert, 1968, is an amusing piece of imaginary historical reconstruction. Finally, Jean-Louis Brau, *Cours, camarade, le vieux monde est derrière toi*, Paris, Albin Michel, 1968, and Jean-Jacques Brochier and Bernd Oelgart, *L'internationale étudiante*, Paris, Julliard, 1968, attempt in their different ways to put the French student movement in its international context.

A large number of periodicals devoted special issues to May-June 1968; the best is probably *Esprit*, **372**, June–July 1968 (it certainly has the best and most reliable summary of events), but *Les Temps Modernes*, **266–7**, August–September 1968 (three of the articles, by Ernest Mandel, Jean-Marie Vincent, and André Gorz, have appeared in translation in *New Left Review*, **52**, November–December 1968), *Partisans*, **42**, May–June 1968, *L'Evénement*, **29**, June 1968, and the Communist *Démocratie Nouvelle*, June–July 1968 (now defunct, a casualty of the crisis in the Party provoked by the Russian invasion of Czechoslovakia) all contain interesting primary material.

INDEX

Krivine, Alain, 57, 79, 259

Lecanuet, Jean, 245–6
lycées, 35, 36, 39, 40, 45, 48–51, 58–62, 209
reform, 123–5, 134–6

Matignon agreements (1936), 192–3
Mendès-France, Pierre, 88, 178, 194, 195, 247, 266–7, 287
Mitterand, François, 178, 195, 248, 253, 254, 260
Mollet, Guy, 178, 247, 251, 253, 258
Mouvement d'action universitaire (MAU), 81
Mouvement de la jeunesse révolutionnaire (MJR), 92–3, 96, 98–9, 103
Mouvement républicaine populaire (MRP), 70, 233, 246, 250
Mouvement pour la réforme, 263
Mouvement du 22 mars, 78, 80, 91, 92, 101–4, 108, 200

Nanterre, 72, 75–81, 82, 86, 91, 103, 104, 108
Nantes, 208–10
Napoleon, 21, 23, 33
nation, idea of, 21–3
newspapers, 85, 295–8

Occident, 79, 80, 81, 82, 83, 92, 99–100, 198, 282
Office de radiodiffusion et télévision française (ORTF), 88, 186, 187, 196, 198, 264, 293–5
Organisation de l'armée secrète (OAS), 93, 98–9, 161, 264, 302

Parti républicain et radical-socialiste, see Radical Party
Parti socialiste français, see Section française de l'internationale ouvrière
Parti socialiste unifié (PSU), 71, 89, 90, 103, 105, 178, 194, 258–9, 264–5, 266, 271, 283, 286
Patronat, 139–42, 154, 161, 162, 190, 191, 213, 224–6
Peyrfitte, Alain, 74, 78, 82, 84, 94, 195
Pompidou, Georges, 85, 94, 167, 179, 182, 186, 195, 196, 197, 243, 259, 302
population, 24–5, 27–30
Progrès et démocratie moderne, Centre de (PDM), 240, 243, 245–7, 260, 261, 264–5, 266

Radical party, 248–50

Rassemblement du peuple française (RPF), 232, 236, 237
Républicains indépendents, 232, 240, 243
Rochet-Waldeck, 178, 256, 259–60, 265

Salaire minimum agricole garanti (SMAG), 191
Salaire minimum interprofessionnel garanti (SMIG), 191
Sauvageot, Jacques, 89, 95, 110, 186
Section française de l'internationale ouvrière (SFIO), 178, 251–3, 254, 258, 286
Séguy, Georges, 177, 190, 191
Sorbonne, 57, 81–4, 93, 94, 95, 117, 118, 119, 121, 124, 188, 200
strikes, 160–1, 169–70, 202, 205–6
general (1968), 176–201, 207–26
in Grenoble, 284–8
Le Mans, 166–7
Renault, 57, 180–1, 217, 219–20
Rhodiacéta, 164–6
Técalémit, 210–15
students,
movements, 56–7 105–8
social origins, 65
Syndicat national des instituteurs (SNI), 90, 269
Syndicat national de l'enseignement secondaire (SNES), 90
Syndicat national de l'enseignement supérieur (SNESup.), 90, 93, 94, 95, 184, 282, 283

teaching profession, 36–7, 51–3
Touraine, Alain, 80
Truffaut, François, 101–2

Union des démocrates pour la République (UDR), 237, 242–4, 264–5, 266, 267, 268, 272, 281, 283
Union des etudiants communistes (UEC), 56, 57, 71
Union de la jeunesse communiste marxiste-leniniste (UJCM-L), 57, 199
Union national des étudiants de France (UNEF), 56, 57, 68–72, 74, 75, 89, 90, 92, 93, 94, 95, 103, 107, 109, 110, 111, 184, 185, 194, 208, 282, 283, 285
Union pour la nouvelle république (UNR), 237, 238
universities, 35, 39, 40, 41, 54–7
reform, 117–23, 126–34

worker-management committees, 141, 149–51

320